This book was first published in the United Kingdom in 2022

The Lulworth Cove Press
The Well House
Chaldon Herring
Dorchester
Dorset DT2 8DN
www.phoenicia.org.uk
Copyright@2022 Philip Beale

ISBN 978-1-911098-00-3

Further copies of this book and the hardback edition can be ordered from www.AtlanticBC.net

This book is dedicated to the modern-day descendants of the Phoenicians and Carthaginians. May you be proud of your predecessors' achievements in all things related to their supremacy in trade and maritime skills in the ancient world.

Atlantic B.C.

An epic recreation of a Phoenician voyage
2000 years before Columbus

Philip Beale

The Lulworth Cove Press

Commendations

"History is always being rewritten. But few people have the imagination and sheer guts of Philip Beale and his crew to demonstrate the seemingly impossible. This book is the most interesting and inspiring I have read in a long time."
Sir Ranulph Fiennes OBE,
The World's Greatest Living Explorer

"Philip's dedication and determination to elevate the role of the Phoenicians in the history of exploration knows no parallel. This is a modern-day classic in the style of Thor Heyerdahl's Kon-Tiki and describes his epic 6000-mile voyage from Carthage to the Americas. Well researched, this is a fascinating, inspiring and enjoyable account of an adventure with a purpose."
Col John Blashford-Snell CBE,
President of the Scientific Exploration Society

'Truly a voyage of bravery and wonder – I loved this book. Philip Beale is a sailor in the great tradition of Thor Heyerdahl and Tim Severin, those who navigate their way across oceans to test their theory – and themselves. It's an inspiring tale, one steeped in history, insight and maritime daring-do.'
Benedict Allen, Explorer, Author and Film Maker

"Philip Beale has the foresight, passion, and fortitude to do what others might only dream about. In the spirit of a true adventurer and explorer, his daring opens our minds to the history we were never taught in school. Philip talks the talk and walks the walk…he literally risks it all to prove that Phoenicians of 2500 years ago could sail to the Americas."
Steve Elkins,
Leader of Lost City of the Monkey God Expedition

"Beale's account of his epic 6000-mile voyage from Tunisia's Carthage to the east coast of North America is proof-positive that Christopher Columbus may have been following in the wake of Phoenician

voyages some 2000 years earlier – and that modern-day adventures can shine new light on big questions in human history … and deliver capacity-building experiences for all those involved. A brilliant read!"
Pen Hadow, Polar Explorer and Environmentalist

"An epic journey and incredible achievement. Read Atlantic BC and you'll be motivated to get out into the world and explore. This is what adventure is all about."
Levison Wood, Explorer, Writer and Photographer

"Recreating historical journeys has always fascinated me, as they bring to life the geography, the hardship and the endeavour of early pioneers. This Phoenician expedition is a gripping story of human endeavour and triumph over adversity. An odyssey and a page-turner of a book, that flits between the real life present day adventure and the great unknowns of the legend that inspired it."
Mark Beaumont, Endurance Cyclist and Adventurer

"History, Tradition, Myths and Tall Tales have always fascinated me, Captain Philip brings us an exciting new perspective with Atlantic B.C. This makes you wonder how many times have legends or myths brought about drastic changes in historical perspectives? With new discoveries made almost every other day, anything is possible.

Captain Philip and his crew on the *Phoenicia* take us on an admirable adventure, that portrays courage, bravery, and resilience, just like the ancient Phoenicians did in their many adventurous journeys. This journey with the *Phoenicia* enlightens us with unique possibilities and theories on the history of navigation. Hurrah, Captain Philip! What a delightful contribution!"
Dr. Habib Chamoun-Nicolás, Professor, Author and Consultant of Cross-cultural Negotiations and International Business Development

Phoenicia's Voyage 2019-2020

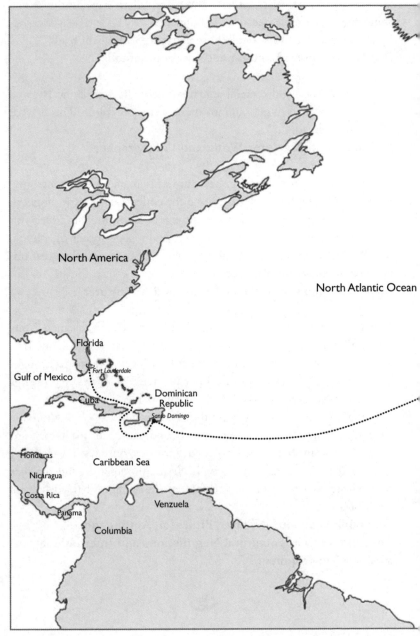

The Phoenicians in the Mediterranean

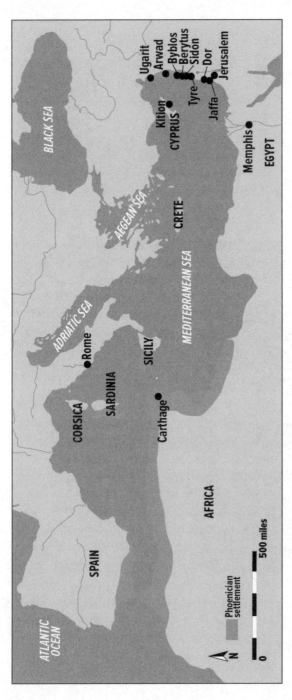

The map shows the original Phoenician city-states in the Eastern Mediterranean, from Tyre in the south to Arwad in the north. The map also shows some of the other important cities and islands in the ancient world. From about the 8th century BC the relative power of eastern city-states began to decline, as Carthage became the dominant economic power in the Western Mediterranean.

Foreword

"And where science stopped, imagination began."

Thor Heyerdahl, The Kon-Tiki Expedition

The following pages are an account of my 2019 voyage across the Atlantic Ocean from Tunis (ancient Carthage) in the Mediterranean to Florida in North America aboard the *Phoenicia*, a wooden replica of an ancient Phoenician sailing ship, of which I was the captain and expedition leader.

Inspired by the example of previous maritime adventurers including Thor Heyerdahl and Tim Severin who had themselves both constructed replicas of sailing vessels used in ancient times – the balsawood raft, *Kon-Tiki*, and the leather currach, *Brendan*, respectively – I wanted to prove that a contested historical theory was, at the very least, a practical possibility.

In this regard, I already had form. In 2003, I reconstructed an 8th century double outrigger which I had first seen etched onto a stone on the Borobudur stupa in Java and sailed it with my gallant crew from Jakarta in Indonesia, more than 4000 miles across the Indian Ocean, to Africa. Our objective was to demonstrate that the types of ship known to exist at the time were perfectly capable of reaching Madagascar, and navigating around the Cape of Good Hope and up to West Africa. If such voyages were possible, it would explain how Asian rice, plantains and other Asian cultural items reached as far as West Africa over a thousand years ago.

This successful expedition was followed by my first voyage aboard the *Phoenicia*. The ship was built in 2007/8 in Arwad in Syria using materials and construction techniques developed by the ancient Phoenicians, a race of master mariners and traders from the eastern Mediterranean whose civilisation was at its height between 1100 and 200 BC. This region, traditionally known as the Levant, was a geographical area centred around modern-day Lebanon and I shall summarise the extraordinary history and achievements of these largely forgotten people in due course.

The goal for this first expedition aboard *Phoenicia* was to demonstrate that an account by the Greek historian Herodotus, recording that the ancient Phoenicians had circumnavigated Africa in around 600 BC was not only perfectly possible, but in all likelihood true, despite the lack of concrete proof. Physical evidence, it should be noted, from a maritime voyage of discovery would be highly unlikely to have been left behind, let alone discovered, more than 2500 years later.

The seeds of my most recent expedition, the second aboard the *Phoenicia*, had been sown long before the crew and I arrived back in Arwad in October 2010, having achieved our objective. This time I wanted to test a theory that the Phoenicians had not only sailed around Africa, but had also been the first to sail across the Atlantic, perhaps as much as 2000 years before Columbus.

Stories, legends, theories, call them what you will, that the Atlantic had been crossed many centuries before Columbus are far from new. A 9th century Latin text, *Navigatio Sancti Brendani Abbatis* (The Voyage of St Brendan the Abbot), for example, records the legend of St. Brendan's 6th century voyage across the Atlantic. Indeed, the objective of Tim Severin's epic *Brendan Voyage* aboard a handcrafted reconstruction of a traditional Irish currach made of tanned ox hides was to show that the legend may well have been the truth. Again, while physical evidence would hardly be likely to have survived, the success of his voyage has only served to demonstrate the folly of outright dismissal.

I had also known for a long time about the distinct likelihood, many would say categorical proof, that the Vikings not only reached the North American continent in the 10th century but also built settlements on the mainland. This time there is hard physical evidence to corroborate this theory and not just the famous 13th century Icelandic sagas recording the epic voyages of the explorer, Leif Erikson. These record that after his father, Erik the Red, discovered Greenland, Erikson himself sailed west to a place referred to in the sagas as 'Vinland'. Archaeological evidence of Norse settlements in what is now the Canadian province of Newfoundland have shown that these sagas reflect fact, rather than fiction.

Yet another theory suggests that the Chinese arrived in America in the 15th century, just 70 years before Columbus. More pertinent to me, however, and brought home forcefully during my experiences of the winds and currents around the coast of West Africa during the circumnavigation of Africa, was my belief that the Phoenicians may have reached mainland America – either by accident or design – towards the end of the first millennium BC.

While the archaeological and scientific evidence to prove this theory was lacking, as was the case for both Heyerdahl and Severin before me, like them I wanted to prove that it was not only a practical possibility, but also extremely likely. Especially when the extent of the known Phoenician colonies in both West Africa and the Canary Islands, and quite possibly the Azores, nearly 1000 miles into the Atlantic off the coast of Portugal, is taken into account.

The fact that a second expedition aboard the *Phoenicia* became a mission I simply had to attempt was because of my conviction that ancient history, beyond the names and dates of kings, tyrants, and emperors, is rarely, if ever, written in stone. The aphorism attributed wrongly to Churchill that "history is written by the victors" is an expression of the truth that history is not a fixed entity, whoever writes it. New scientific discoveries undermine previous certainties, while re-interpretation of the past through the lens of the dominant ideology in any given era, inevitably results in a process which is forever in flux.

Indeed, in the face of many of the re-interpretations of history brought about by the scientific discoveries of the 20th and 21st centuries, many previously accepted versions of the ancient world have been shown to be inaccurate, or just plain wrong.

The history of the 'discovery' of America is one such example. For centuries, it never occurred to the historians of the Old World that the ancestors of the 'Indians' encountered by Columbus in the New World might have discovered it for themselves. Putting aside the very likely human crossing of the Beringia land bridge which once connected Asia to America around 20,000 years ago, the belief that Christopher Columbus was the first to set foot on the American mainland in historical times is now itself open to very serious doubt.

The very idea that a civilisation which grew up well before the Greeks and the Romans could have reached America 2000 years before Columbus would, until recently, have seemed a naïve fantasy. But the same attitude once prevailed about the theory that the ancient inhabitants of South America crossed the Pacific to reach Polynesia and, in particular, Easter Island.

Thor Heyerdahl, during his time living wild with his first wife, Liv (later Rockefeller)[1], on the South Pacific island of Fatu Hiva before World War 2, conceived the idea that contact had been made between South America and Polynesia. Their observations of the local people and their culture, as well as the zoological and botanical specimens they collected, convinced them that contact had indeed been made in the distant past.

The success of the Kon-Tiki Expedition opened up debate in an area which had previously been considered a closed book by anthropologists and historians. Although Heyerdahl's theories have since been questioned to the extent that many believe they have been proved wrong, the most recent contribution to the debate, an article in the peer-reviewed scientific journal *Nature* in July 2020, reaches the opposite conclusion.

The summary of the study states:

> "We find conclusive evidence for prehistoric contact of Polynesian individuals with Native American individuals (around AD 1200) contemporaneous with the settlement of remote Oceania. Our analyses suggest strongly that a single contact event occurred in eastern Polynesia, before the settlement of Rapa Nui [Easter Island], between Polynesian individuals and a Native American group most closely related to the indigenous inhabitants of present-day Colombia."

At the very least this latest discovery demonstrates that the pendulum of academic opinion still swings one way and then another. Without Heyerdahl's epic voyage, the pendulum would probably not have swung at all.

I hope you will enjoy the story of the *Phoenicia* and her crossing of the Atlantic. It is a story that would not have been possible without the support and hard work of many others, stretching back over a number of years to the genesis of the first expedition around Africa. While I

1. Liv later married the American adventurer and author James Stillman Rockefeller Jr.

hope I have acknowledged them all in the credits at the back of this book, the success of the expedition was primarily down to vital members of the crew who sailed the ship on all the key legs of the voyage.

When I sat down to write this book, I asked each of them to give me a record of their version of the voyage so I could include their memories and stories as well as my own. In the course of the narrative the reader will be introduced to all of them in turn, with an explanation of how they came to be involved with the project in the first place. The success of the project – establishing conclusive proof that the ancient Phoenicians were capable of crossing the Atlantic – was down to their dedication, hard work, and bravery.

It was an expedition that enriched my life immeasurably and left me with a lifetime of inspirational memories. I can only hope that they feel the same.

Philip Beale, January 2022.

Introducing My Crew – My Pillars of Hercules

I fear some of my brave crew may be disappointed that they have not featured more in this account of the voyage. However, I know from experience in the writing of my book *Sailing Close to the Wind*, about Phoenicia's circumnavigation of Africa, that in order to make the story lucid and compelling for the reader, it is important to keep the number of key dramatis personae to a minimum.

The crew members below were all central to the success of our mission. In fact, without the efforts of this core group, the expedition would firstly never have set sail and would certainly never have made it across the Atlantic. This book is as much their story as it is mine, which is why I have asked them all to share their memories with me to create this narrative of the voyage, and perhaps lend a different perspective on events from my own.

All of them have contributed their memories, so while responsibility for its accuracy is my responsibility alone, their input has added perspectives, details, and I hope a far deeper testimony of our shared experience than I could have achieved on my own.

Steinar Lillås

Steinar lives on the island of Tjøme in Oslof-joyd in south-eastern Norway and works as a Viking ship captain in Tønsberg on the replica Viking ship, *Saga Oseberg*. He has sailed Norwegian traditional boats all his life and his ancestors came from the islands at the far end of the Oslo Fjord where they made a living as pilots  and sailors. Boats and the sea are part of his DNA. He grew up near the Oseberg Mound, which covered an almost complete Viking ship and was the richest archaeological Viking find in history, and dreamed of being at the helm of a Viking ship since he was a boy.

After hearing a lecture of mine about *Phoenicia*, he realised he had the opportunity to take part in an expedition like his hero, fellow Norwegian Thor Heyerdahl, and I was delighted to ask him to be my deputy. Steinar is now working with the *Saga Farmann* and planning the re-creation of a Viking journey through Europe and Russia.

Abdul Aziz

Aziz was born in Medan, the capital city of North Sumatra Province of Indonesia on October 11, 1976. Since he was a child Aziz has loved to travel, perhaps because some of his family members changed jobs every few years and he therefore got used to moving from place to place.

His adventures continued whilst studying at Muhammadiyah University in Jakarta by joining the outdoor activity club. At the club, he participated in mountaineering expeditions in Indonesia as well as overseas trips to Kilimanjaro in Tanzania and Elbrus, Russia in 2002.

The journey in adventure continued when the Indonesian Ministry of Tourism opened the registration for the crew of the Borobudur Indonesia-Ghana 2003/2004 ship expedition in 2003. He passed the selection tests, even though he thought his English wasn't good enough. Aziz received Indonesia's state medal from President Megawati in 2004 in recognition of the success of the expedition. To make a living he became a journalist, writing various articles and took photos to support them. Due to his unique qualities and work ethic, he was invited with Dirman to participate in *Phoenicia's* circumnavigation of Africa in 2008/2010 and again in 2019/2020 for the Atlantic expedition.

Charlie Mannix Beale

It was in 2012, when he was 18 years old, that Charlie experienced life on board *Phoenicia* for the first time. As his uncle, I persuaded him to live and work on the ship while it was moored in St. Katharine's Dock, London. Charlie gave tours of the ship and it was during this time that he developed a passion for teaching and educa-

tion. Later, Charlie studied Politics and Philosophy at the University of Liverpool and spent weekends aboard *Phoenicia* assisting with repairs and hoping one day to be a part of her crew.

At that time, Charlie's sailing knowledge and experience was minimal, but while living on the *Phoenicia* for more than nine months, he soon became proficient with ancient sailing techniques. Throughout the voyage, Charlie managed the expedition's social media pages and wrote regular blog posts. Charlie now lives in London and works in the UK Parliament as a manager of the Parliamentary Education Centre. Since returning from the expedition, he has recorded a podcast series inspired by Phoenician history and worked for an economic think-tank.

Maran Fazzi

A doctor from the Netherlands specialising in global health and tropical medicine, Maran was the expedition doctor aboard *Phoenicia*. Maran loves working in the world's most remote locations and after taking an Advanced Wilderness Life Support (AWLS) course with Outdoor Medicine and later becoming an instructor, she felt ready to put the theory of expedition medicine into practice. It also gave her the opportunity to experience life as part of a ship's crew and to learn about sailing.

Maran is the ultimate outdoor enthusiast, enjoying adventure sports in the air, on land and on water. As a keen surfer, she has always enjoyed the sea, but prior to joining the expedition, her experience of sailing was limited to weekend trips on lakes in small sailing boats.

Sheimaa Oubari

Sheimaa is Lebanese French, who until the expedition worked in communication and project management in Lebanon. In 2013 she founded *Achillea*, a cultural events company in Lebanon with a mission to promote arts and culture. The company has supported many Lebanese talents and hosted international artists at major events. She's also a French literature graduate from the Lebanese University in Beirut and is now focussed on a Master's degree.

Through her NGO work promoting Phoenician heritage, she first made contact with me in 2016. After three years promoting the expedition with the Lebanese diaspora, finding sponsors and building partnerships, she volunteered to be part of the crew, even though she had no experience sailing. She initially volunteered for a short leg in the Mediterranean, but after taking part in the Lebanese uprising in October, 2019, she re-joined the expedition, proudly displaying the Lebanese flag whenever we made landfall.

Sudirman

Sudirman, or Dirman as he is known, is Indo-nesian and was born and has lived most of his life on the Indonesian island of Pagerungan Kecil, which is located 60 miles north of Bali. Dirman is one of the most multi-talented and nicest guys you are ever likely to be meet. First and foremost he is a shipwright, previously  building traditional wooden fishing and leisure boats. However, he is a natural sailor, helmsman and magical mechanic who can turn his hand to most challenges. He has a passion for fishing and making his own traditional lures. He is always happiest when he has caught a fish and then has a smile a mile wide.

He worked on the building of the Borobudur ship (*Samudra Raksa*) and went on to sail with her from Indonesia to Madagascar and Ghana in West Africa in 2003/04. Following the success of the expedition, Dirman received Indonesia's state medal from President Megawati in 2004 as recognition of the service to his country. He was also instru-mental in the success of *Phoenicia's* circumnavigation of Africa from 2008/2010. In terms of boatbuilding, in recent years he has been com-missioned to build a number of historic replica south-east Asian boats. He is married with one daughter and one son.

Yuri Sanada

Yuri was born in Brazil where he studied to be a biologist while spending his free time travelling and adventuring. Later he moved to England where he met his wife, Vera. After travelling in Europe and the Middle East, they moved to the Florida Keys, training as a NAUI Scuba Diving instructor, before moving to Japan to open a  diving school for foreigners. Back in the US, he lived aboard a sailboat on the West Coast and started working as a writer and a film producer.

After crossing the Pacific, he returned to Brazil and opened his production company, Aventuras Produções, while still living and working aboard his sailboat.

Since then, he has produced and directed many award-winning TV series and documentaries about scientific and adventure expeditions. He made the first Brazilian IMAX Amazon Adventure 3D which was awarded seven international awards. Yuri was a member of the *Around Africa* expedition and has made documentaries about both expeditions. His latest project is an expedition on the Amazon on hybrid boats powered by solar panels and pedals. Yuri is a Fellow of the NY Explorers Club which promotes scientific exploration and field study around the world.

Philip Beale

Philip Beale was born in England in 1960 and after graduating in Politics from the University of Hull became an officer in the Royal Navy. From 1987 to 2003 he pursued a successful career in the City of London. Having had an interest in ancient seafaring migrations from an early age, he left the City in 2003 to pursue a dream of building an 8th century Indonesian ship, known as the Borobudur Ship. With an international crew he sailed her from Jakarta, 12,000 miles across the Indian Ocean to Madagascar and then around the Cape of Good Hope to Ghana.

During the Borobudur Ship expedition, Philip conceived the idea of building a replica Phoenician ship to recreate the voyage that Herodotus described the Phoenicians making – a circumnavigation of Africa in 600 BC. Not content with demonstrating that the Phoenicians could have circumnavigated Africa, he set out in 2019 to show that the Phoenicians could have reached the Americas. Philip is a Fellow of the Royal Geographical Society, a member of the Scientific Exploration Society and a Director of Pioneer Expeditions.

List of Contents

The Riddle

Did the Phoenicians reach America 2000 years before Columbus?

"It is one of the greatest voyages of mankind and if anyone could have done it before Columbus, it was the Phoenicians. Of all the ancient civilisations, they were the greatest seafarers – Lebanon had cedar trees perfect for building strong boats, they were the first to use iron nails and they had knowledge of astronomy and currents."

Philip Beale
Phoenicians Before Columbus Expedition Leader (2019)

It can be a sobering experience to look back at statements we have made, or words we have written in the past. But as I look back at the sometimes seemingly insurmountable challenges we faced in mounting the *Phoenicians Before Columbus Expedition*, I realise now that without the strength of my belief that the ancient Phoenicians had the capability of reaching America, we would probably never have embarked on this epic voyage, let alone achieved our ambition.

It is, after all, one of the great unanswered riddles of history. Alongside the mysteries of who built Stonehenge, what happened to the Roman Ninth Legion, who killed the Princes in the Tower, and what happened to the crew of the Mary Celeste, should be the simple, tantalising question: "Did the Phoenicians reach the Americas nearly 2000 years before Columbus?"

This question had nagged away at me ever since I first seriously considered it in 2003. Back then, I was leading my first maritime expedition

– the *Borobudur Ship Expedition* – when, with the aid of a hugely talented team, I reconstructed an 8th century double outrigger which I had first seen sculpted on a stone relief on the Borobudur stupa in Java.

Our intention was to demonstrate the many cultural influences on Africa derived from its ancient maritime links with Asia. In the great tradition of previous experimental voyages like Thor Heyerdahl's *Kon-Tiki Expedition* and Tim Severin's *Brendan Voyage*, we sailed her from Indonesia to Madagascar and around the Cape of Good Hope to Ghana.

In the absence of written records or archaeological proof, political affiliations in the modern world have a habit of filling the vacuum. And so it was on the *Borobudur Expedition*. When we reached Cape Town, we were greeted with headlines in the *Cape Times* asserting that the Indians, and not the Asians, had been the first maritime traders with the African mainland.

Although I had never claimed the Asians were the *first*, my curiosity was piqued. It was then that I discovered that in all likelihood this accolade should be bestowed on neither the Asians, nor the Indians, but those enigmatic master-mariners of classical times, the ancient Phoenicians, whose origins pre-date both the Greek and the Roman civilisations. The history of the Phoenician civilisation, their achievements, and the legacy they have handed down to us, is a fascinating one which I shall return to in more detail. But the mystery of how sailors, from this loose affiliation of city states surrounding the eastern Mediterranean in pre-Biblical times, somehow reached the southernmost tip of Africa and then completed a circumnavigation of the continent, set me off on an historical quest along the highways and byways of ancient classical history.

The source of this hypothesis, I discovered, was to be found in the writings of the renowned Greek historian, Herodotus. Writing in the 5th century BC – around 150 years after the events described – Herodotus recorded that Phoenician sailors had sailed around the entire continent of Libya (modern-day Africa) in around 600 BC, the first to achieve this extraordinary feat of navigation and seamanship. Interestingly, this was more than 2000 years before the Portuguese explorer, Bartolomeu Dias, became the first recorded European to round the Cape of Good Hope in 1488.

Below is Herodotus' account of the voyage in Aubrey de Sélincourt's celebrated 1954 translation:

> *"The Phoenicians sailed from the Arabian Gulf into the south-*
> *ern ocean, and every autumn put in at some convenient spot on the*
> *Libyan coast, sowed a patch of ground, and waited for next year's*
> *harvest. Then, having got in their grain, they put to sea again, and*
> *after two full years rounded the Pillars of Heracles in the course of*
> *the third, and returned to Egypt. These men made a statement which*
> *I do not myself believe, though others may, to the effect that as they*
> *sailed on a westerly course round the southern end of Libya, they*
> *had the sun on their right - to northward of them. This is how Libya*
> *was first discovered by sea."* [2]

The Phoenicians were funded by the Egyptian pharaoh, Necho II, who was responsible for building the earliest precursor of the Suez Canal. Necho's motivation had in all likelihood nothing to do with exploration for its own sake, but more probably to make a reconnaissance for a surprise attack from the south on his enemies, the Babylonians, who occupied much of modern-day Iraq.

With a monopoly on maritime trade throughout the Mediterranean for many centuries, the Phoenicians needed to be, and were, the most talented sailors and ship-builders of the age, admired for their skills by both the Greeks and the Egyptians. They are recorded by Aratus,[3] a Greek writer on astronomy, as having used both the sun and the stars for navigation, in particular Ursa Minor which contains Polaris, the Pole Star. This enabled them to sail out of sight of land and at night. With favourable winds they could have reached speeds of between three and six knots, covering up to 100 miles in a 24-hour period.

Necho's expedition took three years and finally returned to the Mediterranean through what were known in the ancient world as the 'Pillars of Hercules', but known today more prosaically as the Straits of Gibraltar. As we have seen, and although Herodotus himself doubted the claim which was passed down to him orally, he records that the

2. Herodotus, De Sélincourt, A. and Marincola, J., 2003. *Herodotus the histories.* London: Penguin Books.
3. Aratus and Bekkerus, I., 1828. *Aratus.* Berolini.

sailors stated that they: "had the sun on their right, to northward of them."

Knowing this kind of detail seems extremely unlikely unless it was handed down from an eyewitness account and it was this crucial piece of information which suggested to me that the story was in all likelihood true. Without making the expedition, the Phoenicians would not have known about the position of the sun in the southern hemisphere.

It is similar in kind to the observations of the Greek mariner, Pytheas, who in 330 BC sailed north beyond Orkney to more than 60 degrees north, where he recorded that the summer sun never set at night. Again, this is a detail that is highly unlikely to have been recorded based only on the sketchy scientific knowledge available at the time.

What is recorded however, is that following on from their successful circumnavigation of Africa, the Phoenicians established colonies on the west coast of Africa. The Roman author and naval commander, Pliny the Elder,[4] records that Carthage dispatched Hanno the Navigator with sixty ships, repopulating or founding seven colonies along the coast of Morocco in the process. At the time Carthage (modern Tunis) was one of the most powerful city-states in the Mediterranean, which had itself been founded by the Phoenicians in around 814 BC.

Although there is a consensus among scholars that Hanno reached as far south as Senegal, many of the locations described in his account of the voyage, which was translated into Greek from a tablet Hanno is reported to have placed in the temple of Ba-al Hammon in Carthage, are impossible to locate with any accuracy. One possible reason for this is that these locations were deliberately disguised in their descriptions of geographical features in order to keep them secret from the Greeks, who at that time were the Phoenicians' direct competitors as a trading nation.

Researching the history of the Phoenicians was a fascinating journey, not least because few written records survive. Nonetheless, Greek and Roman accounts, alongside archaeological discoveries in the 20th century, reveal the huge influence they had over the Mediterranean world in classical times. And the more I discovered about the achievements of the Phoenicians, and how little we know about them compared

---

4. Pliny, Rackham, H., Jones, W. and Eichholz, D., 2012. *Pliny natural history*. London: Folio Society.

to the Greeks and the Romans, the more I began to speculate about how much more of the globe they may have reached that has escaped recorded history.

In one way or another, these investigations were to change my life, and led to the genesis of my next expedition: to build a ship as near as possible to an ancient Phoenician design and sail it around Africa to show that the circumnavigation was, at the very least, a practical possibility.

Circumnavigation of Africa Expedition

The story of our epic voyage around Africa between August 2008 and October 2010 is told in my first book, *Sailing Close to the Wind*. I will describe later how our ship, *Phoenicia*, came to be designed and built, but in essence it is as accurate a replica of an ancient Phoenician single-masted, square-sailed sailing ship as it was possible to reconstruct. To achieve this, we employed the traditional skills of contemporary designers and ship-builders living and working in one of the Phoenicians' original city-states, that of the island of Arwad in Syria.

The ship was built using both the wooden materials and pegged mortise and tenon technology of the ancient Phoenicians. Our original intention was not to have an engine, however after reaching the Red Sea it became clear that with a vessel of 50 tons displacement we would have needed an Olympic calibre rowing team to get us into and out of ports. So later in the expedition we reluctantly installed an old truck engine that we came across in a scrap engine warehouse in Port Sudan. On board we also used modern satellite navigation and communications technology. Their use was a necessity both for the safety of my crew and those other ships and boats we would encounter at close quarters, particularly while sailing in and out of harbour. While ancient Phoenician technology did not include the internal combustion engine, neither did they have busy shipping lanes, massive container ships travelling at over 20 knots or high standards of health and safety.

We started the voyage by sailing through the Suez Canal and down the Red Sea to Yemen and on to Salalah in Oman. From here we negotiated the pirate-infested waters of the Indian Ocean, sailing to Mayotte in the Comoro islands and then to Beira, Mozambique, before sailing around the coast of South Africa and the Cape of Good Hope to Cape Town.

On the return leg, we crossed the South Atlantic visiting Saint Helena, Ascension Island, and Flores in the Azores before returning once more to the eastern shores of the Mediterranean where we arrived back in Syria to a hero's welcome in October 2010. In all we had completed more than 20,000 nautical miles in 26 months and, most significantly for my next expedition, the Ascension to Azores leg alone was twice as far as a transatlantic voyage. At one point we even came within 6400 miles of the Americas.

After the euphoria of our circumnavigation of Africa began to fade, I still found myself fascinated by the question of whether the Phoenicians had actually reached America. Among many other observations about the realities of being aboard a sailing ship of ancient design and construction, it had become increasingly obvious to us that even if they had not set out with the intention of sailing further west on a voyage of discovery, the Phoenicians could very easily have made landfall in the Americas simply by accident. Atlantic storms, the trade winds, and the currents may be familiar to us, but they could so easily have taken the ancients by surprise.

As we shall see, it is also highly probable that they had settlements in the Canary Islands, 600 miles off the coast of Morocco, and possibly in the Azores, 900 miles off the coast of Portugal. But before we consider the evidence for a Phoenician crossing of the Atlantic in the first millennia BC, I should first give a short account of the history and achievements of this extraordinary, and far too often overlooked, race of seafarers, traders and explorers.

Who were the Phoenicians?

The general assumption of the origins of the Phoenicians is that they did not suddenly arrive from anywhere and were, in fact, the very same biblical Canaanites who inhabited the Eastern Mediterranean in ancient times. With limited agricultural resources, they turned their attention to the sea for fishing and trade, and so became pre-eminent in all aspects of maritime trade and culture.

Surrounded to the east by mountains, and to the west by the sea, their homeland centred around this coastal strip which included modern-day Lebanon and parts of Syria and Israel/Palestine. They cannot be described as a nation in the modern sense, but were more a collection of city-states with a shared language and culture. These city-states included Aradus (Arwad), Byblos, Tyre, Sidon and Beirut. Of these, Tyre – built on an off-shore promontory – became the most powerful, followed by Sidon and Byblos.

A common interest in maritime trade united these disparate city states, whose economies were unable to depend on the limited land-based resources available in the narrow coastal strip along which their ancestors first settled. Their accomplishments and influence on the classical world, most notably the Greeks and the Romans, were made possible by their later achievement in becoming the dominant maritime traders in the classical world.

As their prosperity grew, the Phoenicians soon attracted the attention of the powerful Egyptian empire who coveted their forests of cedar wood – a building material conspicuously absent from the deserts of north Africa – and access to Mesopotamia, an important trading partner, to the east. But instead of subjecting them to the position of vassal states, they were given favoured status and allowed to prosper independently, competing more with each other than their powerful neighbours.

Between 1200 and 900 BC, during the historical period known as the Late Bronze Age Collapse, the Eastern Mediterranean and the surrounding regions came under attack from the infamous Sea Peoples whose origins are not fully understood.[5] This was accompanied by a decline in agricultural productivity due to climatic conditions. However, after a period of retrenchment, the Phoenician city-states bounced back to take advantage of the power vacuum created by the weakening of the neighbouring civilisations of the Egyptians to the west and the Hittites to the north.

The Phoenicians re-established contacts with nearby Cyprus and then expanded west to Rhodes, Crete and Sicily before establishing colonies, including Utica in Tunisia which acted as a stepping-stone to Gadir (Cadiz) in the western Mediterranean and Lixus on the Atlantic coast of Morocco.

5. Cline, Eric H., 2021. 1177 B.C: *The Year Civilization Collapsed*. Princeton: Princeton University Press.

This period in their history has been described as the 'Phoenician Renaissance.' This was the era when the Phoenicians created colonies all across the Mediterranean as far as the Iberian Peninsula and the coast of North Africa, building harbours and warehouses and creating settlements wherever they went. It was now that Tyre became the dominant city-state during the reign of Hiram I (c. 980 to 947 BC) and the Phoenicians established themselves as the dominant seafarers and traders in the ancient world.

In doing so they built ports with trading facilities all across the Mediterranean and beyond, reaching as far as Morocco on the west coast of Africa. These included the largest islands in the Mediterranean including modern-day Cyprus, Sardinia, Corsica and the Balearic Islands. The colony of Carthage (modern-day Tunis), founded in the 9th century BC, later superseded the earlier city states as one of the most dominant powerhouses in the region. The founding of Carthage, as told by Roman historians, is traditionally credited to Dido, Queen of Tyre, the tragic heroine of Virgil's epic poem the *Aeneid*.

The Carthaginians are today much better known than their earlier Phoenician predecessors, and Carthage itself later became the capital of its own Punic Empire. Punic, the Latin version of the Greek word Phoenician, included the people of Carthage and Western Phoenicia as well as its colonies in the islands of the Mediterranean (Sicily, Sardinia, and Malta among them) and the north coast of Africa.

It was the Carthaginians who extended the influence of the Phoenicians still further west. In the 5th century BC, Hanno the Navigator explored the coastal areas of Africa beyond the Pillars of Hercules to present-day Morocco, establishing settlements all along the Atlantic coast of West Africa, most notably at Mogador (modern-day Essaouira).

As they steadily built their reputation as master seafarers and traders, they created what can accurately be called the first navy in history. While never establishing an empire in the Roman sense with vast areas of conquered territory, they certainly prospered and undertook many voyages of exploration in their drive to establish trading links beyond the Pillars of Hercules, some of which may have extended all the way across the Atlantic.

Their exports included building materials like the legendary Cedars of Lebanon, which were famously used in the construction of Solomon's temple in Jerusalem and which, according to the Bible, was also built by Phoenician craftsmen. They also imported materials such as linen, cotton, wool and silk in order to create fabrics (clothes, embroideries and carpets) which they would then, in turn, export. Metals were also acquired including copper (Cyprus), silver, iron, and brass (Spain), tin (Cornwall, UK) and gold (Ethiopia). The Phoenicians also developed technology for producing both transparent and coloured glass products which they exported all over the Mediterranean – everything from drinking glasses to vases and perfume bottles.

But the product with which the Phoenicians are most famously associated is the purple dye, known as Tyrian Purple, which was produced from the secretion glands of a species of sea snail known as the murex. This dye was first produced as early as 1500 BC and became associated with them so strongly that the Greeks started to call their trading partners 'phoinix' (meaning red-purple) and from which we subsequently inherited the word Phoenician. However the Phoenicians themselves did not immediately adopt their new title, but went by the names of their respective city states, such as Tyronians (Tyre) or Sidonians (Sidon).

Over the centuries the dye became a source of enormous wealth and is estimated by modern experts to have been worth ten to fifteen times its weight in gold. The complicated techniques for making the purple dye were one of antiquity's best-kept secrets because it was a source of so much wealth. Understandably, the Phoenicians jealously guarded their recipe and its production processes, full access to these secrets being kept to a very small circle of skilled dyers who were sworn not to reveal their knowledge.

Over the centuries they improved their techniques, and the deep red-purple colour they produced became an integral symbol of Phoenician culture and identity. It was a greatly sought after commodity, and even today the Phoenicians are always associated with the colour purple. Remains from the production of the dye, in the form of discarded murex shells, continue to be found, the most notable being a mound discovered by archaeologists in Ibiza approximately 105 metres long and 30 metres wide.[6]

6. Allanah MacDonald, 2017. Master's Thesis for Marine Archaeology.

There was a huge market for fabric dyes in the ancient world, and because this purple pigment was complicated and difficult to produce, involving tens of thousands of snails, only the rich were able to afford it. It was also resistant to fading and appeared brighter in strong sunlight. Its association with wealth and power became so established that a thousand years later, during the Roman Empire, Tyrian purple was only permitted to be worn by the emperor himself. During the reign of the tyrant, Caligula, it is recorded that the emperor had the King of the Moors killed for daring to wear a purple cloak while attending a gladiator fight.

To this day among religious hierarchies, most notably in the Catholic Church, purple denotes spiritual purity, while purple as a symbol of royalty is a tradition displayed in the gowns and crowns worn by the British royal family on state occasions.

Despite their relative obscurity in the collective memory, the legacy of the Phoenicians remains with us in other ways. Were it not for them the words you are reading now would look and sound very different. As the written Phoenician language developed over time, it moved from being a purely pictographic script to the phonetic one we have inherited today. The alphabet they created spread around the known world and later formed the basis of both the Greek and Latin alphabets. It is from the latter that we have derived our own alphabet, the most widely used in the modern world.

Although the Carthaginian republic was one of the most long-standing and wide-spread civilisations of the ancient world, its existence as a purely Phoenician entity came to an end at the conclusion of the Third Punic War against Rome in 146 BC, when Carthage itself was razed to the ground. The Romans later rebuilt it and the surviving Carthaginians, living in the surrounding cities, were integrated into the Roman Empire and Carthage once again prospered and became an important trading city. The last remains of a specifically Punic culture, however, came to an end with the fall of the Roman Empire in the 5th century AD.

Pre-Columbian Transatlantic Crossings

It is thought that the first discoverers of America were Palaeolithic hunter-gatherers from what is now Asia, who crossed what we know today as the Bering Strait at least 20,000, and maybe as much as 33,000 years ago. Claims have also been made that the Irish and the Chinese reached America centuries before Columbus, while archaeological proof has now been found which shows that the Vikings settled on the American mainland in 1021 AD.[7]

So, what is the current evidence for pre-Columbian transatlantic crossings? Although the evidence for Irish and Chinese crossings falls below the standards needed for scientific proof, there is now very substantial archaeological proof that the Vikings reached North America. Thirteenth century Icelandic sagas record tales from Viking history of the voyages of Leif Erikson who is said to have discovered a brave new world in the west called 'Vinland the Good.'

Much to the surprise of many who believed these stories referred to the discovery of Iceland and Greenland, archaeological proof that the Vikings reached North America hundreds of years before Columbus was discovered in the 1960s. The Norwegian explorer, Helge Ingstad, and his wife, archaeologist Anne Stine Ingstad, excavated the remains of eight turf longhouses at L'Anse aux Meadows in the far north of Newfoundland.

At the time, some were sceptical of the findings because longhouses were also built by the local Inuit. However conclusive proof was to follow, with the discovery of a Scandinavian bronze ring pin and many other metal objects, along with evidence that weaving also took place at the site. Radiocarbon from organic matter was also dated between 980 and 1020 AD, which tallies with the dates of known Viking expeditions.

Further proof of Norse settlements in North America was discovered in 2015 when satellite imagery revealed irregularities in the soil at Point Rosee, 400 miles south-west of the earlier site. The on-site dig that followed revealed a hearth for roasting iron ore and a turf wall of the kind built by Viking settlers all across the North Atlantic.

7. Nature October 2021 https://www.nature.com/articles/s41586-021-03972-8
8. Jett, S. C. (2017). *Ancient ocean crossings: reconsidering the case for contacts with the pre-Columbian Americas.* The University of Alabama Press.

Crossings in the ancient world

In 2017, Stephen C Jett, Professor Emeritus of Geography at the University of California, published *Ancient Ocean Crossings*.[8] In this ground-breaking book, he lamented the hostile intellectual climate for the theory that both the Atlantic and Pacific oceans had been crossed, perhaps many times, before the first documented crossings by Christopher Columbus (1492) and Ferdinand Magellan (1521) respectively.

Jett likened this hostility to the ridicule poured on the theory of Continental Drift, which has since been proved through the process of plate tectonics. Despite the existence of considerable circumstantial evidence – including the fact that the continents of Africa and South America looked as if they would fit together like the pieces of a jigsaw puzzle, with identical rock strata, fossils and plant distribution – there was initially no theory as to how this could have happened. The prevailing view, therefore, among the academic elite was that it was impossible, and ridicule was the price for stating otherwise.

Jett sums this up as a "classic demonstration of the dictum that all truth passes through three stages: initial ridicule, subsequent violent opposition, and ultimate acceptance as self-evident fact." Although in the case of pre-Columbian crossings of the Atlantic we are still at Stage Two, the weight of evidence is continuing to build.

The arguments against this possibility include the false assertion that people believed the world was flat until Columbus' time and that they might sail over the edge. In addition, before the 16th century sailors did not have the capability to build ocean-going vessels or have sufficiently sophisticated navigation techniques. The latter I had disproved, certainly to my own satisfaction, during my circumnavigation of Africa. Indeed, summarising my first expedition aboard the *Phoenicia*, Jett concluded that: "clearly a ship of this kind could have traversed the entire Atlantic with ease."

The evidence of European civilisations reaching the Americas in the classical period is by no means conclusive, but there is much to suggest that it did in fact take place. Based on incompletely researched conclusions concerning both physical geography and human capabilities, many scholars simply accepted that pre-Columbian, pre-Norse transatlantic voyages were impossible and thus never investigated further.

One of the first things that sceptics ask for is archaeological evidence of human contact. Why is there no evidence of Old World objects in New World sites? Given that the vast majority of materials that might have been carried across the oceans would have been perishable – from the wood of the ships, to foodstuffs and even the bones of the crew – stone objects and ceramics are the most likely objects to have survived.

The archaeological remains of historically documented post-Columbian transatlantic journeys are themselves very scarce, so it is hardly surprising that the evidence for voyages that took place nearly 2000 years earlier should also be hard to find. The other factor is the likelihood that early voyagers would have been unwilling to carry many unnecessary objects, as space aboard ship would have been at a premium, with food and water supplies given priority. However, as Jett reports, some artefacts have in fact been reported but often by people who are not archaeologists and whose discoveries do not therefore count as real evidence.

Other arguments dismantled by Jett include the idea that nautical technology of ancient civilisations in the form of ship-building skills and navigational techniques were by no means sufficiently advanced to survive such voyages. I, and others before me, have now surely done enough to demolish such prejudice.

Significantly, recent biological studies do strongly suggest that Old World pathogens and plants crossed the oceans millennia ago. The former include microbial diseases and intestinal parasites and worms that were widespread in the Americas before Columbus, and can only have been introduced by pre-Columbian explorers.

As Jett writes: "A species of headlouse was also shared. Cultivated plants and domesticated animals including chickens have also been found which would not have been possible without human interaction. The sharing of so many species implies that pre-1492 trans-oceanic contacts were intensive. Geographic patterns of DNA also appear explicable only in terms of early New World introduction by voyagers from the Old World."

Jett concludes that this calls: "for a major rewriting of traditional history".

Did the Phoenicians discover America?

As we have seen, the success of the Phoenicians was in no small part due to their skills as mariners and their knowledge of the prevailing winds and currents. Significantly, as we turn to the key issue of how far the Phoenicians sailed into the Atlantic or whether, indeed, they actually succeeded in reaching the other side, there is the fact, surprising to some, that the Atlantic is actually much easier to sail than the Mediterranean.

The latter, being land-locked and dotted with thousands of islands both large and small, has many challenging currents, especially close to land. These vary considerably from season to season and year to year. Widely differing landforms on its hugely varied coastlines also make its winds notoriously fickle. Storms can run a ship aground, fog can hide rocky outcrops, and unpredictable winds can easily blow a ship ashore. Its shallow seas, with an average depth of around 5000ft, are also full of invisible geoforms that create unexpected swells and currents.

Any serious sailor who is familiar with both will agree that the currents and winds in the Atlantic are actually much more consistent and predictable, except of course during the hurricane season between August and October. Importantly, the Phoenicians regularly sailed the length and breadth of the Mediterranean, voyages that would have been longer and more dangerous than sailing from the Canaries to the Americas.

As we have seen, they also circumnavigated Africa in around 600 BC, a coastline that I know from experience is full of hidden hazards, from treacherous currents to unpredictable winds that can suddenly run a ship aground. However counter-intuitive it may seem to non-sailors, hugging the coast in an ancient square-rigged vessel while sailing around Africa could have been a recipe for disaster.

Why struggle against the elements when following the prevailing winds and currents five to ten miles offshore would have been the easier option?

One of the key questions in the search for a solution to the *Phoenicians Before Columbus* riddle, therefore, is how far west into the Atlantic the Phoenicians can be proved to have reached? This question focuses on the Canary Islands, located 600 miles west of Morocco on the west coast of Africa, and the Azores, 950 miles west of Portugal on the European mainland.

The Canary Islands

The evidence for the Phoenicians having reached the Canary Islands is strong, although it is disputed whether they are the originating ancestors of modern Canarians who were more likely to have been North African Berbers. Pliny the Elder records that Hanno is likely to have visited the islands during his voyage around the west coast of Africa in the 5th century BC and, like both the Greeks and the Romans at a later date, it is probable that both the Phoenicians and later the Carthaginians traded with the islands.

The Canaries were also a source of the murex sea snails from which the Phoenicians made their trademark purple dye and which helped give them a monopoly on trade around the Mediterranean for many centuries. In 2009, a possible Phoenician warehouse and pottery were found at Teguise on the island of Lanzarote in the Canaries by Pablo Atoche, Professor of Archaeology at the University of Las Palmas, Gran Canaria.

Previously it was thought that the Romans were the first to reach the Canaries in the 1st century AD, but Professor Atoche's discoveries put this date back by up to a thousand years to the 10th century BC. His finds included a structure of about 100 square metres with the remains of ceramics, personal adornments and a stone stela with engravings. Atoche believes that: "the construction could be a warehouse where different elements would be deposited for export."

The remains seem to suggest that the settlers were ranchers and farmers, while the bones of the goats, pigs and sheep also discovered could have been used to produce items for export such as hides and meat. Elsewhere in the Canaries, a small cave in Icod de los Vinos, in Tenerife, where remains of human activity have been found, also dates from the same century.

Other accounts of voyages to islands that may well be part of the Canaries archipelago have also been handed down. In the 4th century BC, the famous Greek philosopher, Aristotle, records that the Carthaginians sailed for four days beyond the Straits of Gibraltar: "they say that an island was discovered by the Carthaginians ... having wood of every kind, and navigable rivers, and admirable for the fruits besides."

The Azores

Finding proof that the ancient Phoenicians reached the Azores was a more difficult proposition entirely. Then in 2012 I learned of a fascinating research project which appeared to shed further light on this issue. On the islands of Corvo and Terceira, three members of the Portuguese Association for Archaeological Investigation discovered extensive evidence of what they strongly believed were the remains of 4th century BC Carthaginian underground temples. They described their findings to me as irrefutable evidence of the existence of a pre-Christian occupation of the Azores.

This gave credence to the previously dismissed evidence of Damien de Goes, a Portuguese who in 1567 recorded a story that he claimed to have heard from the Portuguese explorers who first reached the Azores. When they arrived on Corvo they were said to have found a statue of a man seated on a horse, on a rock towering above them. His right arm was extended, and one finger was pointing west to the ocean beyond. On the base of the statue was an inscription, almost worn away, in a language they did not understand.

The image was sketched and taken to King Manuel in Lisbon who, on seeing it, sent an emissary to the island to remove the carving and bring it to Portugal. However, by the time the king's man arrived, he found that it had been destroyed by a winter storm. The remaining fragments were duly presented to the king who kept them in his wardrobe. From where the trail – sadly, but perhaps rather predictably when it comes to royal closets – goes cold!

Father Gaspar Frutuoso, a native of the Azores, also records the monument in a document dated 1590. Local inhabitants he spoke to describe the:

> "...*figure of a large man of stone, standing on a slab or support, and in the stone were sculpted some letters, and some people say that his hand was pointing... as if indicating the great coast of America with two extended fingers... In their opinion the builders were Carthaginians, as they travelled these parts... and returning from the Antilles, they would have left this stone monument with the letters as marks and signs of what they had discovered back there."* [9]

9. Gaspar Frutuoso (c.1522-1591) was a Portuguese priest, historian and humanist from the island of São Miguel, in the Azores. He published six volumes (Saudades da Terra) of descriptions of the history and geography of the Azores, Madeira, Canary Islands.

It wasn't until two hundred years later that a clay pot emerged from the ruins of a stone building, also on Corvo. Inside were a large number of gold and copper coins. What made these coins interesting was their origin and date. Two were from Cyrene, an ancient Greek colony in what is modern day Libya, and seven others, two gold and five copper, were Punic coins. From the features on the coins, every one of them was dated to the 4th century BC.

Had these coins been left by the Phoenicians, or another ancient civilisation, nearly 2000 years before the Portuguese arrived? If ancient seafarers had got this far, how much further had they already gone? Due to the prevailing westerly winds at this latitude, the Phoenicians would probably have had to circumnavigate a large part of the Atlantic before reaching the Azores, thus making their discovery of the Americas that much more likely. Was this the reason the stone horseman was pointing west into the Atlantic towards the New World?

Given that the Phoenicians were expert seafarers, and had visited and traded with the Canary Islands from their colonies along the Atlantic coast of North Africa, the available evidence would seem to suggest that they were the most likely to have discovered the Azores. If correct, it would confirm my theory that the Phoenicians used the islands as a staging post when returning to the Mediterranean from their African colonies.

While there is no firm documentary evidence, Diodorus of Sicily, the 1st century BC Greek historian, records that the Phoenicians, after being caught in a storm, made landfall on a 'vast island' many days west of Africa with navigable rivers and inhabited by people living in well-built homes and irrigated groves: "after being storm-tossed for many days they were carried ashore on the island... and when they observed its felicity and nature they caused it to be known to all men."

It would also explain how the Phoenicians could have circumnavigated Africa from east to west while avoiding the treacherous currents and winds that are so dangerous near to the coast. The debate that still rages is how far the Phoenicians reached in their attempts to establish new trading routes and whether they crossed the Atlantic to the Americas either by intention or accident.

As we have seen, there is substantial evidence that they reached the Canary Islands and probably the Azores. But what is the current evidence that they reached the mainland of the Americas, either north or south, or some of its outlying islands, as Christopher Columbus did at the end of the 15th century?

There is no evidence at the current time that the Phoenicians, or their descendants the Carthaginians, left behind any permanent settlements or colonies. But this in no way negates the possibility that they reached the Americas by accident, after being caught in a storm or the wind-driven Canary current that flows south-west along the west of Africa and then joins the North Equatorial current which sweeps west towards America.

Sadly, a vast library of Phoenician documentary evidence was comprehensively destroyed when Carthage was sacked by the Romans at the end of the Third Punic War in 146 BC. The nearest we get to documentary evidence is in the writings of Diodorus of Sicily who, in the first century BC, wrote in his encyclopaedic 40-volume work of world history, the *Bibliotheca Historica*:

> "...in the deep off Africa is an island of considerable size... fruitful, much of it mountainous... Through it flow navigable rivers... The Phoenicians had discovered it by accident after having planted many colonies throughout Africa." [10]

The ship, he records, was one of ten that had originally sailed from the Gulf of Aqaba to the west coast of Africa where they became separated by a violent storm:

> "...after they had lain under this violent tempest for many days, they at length arrived at this island, and so they were the first that discovered it..." [11]

Although some commentators have suggested that the island was part of the Azores, the Canaries, or even Madeira, this is unlikely. All of these islands are located many hundreds of miles further north in the Atlantic from where the currents and winds would have taken them out

10. Bekker, Immanuel, et al.1888 *Diodorus Bibliotheca Historica*. B.G. Teubner.
11. Ibid.

to sea. Also, the Canaries and Madeira, being the most southerly, are the most likely candidates but do not have any navigable rivers.

Brazil, South America

Many theories have been put forward suggesting that the Phoenicians reached Brazil. Its distance from the west coast of Africa where the Phoenicians are known to have had settlements is only about 1600 miles, the closest point between the two continents. The evidence is frustratingly fragmentary, however, and lacking in the physical evidence that excites archaeologists and is critical to scientific proof.

These theories have been through a number of incarnations and researchers have pointed out that pre-Columbian civilisations like the Mayan built flat-topped pyramids that are very similar to Mesopotamian ziggurats and that their representations of high-status individuals were very similar to those of Phoenician figures with their beards and prominent noses.

Parallels have also been drawn between measurement systems used by the Mayans, the ancient Israelites and ancient Egyptians, which researchers believe could only have reached South America on a Phoenician ship. Claims of the discovery of the remains of Phoenician shipyards were made by the archaeologist Raimundo Lopez in the 1920s around the edge of Lake Pensiva in north-eastern Brazil. These were reported to have contained the surviving remains of petrified wood, nails and dowels along with traditional Phoenician tools.

Ludwig Schwennhagen, an Austrian professor, also excavated the banks of Extremoz Lake in Rio Grande do Norte state. Schwennhagen believes that the Phoenicians used Brazil as a base over an 800-year period leaving behind, as well as physical evidence, important linguistic clues among the languages of the modern-day inhabitants.

The most famous discovery in the history of the 'Phoenicians in Brazil' theory, however, was the discovery in 1872 of an inscription on a stone tablet in Paraiba state. It was discovered by a slave on a plantation and the son of the plantation owner sent a copy of the inscription to the National Museum of Brazil in Rio de Janeiro. Inconsistencies in the lettering and the word usage led it to be dismissed as a forgery, a decision that was further supported by the failure of the tablet to materialise.

In 1968, however, the story surfaced again when a copy of the inscription was found in a letter that had been sent to Wilberforce Eames, head of the New York Public Library during the late 19th century. It had been sent to him by Ladislau Netto, Director of the National Museum in Rio de Janeiro, who had made the original translation of the inscription found on the tablet.

Another translation was made by Cyrus H. Gordon of Brandeis University in Boston which revived the theory and revealed similarities to the original account of Diodorus and refers to the Egyptian pharaoh, Necho II, who commissioned the expedition around the continent of Africa recorded by Herodotus.

However, according to Frank Moore Cross, Professor of Hebrew and Oriental Languages at Harvard, the inscription is a forgery, a conclusion he reached while noting that the grammar is a mixture of Hebrew and Phoenician: "Everything in the inscription was available to the forger in nineteenth century handbooks or from uninspired guesses based on these easily available sources... knowledge of the ancient language was largely derived from biblical studies."

Theories and studies in support of an ancient Phoenician contact with South America are still ongoing. A contemporary researcher, Austin Whittall, records on his website that engraved stones in Patagonia are unlike ancient indigenous carvings and that the symbols appear to be of Phoenician or Hebrew origin. Some also show snakes, which he believes may have a Phoenician origin. Whittall, an acknowledged expert on Patagonia's geography and history, also believes the Paraiba inscription may well be genuine.

North America

Evidence for Phoenician contact with North America was put forward in the 18th and 19th centuries and again in 1913 by Thomas Crawford Johnston[12] and in 1941 by Philip Beistline, a schoolteacher from Pennsylvania. While looking for indigenous Indian artefacts, of which he was a keen collector, Beistline found a stone inscribed with what his friend, Dr William Strong of Johns Hopkins University,

---

12. Johnston, Thomas Crawford 1913. *Did the Phoenicians discover America?* James Nisbet & Co, London.

described as a cuneiform inscription. Taking up the search, Strong found many more stones engraved with an alphabet which he at first thought was Greek. After studying them in detail, however, he later concluded they were Phoenician, after consulting Dr George Radom, an expert in Middle Eastern languages.

Strong eventually found more than 400 similar stones with markings, close to creeks that flow into the Susquehanna River. His theory was that the stones were used to spell out words and that they also used letters as numbers which as traders they would have needed to do on a regular basis.

More convincing, were the findings in 1996 of the geologist and palaeontologist, Mark McMenamin of Mount Holyoke College, Massachusetts. McMenamin believed he had found evidence that suggested a Carthaginian presence in North America in the form of gold coins minted in Carthage between 350-320 BC. The symbols at the bottom of some of the coins were first interpreted as a Phoenician script, but after studying computer-enhanced images of the symbols, McMenamin came to a different conclusion:

"The evidence consists of a particular group of early Carthaginian gold coins (called staters) that bear a map (derived from modified Punic letters) showing both the Old World and the New World. Going from east to west, the maps show India, the south coast of Europe above Sardinia and Sicily, and America. The Phoenicians, and especially the Carthaginians, were known throughout the ancient world for their prowess as navigators and seamen. The intriguing possibility exists that the landmass portrayed to the west of Spain represents an area of the Americas, perhaps Brazil. If so, these coins could provide direct and well-dated evidence that Carthaginians had made contact with the New World."[13]

Reflecting on his theories, McMenamin says: "I was just the lucky person who had the geologic and geographic expertise to view these coins in a new light. I have been interested in the Carthaginians as the greatest explorers in the history of the world." Although originally believing that the so-called 'Farley Coins' that were found at a number

---

13. McMenamin, M. A. 1999. *The Carthaginians Were Here: Evidence for an Early Crossing of the Atlantic*. Volume 1. South Hadley, Massachusetts.

of sites in North America might also be evidence of the Carthaginians having reached America, McMenamin later published evidence that those coins were indeed fakes.

Nevertheless, in recent correspondence with me, McMenamin confirmed that he still holds to his thesis that the gold staters (not related to the Farley Coins mentioned above) showing an image of the old and new world are genuine and indicate that the Carthaginians knew of the New World in the period between 320 and 350 BC He wrote that his theory "represents the best explanation based on the available facts."[14] In conclusion, it is true that hard scientific proof that the Phoenicians reached the Americas is still elusive, but in my view the balance of probability is that they almost certainly did cross the Atlantic at least once, either by accident or design, and probably many times. Whether to South or North America, or both, is open to debate. The fact that hard archaeological evidence has not yet been discovered is, to my mind, certainly not proof that they didn't.

As with all theories where proof has yet to be scientifically demonstrated, the sceptics have to be right all the time, the believers only once.

---

14. Personal correspondence with the author 24 July 2021.

Genesis of an Expedition

Sometimes words slip out of your mouth that tell you things about yourself that you have not yet consciously taken on board. And this is exactly what happened to me during an interview with CNN during an exhibition of our Circumnavigation of Africa expedition at St Katherine Dock in London in 2013, when our ship, *Phoenicia*, was opened for the public to explore.

I was asked what I was planning next, so I started to talk about why I had always believed that the Phoenicians had reached America, while outlining the details in the previous chapter. I explained that the only reason I had been able to successfully circumnavigate Africa was because we had sailed out a significant way into the Atlantic. We wouldn't have been able to hug the West African coast because the currents and the wind from the east push you out into the Atlantic anyway.

When the Portuguese, under Prince Henry the Navigator,[15] first arrived in the Azores in the 15th century, they were returning from Nigeria but couldn't sail close to the coast and ended up in the Azores for this very reason. As we have seen, there is some evidence that the Phoenicians had landed in the Azores 2000 years earlier and quite possibly after reaching the Americas.

My interviewer asked: "So you're going to do the trip?" and I found myself replying: "Yes, I'm going to do it." It was only then that I realised I had committed myself. I thought: "Actually I can't not go now. It's OK to delay, but I've got to do something." So I was mentally on the hook. The article appeared the next week and that was it. I thought: "Well, I've got to do it now." And that was where it all started.

---

15. Russell, P. E., and Peter Russell. 2001. *Prince Henry "the Navigator": A Life* (New Haven, CT: Yale University Press).

Building *Phoenicia* – Reconstructing a 2000 year-old ship

Our ship, *Phoenicia*, as I have explained, was originally built in 2007/8 for my expedition around the African continent. It was a massive undertaking. To make the expedition a true re-enactment of a Phoenician voyage, I realised I would have to build a ship as near as was possible to the design of those ancient ships. The journey, from the genesis of the idea to setting sail on the voyage, took three years. This involved a lengthy research and design process, as well as finding craftsmen with the relevant skills for such an ambitious project, combined with the actual construction of the ship. It was a journey that would have been completely impossible without the support of so many others.

Happily I was ably and enthusiastically assisted by Alice Chutter, an arts graduate I had employed to help with the workload. First, we needed to find people who knew about ancient ship construction. After that, I had to find craftsmen who were capable of using these ancient methods to construct as near as possible a fully functional copy of a ship design that had not been built for nearly 2000 years.

For a start, apart from images on a few ancient coins, Greek vases and the odd stone reliefs, there were very few pictorial clues as to what a Phoenician ship actually looked like. More helpful were the wrecks that had recently been discovered, one of which was the Uluburun wreck discovered off the coast of Turkey in 1982 which is thought to have sunk around 1300 BC.

This wreck is the largest ancient cargo vessel ever discovered. Its contents included copper, tin, glass, ceramics, jewellery, ivory, a golden scarab with the name of Queen Nefertiti etched on it, a golden cup, glass, perfume and even hippopotamus teeth. In truth, a magic window onto the valuable trading commodities of a forgotten world. The ship was from a much earlier era than the ship we were hoping to recreate, but it revealed how the mortise and tenon joints were constructed in the earliest known example of such construction, how the planks were butted together, and how the joints and seams had been sealed with pitch or pine tar to prevent water seepage.

A second wreck – the *Ma'agan Michael* discovered off the coast of Haifa in Israel and dating to around 500 BC – used the 'mixed construction' techniques most likely to have been employed by contemporary Phoenician shipbuilders. This revealed that the pine planks of the hull were joined with mortise and tenon joints, while the planks of the stern and stem posts were sewn together by cord and rope.

Finally another wreck, the *Jules Verne 7*, a Phoenician or Agean merchant galley dating from the 5th or 6th century discovered off the coast of Marseilles, proved the perfect match we were looking for. Finally, with the help of research from this wreck carried out by Professor Patrice Pomey from Aix-Marseille University, we were able to embark on our design.

In the end, the design for the *Phoenicia* was produced by two Greeks, Harry Tzalas, one of the foremost authorities on Mediterranean maritime archaeology with a formidable track record in the reconstruction of ancient sailing vessels, and his colleague, Kostas Damianides, who had a background in Mediterranean boat design and was an advisor to various Greek museums. My colleague Nick Burningham from Australia, who had designed the Borobudur ship "Samudra Raksa," reviewed the designs and suggested a few alterations which were made to the final design.

Phoenician ships were constructed using pegged mortise and tenon joints, a method of construction which spread throughout the region and became standard practice for the next thousand years. This allowed them to build ships which were larger, more robust, and could travel further, while carrying more provisions and trading goods than had ever been achieved before. They also invented the keel, a revolutionary advancement in shipbuilding over the primitive dug-out vessels which preceded them.

It was decided that the keel would be carved from Aleppo pine, the planking from Mediterranean pine, and the ribs from oak and walnut. In addition 8000 olive-wood pegs needed to be hand-made and used to join the planks together. In all, the construction materials included Aleppo pine, Mediterranean oak, Mediterranean pine, cypress fir, walnut, olive and iron nails.

While some were very supportive, many experts believed I was mad. The latter included the late Lionel Casson, the eminent classicist and Professor Emeritus at New York University, who had written many books on ancient maritime history. In a reply to my letter to him enclosing detailed plans of the ship I was hoping to build, he told me

I was "undertaking a misdirected project" and suggested my team and I would be better off reconstructing a Portuguese caravel to recreate Bartolomeu Dias' voyage around Africa in the 15th century.

Despite his credentials, I refused to take his advice. Besides, it is historical fact that the Portuguese sailed around Africa, whereas I wanted to prove that it was at least a practical possibility that the ancient Phoenicians had achieved this remarkable feat nearly 2000 years before.

After visiting shipyards in Greece, Lebanon, and Syria – both the latter being at the heart of ancient Phoenician territory – we eventually found a boat-builder on the island of Arwad, off Tartous in Syria, which was once home to a six-hundred strong fleet of ancient Phoenician ships. Here we discovered Kahid Hammoud whose family had been building boats in Arwad for generations.

After many frustrating setbacks, the keel was laid in November, 2007, and the Phoenicia was finally launched in July, 2008. Weighing 50 tons, she measured 20 metres with a beam of 5.8 metres and a draft of 1.5 metres. The height of the mast was 15 metres from the keel. The mast was made from Syria's tallest tree, at least that's what they told me. It was certainly the tallest they could find! The yard that held our sail was some 14 metres long and made of two large pieces of cypress fir joined together at the centre. During this period I had also managed to attract a multi-national, multi-cultural, crew of volunteers who were prepared to take on both me and the ship, as well as the mad expedition I had proposed.

After several weeks of final arrangements and sea trials, we officially set sail on 11th August from Arwad's main jetty in the presence of the First Lady of Syria. This was nearly three years before the start of the devastating Civil War and the event was attended by a huge crowd of invited guests and islanders as film crews and photographers looked on. In fact it wasn't until August 23rd, after more sea trials and last-minute adjustments to the ship, that the circumnavigation of Africa expedition finally began.

Phoenicians Before Columbus Expedition

As often happens with the idea for an expedition of this magnitude, my initial impromptu decision in that life-changing CNN interview was followed by a period of frustration and false starts. Unless you're a billionaire, a modern expedition of the kind I was attempting needs major sponsorship and, initially, there were some hopeful leads.

The first was a curator from the Metropolitan Museum in New York who came aboard *Phoenicia* and spoke to me during the exhibition at St Katharine Docks. She seemed very excited by the idea and invited me to America to give a talk, which I duly delivered. Sadly, this never turned into the financial support we so badly needed to mount an expedition of this size.

The closest we came to a major sponsorship deal was with a French organisation. Unfortunately, I wasn't informed about a crucial meeting when the CEO asked the killer question, "What do we do if the ship sinks?" The question rather floored our spokesman in the company who, without us being there to support him and answer the difficult questions, couldn't come up with a reassuring answer. The CEO was worried that the boat might sink and the potential risk to their brand identity, so the deal fell through. On the other hand, it's hard to know, even with hindsight, whether I could have convinced him that the boat wasn't going to sink!

We did have some successes, of course. Naturally we were talking to organisations in countries who have an interest in showing that Columbus wasn't necessarily the first person to arrive in America. The Lebanon, for example, is a country where the ancient city states of Tyre and Sidon were located, and their culture and people are descended directly from the Phoenicians.

We held a fundraising event in New York, where a Lebanese American invited an audience of private individuals interested in ancient cultures, who kindly donated to the cause. This was very encouraging. We also attended another function in Washington D.C. in 2015 and gave a couple of presentations in Beirut to the American Lebanese University, as well as the Ministry of Information and the Ministry of Tourism.

We actually signed some agreements with the Ministry of Information and Ministry of Tourism in Lebanon but, although they were a morale boost at the time, these turned out not to be worth the paper they were written on. Perhaps, given what has happened since in the afflicted city of Beirut, I should not have been surprised.

I also flew out to talk to a group of 800 Mormons in Salt Lake City. Their founding beliefs are based on the idea that the original Native

Americans, from whom many Mormons are descended, were Lamanites whose ancestor, Lehi, reached America by sea from Jerusalem in about 600 BC. The Book of Mormon includes a chronicle of these events. My expedition had no religious sub-text itself, but I could understand why any evidence that supported the possibility of trans-Atlantic contact from the Mediterranean two thousand years before Columbus would be of interest to them. The talk was well received and I was even given a standing ovation. Sadly, however, no sponsorship funds were forthcoming.

The one organisation that did support us were our great friends, Viking, producers of high-end life-saving equipment. Viking were always happy to help out when we asked for equipment. But, then again, I remember an amusing conversation with them when they said: "Philip, really we just want you to sink so we can get some excellent publicity and show people how good our life-saving equipment is. But that's probably not what you have in mind."

Understandably, when you look at it from the donor's point of view, it is far easier to get sponsorship for something like, say, a medical health charity, than for an expedition that, by definition, carries an element of risk.

It was a period of setbacks and frustrations but I persevered. I had travelled extensively in my efforts to find sponsors, but in the end we were unable to raise the sponsorship we wanted, and time was passing. We were not only trying to fund an expedition, but also to raise enough to gain publicity and raise awareness of the voyage by using a professional PR company. We wanted to ensure that something of great historical interest was known about. It is a matter of regret that we were unable to employ any PR professionals to get the publicity we both needed and, in my view, deserved.

The big breakthrough name we had been hoping for had simply not come through. We had approached all sorts of major brands and had been speaking to some wealthy private interests who were often very enthusiastic about supporting the project but, when it came down to it, were reluctant to give us financial support. We could never quite get them over the line.

Even though we were managing to raise some sponsorship funds, a bigger problem was the state of the ship itself, which urgently needed repairs. By now *Phoenicia* was moored in Portsmouth in the UK and costing £10,000 a year to maintain and pay berth fees. Even raising this amount was proving difficult. In effect, we needed funds just to stand still, because maintaining the ship was becoming expensive and eating up money as quickly as it was coming in. The situation was becoming very challenging.

These kinds of projects are notoriously tough to get off the ground but the one major advantage we did have was that the boat was already built, however much we needed to do in terms of repairs and maintenance. If you're still trying to get the money to build a boat, then that's a much bigger problem.

However, one weekend I had a working party on board ship made up of friends and acquaintances who were happy to help out. One of these was an old friend called Doug Smith. Now Doug is a big guy, tall, strong and well-built, perhaps six feet four inches tall and weighs 14-15 stone. He was checking the boat over as he hadn't seen it for a number of years.

Within a couple of minutes of being on board, there was a huge crash and I realised he was lying flat on his face, having put his foot through a rotten patch in the deck. "Philip," he told me, "I don't want to ruin the weekend but this ship is not in any shape to cross the harbour, let alone the Atlantic. The deck's rotten and the mast looks in very bad shape too. You've just got to accept it. It's gone too far and too much of a risk." Obviously I knew that we had a lot of work to do, but I refused to accept defeat before we had even started. "No, Doug," I said standing my ground. "The hull's good, the ribs are good enough. We can still do it."

By now six years had passed since my interview with CNN, and I had reached the point when I told myself that it was now or never. Even if I needed to go into debt, I had to be prepared to do that in order to get the project off the ground. I had to take the risk that the necessary funds could be recouped after the expedition was over, when people finally began to realise what we had achieved.

With hindsight I should probably have made this decision earlier, perhaps in 2016, but we were worried about the state of the boat. And even when we did finally set sail in 2019 for the start point in Tunisia, the crew were still working on the mainsail. We were just using a storm sail at that time and when we reached a port I would get all the crew working on the mainsail stitching.

We were also still working on the deck and hull, and particularly the mast. If we had managed to raise some more money, we would ideally have constructed a new mast in the UK. With hindsight, it would probably have been better if I had just spent the money, as it would have saved me a lot of worry on the voyage. The prospect of having the mast break in the middle of the Atlantic and being stranded, just drifting around, was not an appealing one, and it gave me more than a few sleepless nights.

So, in late 2018, the decision was made. We had to make some serious repairs to the engine, but I had decided we were going ahead. Nonetheless, I clearly remember the comments from the harbour master at Royal Clarence Marina in Gosport, Portsmouth, where we were docked before the ship set sail for Tunisia.

It was a week before we were due to set sail, and he had asked if I would join him for a cup of tea in his office. "Philip," he said, as we sat overlooking the neat rows of sailing yachts moored alongside each other in the harbour below, "I respect your previous achievements very much, but you wouldn't get me out on the ocean in that boat for all the tea in China."

From his perspective I could see why. Over the previous few years, he had watched the ship gradually deteriorating in front of his eyes and he had been expecting many more repairs to have been carried out before we left. It wasn't a conversation I wanted to share with the crew and, besides, we wouldn't actually be sailing far from shore for a few weeks as we made our way south to the Mediterranean. I had already decided that this would be the best time to make some final repairs with the help of my more experienced crew members from the previous expedition.

At this stage I had all of the key members of my crew lined up. We were a truly international crew, and many more would be joining for the shorter legs around the Mediterranean, before we sailed out beyond the Pillars of Hercules – better known in more modern times as the Straits of Gibraltar – into the wide ocean beyond. Nonetheless I was determined that there should be a core group who I could depend on when things got tough.

My thanks go out to all of the crew who sailed with me from the bottom of my heart. Their support, enthusiasm, hard work, and sheer bravery ensured the ultimate success of the project and I shall always be grateful to every one of them. After the final chapter of this book, I have recorded all of their contributions and the legs of the voyage on which they sailed.

Reaching the Start Line

At the beginning of the fundraising effort, six years before, I had felt quite confident because often for an expedition of this scale a ship would need to be designed from scratch, but we already had our ship, even if it was in need of substantial repairs. We had also proved conclusively that both the ship and its crew were capable of sailing around Africa – a voyage that took us a long way out into the Atlantic – and we had all lived to tell the tale.

By this stage events had also been put in motion that would be difficult to reverse. My nephew Charlie had just arrived, with a huge bag of his belongings and a blow-up mattress. He had just moved out of his flat, split up with his girlfriend, and put his life on hold in order to take part in the expedition. But I could see that he too was worried by the state of the boat. It was obvious to all of us that, at the very least, we had to replace two huge cross-beams supporting the deck. This would be difficult because as anyone knows who has ever done their own DIY, making room to live when you're upgrading your own living quarters is guaranteed to be a logistical nightmare and there were now three of us living on the boat.

The yard, the horizontal spar which takes the full weight of *Phoenicia's* massive square sail when it's hoisted, also needed repair. This became essential when Charlie and I, with the rest of the team, tried to lift it one day and the whole thing split in half as it was completely rotten. This was literally a few weeks before we were planning to leave and the yard was one of the most critical parts of the entire ship. Wind or no wind, the *Phoenicia* wouldn't be crossing the Atlantic without a mast, yard and sail.

Happily, help was at hand in the shape of my brother-in-law, Ricky, who is a genius woodworker and mechanic. Together with another friend of mine, Ian Bond, who had also sailed a leg of the *Around Africa expedition*, they spliced two telegraph poles together to make another yard. A feat which in itself gives an idea of just how large 970 square feet of sail actually is, and why it takes a minimum of five crew to raise it.

At this point, I realised that we simply had no choice but to embark on the expedition even if that meant funding the expedition myself with the help of a few credit cards. The alternative was a funding hole that would have become so deep as time went by that even a sizeable contribution would be gobbled up in maintenance costs. Looking back, I realise now that I probably should have made this decision a year earlier. However, every difficult decision is always easier in hindsight and now I am just so glad I made the decision when I did. Had I left it any longer, the expedition would probably have been impossible due to the Covid-19 pandemic.

As well as repairs to the deck which Doug had so kindly highlighted, I was worried about the mast as there were clear signs of some rot. Naturally I didn't exactly go about pointing out the rot to the members of the crew and convinced myself that the rot was superficial. Indeed regular inspections seemed to confirm my point of view. However if we had the time and money, we would have replaced the old mast in the UK. Again, with hindsight, we probably should have grasped the nettle then and there. The truth was that it was a worry for me as there is just so much pressure on the mast and yard when you are under sail. A broken mast is one problem you don't want to have to deal with during a storm in the middle of the Atlantic Ocean, not to mention the potential dangers to the crew if the mast and yard were to come crashing down on to the deck.

We also needed another sail. But I simply couldn't afford a professional sailmaker to make one, especially if it was to remain true to the ancient design. We already had our smaller storm sail, but in the end we had to make the mainsail ourselves while sailing to the start line in Tunisia. This meant that when we arrived at various ports and harbours, often under quite stressful circumstances, I had to inform the crew that instead of sight-seeing, we would have to do some more stitching. On one occasion, we even had to sew in the bolt rope which reinforces the edges of the sail, a massive task in itself.

The make-up of the crew for the various stages of the voyage also came together quite late in the day. By this stage I had my nephew, Charlie, who didn't have much practical sailing experience but who completely understood what I was trying to achieve and was clearly inspired by the opportunity. He had also shown himself to be a great self-motivator and had been a key part of the team when the Phoenicia was in St Katharine Docks and was open to the public, following the *Around Africa expedition.*

Dirman and Aziz were friends of old and had been part of the crew on both my previous expeditions, the first time across the Indian Ocean and around the Cape of Good Hope and to Ghana in West Africa and the second down the east coast of Africa and again around the Cape of Good Hope and the rest of Africa in the circumnavigation that we were undertaking.. Nothing is as valuable when the going gets tough as the support of tried and trusted friends, who have endured challenging tests in very demanding circumstances.

And if the success of the expedition depended on any one crew member to keep the ship afloat in an emergency, I would nominate Dirman, as I think would all the rest of the crew. Dirman is not only a hugely talented sailor but also a brilliant shipwright. He builds replica sailing ships back at his home in Indonesia and there's no-one who understands the design and maintenance of a wooden sailing ship better. He is also a brilliant carpenter and a gifted mechanic. Give him a broken engine and I would put serious money on him being able to fix it. He's also an inspired fisherman whose contribution to our limited menu was always welcome.

Which is why I was alarmed when, in the spring of 2019, it looked like he might not be able to join the expedition. Aziz, who is always in close touch with Dirman, contacted me and said, "Philip, I want to join you on this expedition but Dirman can't come, he has too many responsibilities back home." I was therefore quite concerned, this put the whole project in jeopardy as I knew he was critical to its success.

While it has always been easy for me to communicate with Dirman at sea when we are face to face, in truth I only speak pidgin Indonesian and Dirman doesn't speak much English, so it's very difficult to have an in-depth conversation. This meant that I had to persuade Aziz to act on my behalf and I realised at that moment that I needed to be a bit brutal. "You can only come if you can persuade Dirman to come," I told him. And I meant it. Luckily, my ruse worked and a few weeks later I received the message that Dirman was coming after all. So now I had both Dirman and Aziz, which was a huge relief.

Another in the 'Can't Do Without' category was Yuri Sanada. Yuri too had been an integral part of the crew on the *Around Africa expedition* and is a film-maker who had documented our earlier voyage, so I knew I could rely on him. In fact, when I travelled to Salt Lake City to make my presentation to the Mormons, he had come with me in the hope that he could strike a deal for making a documentary about the expedition.

So apart from Charlie and the stalwarts from my earlier expeditions, Steinar was the first of the new crew members. I had met Steinar at a conference in September, 2017, when I was invited to Norway to talk to a group in Trondheim who sail replica Viking ships to recreate historic expeditions. They have a very well-funded organisation supporting them and it was fascinating to learn about their voyages. At the end of the conference, after I had given my talk about my first expedition aboard *Phoenicia*, a rugged gentleman, who was clearly a die-hard adventurer, came up to me and introduced himself.

He told me he was the captain of one of these ships and how he had been inspired by my talk and wanted to join us on the expedition. He explained that most of the Viking re-enactments he had skippered were around the seas of Scandinavia and that he had never been on an ocean voyage before, but had always dreamed of doing so ever since he was a boy.

I knew that Steinar's experience and knowledge, as well as his physical and mental strength would be invaluable, so I accepted his offer immediately and later asked him to be my deputy. As an expedition leader, especially when timings are very fluid, it is vital to be pragmatic but I knew I could depend on Steinar. Steinar was the first key crew member to sign up and, even when we delayed a year, he said that it didn't worry him. He simply told me that when we sailed, whenever that was, he wanted to be part of the expedition.

***

Crew Member Story – Steinar Lillås

Steinar, *Phoenicia's* Second in Command and a Viking ship
skipper back home in Norway, recalls a very scary
near-miss… and a violent storm.

I remember only too vividly the night we almost had a collision
with a super tanker which didn't even realise we were there. It
was at night and we were in the vicinity of the Cape Verde islands off the coast of Africa. We could just make out the lights
from another boat and I thought it was a big ship in the distance on our starboard side which I felt sure would harmlessly
pass us by.

It can be very difficult at night to interpret lights at sea as you
have very little sense of perspective. Judging the distance, size,
and direction of travel of another ship is a real art. I was looking
very closely at its lights and it seemed at first as if it was a small
ship going quite slowly in the same direction as we were going.
But what looked like a small ship that was quite close and going
quite slowly suddenly turned into a giant super tanker that had
been far off but was now almost on top of us.

It suddenly became clear that it was crossing right in front of
us even though we had the right of way and were on a starboard
tack. There's no way a ship of that size would have picked us
up on its radar, and if it had hit us no one would probably have
noticed until it arrived in port with the last few remains of the
Phoenicia hanging off its bows. We think, probably, it was a huge
tanker on autopilot in the middle of the night that wasn't going
to change direction for anyone. It was a very scary moment.

Another terrifying situation, for very different reasons, was
the storm we encountered on the other side of the Atlantic. I
remember it so well partly because the days leading up to it,
sailing along the south coast of the Dominican Republic, were
so perfect. Every Saturday during the voyage, we would enjoy
a happy hour at 4pm and on that particular Saturday there was

absolutely no wind. It was completely calm until around 6pm, when the wind started to blow just a little bit. It starts to get dark around that time in the Caribbean whatever the time of year as it's not far north of the equator.

Conditions began to change more dramatically as we entered the channel between Cuba and Haiti. The winds became much stronger and we had to contend with some huge waves as dusk fell. The important thing when the wind gets up is to hold the ship straight into the wind because if it gets just a little bit side on, it will flip the ship broadside to the waves, which isn't a great position to be in when there's a storm brewing.

Suddenly I saw this white wall of water racing towards us and at the same time the ship's stern disappeared backwards into the great chasm that had opened up behind us. Then this gigantic wave broke over the bows. When a storm first breaks at sea, it takes a while to get orientated to the see-saw motion and you soon find yourself clinging on to whatever will keep you upright. I immediately started worrying that the front hatch might still be open and then the next thing I knew the horse's head figure-head was completely submerged and the whole deck was covered in water up to about half a metre, flooding the cabin and the kitchen area.

The storm lasted the whole night and all the crew (apart from Philip, of course!) were really quite scared. I remember talking to Sheimaa afterwards and she said she felt so frightened and seasick she wouldn't have minded if the waves had just picked her up and swept her away. She just wanted the experience to be over and she didn't really care how!

There were others who I could partially rely on, but I could never be absolutely sure, and the impossibility of committing to a time-frame made it difficult for them, as well as me. The start of the expedition was unavoidably put back several times and I knew, from cruel experience, that two questions impossible to answer were how long we would be at sea and when we would finally make landfall on the other side of the Atlantic.

For the first leg, from Portsmouth to the official start of the expedition in Tunis, when we would simply be getting to the start line, most of the crew were young and inexperienced and mostly recruited through online portals like *findacrew.net*. With the exception of Charlie, who knew he would be a part of the crew for the entire expedition, the crew for this section of the voyage knew they would be leaving in Tunisia and were happy with this arrangement.

Although the *Phoenicia* is a stunning sight, with her huge, purple and white-striped sail (she is often compared to a pirate ship) she's not the easiest of ships to sail and has limitations that don't affect most modern sailing vessels. She's a challenge because there's only a square sail which means she can only sail downwind. Tacking, when a ship sails into the wind and changes the side the wind is on is impossible. Gybing, sailing with a following wind and changing the side the wind is on, is possible but involves moving the yard across the boat at the same time as the stern crosses the wind, which can be quite a difficult manoeuvre, especially in high winds.

She's also very heavy, but because she has a broad beam and a lot of ballast, she is also quite stable. Modern yachts can sometimes be knocked over by a fierce side wind, but *Phoenicia* is rarely exposed to strong winds on the beam and is therefore much less likely to capsize.

The Phoenicians also used the first known system of reefing, using eight brailing lines to help change the sail's shape, making it possible to mimic a triangular sail. This partially works, but not totally, because the bottom of the sail is still reefed up, which limits performance. It looks a bit like a triangular sail but is not as efficient. The important thing is that the brailing lines enable the sail coverage to be reduced without lowering the yard during storms or strong gusts. *Phoenicia's* top speed is seven knots at which point she starts to bounce about and the crew need to start taking in the sail with the brailing lines.

Probably due to the fact that there were some young and very inexperienced people aboard, it was a lively atmosphere in the weeks before we set sail. Although I was as familiar with the boat as it was possible to be, I hadn't actually sailed her for five or six years and this combination of a rusty skipper and some very inexperienced crew resulted in an episode a bit like one of those scenes from *Only Fools and Horses* where it all goes horribly wrong for Del Boy and friends.

We needed to move the ship to a neighbouring marina in Portsmouth, about a mile away, where I knew of someone who might be able to advise us on the state of the mast. It was a decision that nearly went badly wrong because on this particular day we had to sail towards the Solent, the famous channel of water which runs between Portsmouth and the Isle of Wight.

The Solent is famous for its double tide, which means that the water is rising for up to 17 hours a day with the ebb tide falling quickly in between. So, while it is very useful for commercial shipping, it also means it has some ferocious currents. Unfortunately, we found ourselves caught in one of these as we made our way into the next marina where we were unable to bring the ship under control fast enough before crashing into a huge billboard.

It's one of those situations that seems very funny in retrospect but which wasn't quite so funny at the time. As well as the damage to the billboard, much more distressing from our point of view was the loss of the wooden figurehead on the bow, in the shape of a horse's head, which was a symbol of the boat's Phoenician heritage. Horses' heads appeared on their coins and were a powerful cultural symbol. But our particular horse's head had broken off and plunged into the harbour. This was the same figurehead that had gone before us on our voyage all around the continent of Africa. Figureheads have a certain magic attached to them, like a guardian angel to keep evil spirits at bay, so initially it felt a bit like the killing of the albatross in Coleridge's *Ancient Mariner.*

We were all mourning its loss, believing it had been irretrievably lost overboard. However, when we finally tied up at the new marina, we realised it was still hanging from the bow of the ship. Luckily for us, Charlie and one of the other crew members had been splicing some rope the day before. They had made some loops which they then stored by throwing them around the horse's head at the end of the day. This meant that with the ropes still attached, we were able to haul it back on board, although not without a struggle, as it was considerably heavier than we had realised.

It was a small incident really, but we were all shaken up a bit, and I felt especially sorry for Charlie. This was his first experience of the open sea aboard *Phoenicia* and within half-an-hour of setting sail he found himself being swept headlong into a harbour wall. Given that we hadn't even managed to leave Portsmouth, he was probably wondering what the Atlantic Ocean had in store for him.

Finally, however, the day of our departure dawned. Our first port of call was Lyme Regis further along the south coast, and then Plymouth, from where we would make our departure from the UK across the English Channel to Portugal. We sailed on Thursday 4th July but once again things didn't go as smoothly as we had hoped.

At this stage we were using our engine, when a Phoenician crew would have used oarsmen. However, the crowded, fast-moving harbours of the 21st century, are a little different from those of the 6th century BC. In fact, it would have been impossible to manoeuvre through the armada of small boats in a typical harbour without one, and we certainly had no qualms using the engine on the delivery leg of the voyage to Tunisia. So, while we never used the motor after we had left Tenerife and were crossing the Atlantic, it was essential at this point.

Our first objective was to navigate our way out into the Solent and around the Needles. On this particular day it was very choppy, with the current turning against us once again. We did eventually make it into Lyme Regis Harbour, but this time the engine kept cutting out. One of the most difficult, and least glamorous, parts of sailing is negotiating busy harbours with which you are not familiar. Knowing the rules of the sea is one thing, a misfiring engine that keeps cutting out is quite another.

It was hardly the most dignified entry and we narrowly missed quite a few dinghies anchored in the harbour inside the famous Lyme Regis Cobb. Just as we were about to moor up against the harbour wall, the engine cut out again and we were thrown up against the harbour wall and into a phalanx of dinghies. There was a small crowd that had come to cheer us in, and I think they were a bit shocked at the sight of us crashing through the moored dinghies, completely out of control, with the harbourmaster shouting instructions which we appeared determined to ignore.

Happily, no real damage was done and the next leg down to Plymouth went off without incident. Our whole journey down the south coast reminded me a bit of the Falklands War when supplies and equipment were still being loaded onto the ships from helicopters after they had left port because they had to leave in such a hurry. So, while we were not planning on fighting any naval battles, we still had equipment being sent ahead of us to Plymouth where we would set sail from a few weeks later.

During our stay in Plymouth, more of the younger crew members came aboard. I always like my crews to be multi-cultural and this crew was no exception. It included a young man called Aaron Barrett. Aaron went on to help design the new Mayflower Autonomous Research vessel. This is now on a global mission of discovery collecting data to help safeguard the future of the oceans and is controlled by Artificial Intelligence while being powered by energy from the sun. We also had a Kiwi and a couple of Belgians on board as well as a young Mexican who had heard about the expedition and turned up at the last minute without warning but determined to join us. And he did.

We finally set sail from Plymouth on our journey to Tunis on July 20th. Teething problems plagued us from the start and the engine kept cutting out as the wind blew us backwards. After sailing for a day and a half without being able to fix the engine, the decision was reluctantly made to turn back. To make matters worse, the mother of one of the younger crew members watching our tracker on Facebook had assumed that because we had turned back there was a serious problem and had alerted the coastguard.

We thought at first that the engine problem was to do with the glow plugs. Glow plugs are elements in the engine that heat the incoming fuel and air to assist fuel combustion. However, as we made our way back towards Plymouth, we discovered that the engine wasn't fitted with glow plugs anyway and the misfire was down to a relatively minor problem with the Kill Switch. What should have been just a frustrating inconvenience had now become a major problem because we had lost two days of sailing time. This delay had completely ruined our carefully planned schedule to hit a crucial weather window when crossing the notoriously uncertain seas of the Bay of Biscay.

Desperate to make up some time, the next day we crossed the English Channel from Plymouth to nearby La Rochelle, roughly halfway down the west coast of France, and waited for the weather window to open once more. The crew were able to relax but it was frustrating for me because we were losing valuable time from our schedule.

However, on our next leg we managed to sail a satisfying distance along the north coast of Spain, parallel to the Asturias region and the Picos de Europa mountains. We had now arrived in the port of La Coruña in Galicia in the north-western corner of Spain, not far north of Santiago de Compostela.

One of the famous sights in the city is the world's oldest lighthouse, built on a peninsula about a mile and a half from the centre. It was built by the Romans in around the 2nd century AD, possibly under the Emperor Trajan, but the interesting feature from our point of view was that the foundations and the design are probably Phoenician.[16]

Some experts believe that alongside their extraordinary feats of maritime exploration, the Phoenicians also built the first lighthouses.[17] If so, the most likely sites would have been in their homeland ports, Gades (modern Cadiz), or of course Carthage (modern Tunis). It is very likely these designs were copied by the Greeks who built the Lighthouse at Alexandria, one of the wonders of the Ancient World, during the Hellenistic period of Egyptian history under the pharaoh, Ptolemy 1.

Bringing us back down to earth, I was still worried about the state of the mast – a recurring theme throughout the voyage – and we discussed the possibility of sourcing a new one from a Spanish company which manufactured telegraph poles. Despite their apparent strength, we were worried that the telegraph poles weren't strong enough for such a critical piece of equipment, although in retrospect I think they almost certainly would have been.

It was at this stage that some of the younger crew members who had joined us in Plymouth had to leave. This meant that the crew was down to six, which is absolutely the bare minimum needed to sail a ship of *Phoenicia's* size and complexity. We were still making a lot of repairs, as well as stocking up on supplies, so there was very little time to relax. To reassure myself about the condition of the mast, we hired a cherry picker and drilled into it to check the condition of the wood which happily turned out to be much more sound than I had thought.

---

16. Trethewey K, Ancient Lighthouses – Part 4: The Phoenicians.. PL11 2LX, UK. Website: https://www.academia.edu/38979566/Ancient_Lighthouses_-_Part_4_The_Phoenicians
17. Ibid.

The next leg was to Lisbon rounding Cape Finisterre – dubbed 'finis terrae' by the Romans meaning the 'end of the earth' – and sailing directly south down the coast of Portugal. Charlie's narrative in the accompanying panel, will tell you more about our arrival in Lisbon, which wasn't exactly the most relaxing experience due to a sail malfunction. It was also a little scarier than it should have been due to the limited manpower available with a skeleton crew.

Unfortunately, after making enquiries about the mast, we ended up wasting another week talking to people who were trying to sell us modern fabricated masts which would have been beyond the technology of the ancient Phoenicians, definitely not what we wanted. Finally, we set sail again and carried on down to Gibraltar, putting our concerns about the mast to the back of our minds, and thinking that if there was still an issue when we arrived in Tunis, we would be able to solve the problem there.

In Gibraltar, we welcomed Sheimaa on board, another of our key crew members, who has also written about her experiences of her first few days aboard Phoenicia. But we were still very behind our intended schedule. My main frustration was that if we had been sailing west by this time from Tunis, at the start of the expedition proper, the wind in the Mediterranean would have been in our favour. Instead we found ourselves sailing east towards Tunis with the wind against us.

As I have mentioned before, sailing in the Mediterranean is often a lot more difficult than in the middle of the Atlantic. The relatively shallow seas cause the waves to whip up much more than they usually do in the Atlantic, so we really struggled to make progress. Eventually we decided that we would sail along the south coast of Spain and put in at Cartagena, which was also an ancient Phoenician port.

Cartagena was founded in 227 BC by Hamilcar Barca of Carthage (father of the famous Phoenician general, Hannibal) after he had conquered the local Iberian tribes. This later became a major Phoenician port and was named Qart Hadasht (meaning 'New Town' in Phoenician), the same name as the original city of Carthage.

With the winds and the weather against us, it had taken about three weeks to do four hundred miles – a ridiculously slow rate of progress – and at this point we were struggling to make any headway at all. Our engine was no match for the wind and the currents – we were beginning to despair that we would ever make it to the start line of the expedition.

It was at this stage that I began to think we would have no choice but to change the plan and start the expedition from Cartagena. It was, after all, an important Phoenician port and its inhabitants are very proud of their Phoenician heritage. I knew this would not go down at all well with the Tunisians – I was aware they were preparing to roll out the red carpet for us, but I was beginning to feel we might have no option but to change our plans.

I had a quiet word with Charlie away from the rest of the crew and told him that I was beginning to think we simply might not get to Tunisia. I showed him all the weather predictions, which were not looking at all good. Sailing into the wind while being constantly blown back was also beginning to become quite a frightening prospect and I was aware we had a very inexperienced crew on board.

I've always trusted Charlie's judgement and I could sense he was very unwilling to change plans having come so far, though he understood that I was the skipper and had the safety of the crew in my hands. I also knew that Sheimaa had been working tirelessly making arrangements for our stay in Carthage, Tunisia, an event which had been in the planning for months. She had been liaising with the port authorities and the mayor's office who were not only planning various welcome ceremonies, but also cultural visits to many of the important Phoenician remains in the old city of Carthage.

After waiting a few more days, a weather window appeared to open up and we decided it was worth making the attempt to sail the final 600 nautical miles east by hugging the north coast of Algeria. As it turned out the weather conditions between Cartagena and Tunisia were among the worst I have ever experienced at sea and there was more rain and lightning in those two or three days than I've ever seen in my life. The thunder and lightning went on for hour after hour and the sea was very rough indeed. It was very frightening, especially for the members of the crew who hadn't spent much time at sea.

We were now sailing around 12 miles off the coast of Algeria, just outside their territorial waters, but some of the crew were understandably very scared. Their feeling was that I should dismiss any worries I had about Algerian port authorities and make a run for a nearby port.

Whether rightly or wrongly, I was very reluctant to make this decision as I knew we would find it very hard to leave once we became bogged down in Algerian bureaucracy.

So I made it clear that we were going to stick it out until the storm passed. To make things as comfortable as possible, we took the sails down and threw out a sea anchor weighed down by mattresses, a bit like an underwater parachute. Even so, we still found ourselves being blown backwards, this time by around 25 miles.

***

Crew Member Story – Sheimaa Oubari

My First Days at Sea

I was quite nervous when I arrived in Gibraltar to meet the ship. I arrived at Queensway Quay Marina with my suitcase and recognised the Phoenicia immediately from the horse's head on its prow. Frankly it would be impossible to mistake it for anything else. An ancient Phoenician ship tends to stand out in a crowd of sparkling modern yachts.

I was a little shocked to be honest. The crew were working on the engine and there was grease everywhere. It was quite disorganised and reminded me of some refugee camps I had seen in southern Lebanon. One of the crew members wasn't talking because of his religious beliefs and then I saw the toilet! That was when I really started to have second thoughts. It was on the deck and had no covering.

So I said to Philip the next day, "Captain, this is a problem for me." And he said, "Don't worry Sheimaa, nobody cares." But I told him it was impossible for me. "I'm not that adventurous, I'm a city girl. I grew up between Paris and Beirut. I never really did any camping or anything like that."

So the next day he came to me and said, "I've got a gift for you." It was just a piece of cloth to clip around the wooden bars but the thought that I was going to have to use this toilet hanging over the side of the deck when we were out at sea was still very horrifying for me.

My first night on board in the harbour was quite an experience gazing up at the Rock of Gibraltar. On my third day, when we left port, I remember standing by the horse's head and thinking how amazing it was with the open sea all around us. But then later I started getting seasick and it was very cold on the first night.

The watches were particularly tough for me. They were six-hour shifts and I knew I had to stay awake. But my body was just so tired. The crew brought me some blankets but even off-watch I simply couldn't go down below because I felt so sea-sick. In fact, I stayed on deck the entire time from Gibraltar to Carthage. I slept and ate and went to the toilet on deck. Mind you, I didn't have much choice about the latter.

And when the wind was against us, which it seemed to be most of the time, it was really difficult to get anywhere. My mood went from one extreme to the other. One moment I felt like I was dying, and then the next I would look up at the Milky Way or be watching dolphins jumping next to the ship. It was still very rough and I remember that first night thinking that as soon as we reach port I'm taking a plane back home. I just can't do this. It's not for me.

There were only eight of us on the leg from Gibraltar to Carthage and with six-hour watches, we could never really sleep for more than four hours at a time, so I became really sleep deprived. But you're pushing your body and your mind. And when you're not on watch, you need to do your own personal chores like washing your clothes or perhaps the captain would need you to fix something or pull something. So when you're supposed to be resting, you're not actually resting at all.

But I was still amazed that I was able to sleep on the wooden deck with no mattress. Sometimes I would sleep on the storm sail and during a storm that was the only way I could stay dry at night when everything on the deck was wet and the smells were so alien. Even the wood of the boat smelt very strange to me. And then the crew would cook something British like corned beef and it would make me retch!

But then the next day the sun would come out and everything felt so much better. I hadn't really told anyone how I felt and when we reached Cartagena, the captain took us all out to dinner. By this time, we had all really started to bond and I had been doing everything I could to be a useful member of the crew. But suddenly here we were in 'New Carthage' and right next to the Marina was a fascinating museum with hundreds of artefacts and inscriptions from the wreck of a Phoenician ship that had been discovered off the coast.

When we embarked again, this time on what turned out to be a very stormy leg to Tunis. We were sailing along the coast of Algeria and I was feeling really ill indeed. I had a couple of very rough nights and I was desperately trying to persuade Philip to make landfall in Algeria where we could see the lights on the coast. I told him that I would speak to the authorities because I speak Arabic and anyway Lebanese people are quite skilful at negotiating their way out of things. But Philip was unwilling. "They're not going to be nice to us, they're not going to welcome us," he told me. "They don't like foreign boats and they don't like foreign people, so we just have to continue."

I could see why he wanted to avoid Algeria but then we had another terrible night when we were hit by terrifying lightning storms and the ship was being thrown around violently and the deck was just surging and rocking under my feet. We threw out the sea anchor but we were still being pushed back.

I remembered reading somewhere that sometimes with seasickness it's the hope that you will actually die that keeps you alive. And that's exactly how I felt. At times I just wanted the next big wave to crush us and put me out of my misery. One of the things I learnt about sailing is that you should never start asking, "When are we going to arrive?" The answer is that you arrive when you arrive and that's an end to it. You can't control the wind and the storms and the currents. You just have to stay on course and keep doing your best. And after a while I got used to being at sea even when at times it felt like we would never arrive in Tunis.

As I was so inexperienced, when I joined the ship I hardly knew port from starboard or bow from stern. On the other hand, I was very keen to be as helpful as possible. Whenever there was something that had to be done, I wanted to be the person to do it and I would always say 'Yes' even if I didn't know how to do it. I could always give it a try. On one occasion the captain gave us some Phoenician purple paint and we painted the purple stripes of the sail.

For about a week during this leg, we had no fresh food, no vegetables and we really wanted to catch fish. I remember we came close to a fishing boat and I stood at the bow of the ship and I called them for about ten minutes and finally they came close. Philip had brought a case of cigarettes for bartering, so we asked them if they could exchange them for some fish.

But unfortunately they didn't have any fish. Instead they gave us some ice because during the day it was unbearably hot and the fresh water we had was lukewarm, like 'sock juice' as my mother used to call it. It was already September but it had been a very hot summer sun and we were all fantasising about ice cream and ice cubes. But the ice they gave us must have been used to store fish and it smelt disgusting. Even so, for us it was like gold dust and we were so happy just licking it and putting it on our faces.

They also gave us a very specialised hook and told us that with this we would definitely catch some fish. This hook and its lure looked like a rubber octopus. Then we spent two days trying to catch a fish but we didn't catch anything at all. We probably should have put a weight on the line and made it longer so it was further away from the boat, but as we were moving so slowly it was hopeless. So we just ended up eating out of cans. Canned olives, canned tomatoes, canned everything. You had to become pretty creative mixing up the different combinations.

As I said, some of the time the winds in the Mediterranean were against us, but not always. And one day the captain gave the order to use the storm sail, which is much smaller than the mainsail so that it wouldn't break the mast in heavy winds. Usually, it's much easier to pull up, but with only eight of us, it was still a superhuman effort with just the strength of our arms. But then the next moment I was at the helm and the wind was blowing us forward and suddenly I was having the most wonderful, euphoric experience. I was in control of this mighty Phoenician ship and it was the most amazing feeling of freedom I had ever experienced in my life.

I am happy to say that on this occasion fortune favoured the brave and we avoided both being blown into Algerian territorial waters or, even worse, onto its rocky coast. Eventually the weather changed and we managed to slog our way east along the coast and into the harbour at Tunis. It had been touch and go, but when we finally arrived the welcome we received made us feel it had all been worthwhile. I had been to Tunis before with *Phoenicia* in 2010, so once we had rounded the headland of the Bay of Tunis and came sailing into the harbour it felt a bit like arriving home.

There was a substantial crowd waiting to meet and greet us. This was, after all, the starting point of the expedition and there were journalists waiting to interview us, alongside some of our partners and sponsors, so it was important to give the crowd as good a showing of the ship as possible. Naturally they all wanted shots of us coming into harbour, so we had to delay our actual arrival until about 8 a.m.

We had to try to let the photographers and TV crews get the best pictures of *Phoenicia*, which meant leaving the sail up for as long as we could, while at the same time dropping it quickly enough that we didn't crash into the harbour wall. Unfortunately, as we came into the harbour, the wind completely dropped off, so I had to resort to the old trick of getting close to the marina and putting the engine into reverse to fill the sail and look good on camera. After doing this a couple of times, we eventually made it into the harbour.

Our formal arrival was actually quite a thrilling moment as in this part of the world it is traditional to greet honoured guests with a sound that we would call ululating. It's called Zaghārīt and is often performed at weddings. It's a wavering, high-pitched sound, a bit like a yodel, trilling between two high-pitched notes which makes the hairs on the back of your neck stand on end.

We could hear it from quite a long way off as we sailed into the harbour and came in next to a very long walkway. Many people were running alongside us, smiling and shouting a greeting. It was a real morale boost for all of us as it had been such a challenging crossing from Cartagena.

Inevitably, though, our arrival had its stresses as my French is basic school-boy standard and my Arabic worse, so Sheimaa was talking to the harbourmaster over the radio in French and Arabic. At the same time we were trying to make sure we didn't get on the wrong side of the Tunisian port authorities. Keeping everything safe and under control in a situation like this is not always easy, and in many ways a lot more difficult than out at sea.

As well as oil rigs and huge cargo ships to avoid, there were many more obstacles, some moving, some not, some visible, some not. There were also the usual misunderstandings with the port authorities as to where exactly we were meant to be moored.

Even after we had tied up, we weren't immediately allowed to step out of the ship as our papers hadn't been checked by the Border Force. At the same time, the crew were being interviewed by journalists alongside and Sheimaa was translating between Arabic and English. One of the journalists asked how we liked Tunis when we still hadn't left the boat. Someone replied that it was fabulous and he loved it. We all found this hysterical.

It was a very hot day and some people on the dockside were drinking from a water bottle. Sheimaa asked if we could have a drink. One man wanted to go and buy us all a bottle each but we were just so thirsty we told him that his bottle would do just fine. Everyone said it was the best water they had ever tasted and so cool. When you have been at sea for a while you learn to value the basic necessities of life so much more, and there's nothing so basic or so necessary as water itself. The elixir of life.

The crew also really enjoyed being able to have a proper shower. Unfortunately, the women's shower didn't have any hot water and Sheimaa had to use the men's shower. She enjoyed it so much that the others were starting to complain that she was using up all the hot water. I think she was just so happy to wash off the salt water and feel clean again.

The Tunisians were charming hosts and rolled out the red carpet for us in style. We were entertained with all sorts of lunches and dinners which all the crew hugely enjoyed, not least one of our crew members from Mexico who had caused considerable friction during the difficult leg from Spain along the Algerian coast. He was actually quite a competent sailor and he had seemed a very pleasant, easy-going, young man when he joined us.

However, in the middle of the Mediterranean when things were at their toughest, he told us that he couldn't talk or eat for several days for spiritual reasons. This was a routine that he apparently observed four times a year. Under normal circumstances, back on terra firma, we would all have accepted this as being his personal choice and it would have been fine.

Unfortunately, he hadn't told me or any of the other crew members that this is what he intended to do before we set sail. Sign language can be very frustrating under stressful circumstances, especially when you know the person you're talking to is quite capable of speech.

Understandably in my view, the rest of the crew became very annoyed with him and tempers began to boil over, causing a lot of friction on board. When you're working in a team and you have to communicate with each other, work together and think about each other, it was quite a selfish attitude to take. It also began to border on the farcical when he started to knock on things and write notes and then pass them to you when we were standing right next to each other.

The final straw, though, was in Tunis. The moment we were being entertained and provided with gourmet food on the first day of our arrival, he broke his fast and vow of silence and was suddenly eating and drinking everything in sight and chatting away quite happily. This didn't go down at all well with the rest of the crew who had found him almost impossible to communicate with when we were in dangerous situations at sea.

Up until we arrived, he had indicated that he was going to get on a plane the moment we reached Tunis, but now he wanted to stick around and even started talking about sailing with us on the next leg. This from the same person who a few days before had said that he would be quite happy to be towed behind the ship in one of the lifeboats so that he could keep his vows. In the end, I have to admit that we were all glad to see the back of him.

In Tunis, many of the key crew members for the expedition were waiting for us, including Steinar and also Yuri, who was making a documentary about the expedition and filmed our arrival. Meanwhile, the two Indonesians, Dirman and Aziz, flew in a couple of days later. At the same time, it was proving difficult for the delivery crew of eight members who were a bit taken aback by the razzmatazz of Tunis and were obviously wondering if they had made the right decision to be leaving the expedition just as it was starting. Some of them were asking me if they could stay on and complete the expedition, which made it a difficult balancing act as captain, so I had to make some tough decisions.

The other pressing issue when we arrived was to make sure the ship's structure and equipment was in as good shape as possible. There were a few problems with the alternator about which we were given conflicting advice. Another priority was to mend one of the rudders which had been broken in Lyme Regis. We had actually done a lot of work on the sail during the voyage over and had hoisted it fully for the first time coming into Tunis. Nonetheless, there was still a question mark over the mast which we had been worried about from the start.

I know Steinar especially was a bit shocked when he saw the condition that the *Phoenicia* was in when he joined the crew in Tunis. He told me later that he was very excited to see the ship when we first moored in the harbour and that he thought she was a really beautiful sight. Close up, though, he definitely became more concerned. He told me that the mast looked in very bad condition with all the metal plates attached to it, and we both knew there were some rotten planks on the deck.

Thankfully Dirman managed to build a new rudder within a few days of joining us, as well as completing numerous other repair jobs. His craftsmanship was indispensable at every stage of the voyage.

***

Crew Member Story – Dirman

Once Aziz had persuaded me to join the expedition, I was really looking forward to seeing some new countries and making the voyage. I knew I would be making an important contribution to the expedition as I have a unique skill set which I knew would be invaluable for the rest of the crew. Philip always used to tell me I was a shipwright, sailing guru, senior fisherman and master mechanic all wrapped into one.

I had previously sailed with Philip on both the Borobudur ship expedition and on the Around Africa expedition aboard *Phoenicia*, so I knew crossing the Atlantic in the footsteps of the Phoenicians would be the ultimate Kon-Tiki type expedition. So I was thrilled to join the team.

Of course, with the ship being nearly 12 years-old by the start of the expedition in 2019, I knew there would be a lot of work to do. And sure enough, within hours of me arriving in Tunis, Philip was driving me to a lumber yard to select timber to make a massive new rudder. And similarly, when we diverted to Algiers to reduce the height of the mast, the operation needed someone at the top of the mast drilling into it – me! – so the rest of the crew on the deck below could pull the top few feet off. This took several attempts, as it was stronger than we had realised, but by this time the decision had been made and we had no choice but to get the job done.

There were many other occasions where I was able to win some plaudits for helming and parking *Phoenicia* in some tricky harbours and conditions. In truth, I greatly enjoyed being able to carry out these tasks and play my part.

As an Indonesian who has spent most of my life on a remote island with very basic facilities, some 60 miles north of Bali, making do with the little we had in the way of creature comforts came naturally to me. As in Indonesia when something doesn't work, we sit down and repair it. Only as a last resort would we ever throw away an electrical or mechanical item that doesn't work. And as a shipwright by trade, I knew that anything wooden on Phoenicia could always be repaired with a splint or replacement, as I had done many times before in my own ship-building career.

In terms of sailing, and contrary to popular understanding, conditions around the Java Sea in Indonesia can be very rough, as the depth of the sea is quite shallow and whips up easily. So I was quite at home with rough seas and challenging conditions as I had been experiencing them since I was a little boy. Indeed, whilst I was on the expedition, one of my best friends lost his life on a fishing boat, which made me sad for a time and brought home to me the risks that all sailors take. That said I enjoyed being part of the expedition immensely.

However, when I look back now, I know that the only options were either postponing the expedition indefinitely or setting sail knowing that the ship was structurally sound and that we had all the safety measures in place. But it was not the ship it had been when it was first built in 2008. The truth was that in high seas or when it was raining, the deck leaked into the hold and unless everybody had their clothes and hammocks protected, they would get wet and there was nothing we could do about it.

I had told Steinar this beforehand, but I think he was still a little shocked at the condition of the boat. With all his huge experience of sailing replica ships, I think he was reassured when he saw that the underlying structure of the ship was very solid and that the safety equipment and life rafts were brand new. Nonetheless, I wouldn't have blamed him if he had decided to back out at this stage if he really thought the ship might not be strong enough to survive the voyage. After all, I knew the whole expedition depended on the good will and total belief of this core crew of experienced sailors who had put their trust in me.

Meanwhile, back in the world of drinks and reception parties, the Mayor of Carthage put on a civil ceremony for us which the Minister of Tourism attended. This was followed by another big evening ceremony and a lavish party. The Tunisians were amazingly hospitable and insisted we stay longer than the two weeks we had planned. We had a number of contacts from our previous visit aboard *Phoenicia* before the Arab Spring. At that time the army was in control. Back then, if we needed anything done it was a matter of doling out back-handers. This time it was much more personal and welcoming and Sheimaa had done a lot of work making contacts and setting up all the events.

Leading the welcoming committee were two very charismatic individuals who were incredibly supportive. Eryj Ben Sasi is the President of Didon Carthage, an organisation that supports and promotes Carthaginian culture, while Mohammed Ghassen Nouira is the world's leading expert on Phoenician Purple Dye. They arranged everything for us, including receptions with the Mayor of Tunis, seminars on all things Ancient Carthage, and visits to museums and archaeological sites. Every single day we were there, there was a visit, an event, or an experience they wanted to share with us.

The Naval Officers Association of Carthage was also very good to us and gifted us all the extra equipment we needed for the expedition. One day they arrived at the dockside in a couple of trucks stacked with huge amounts of tinned food, pulses, and many other dried staples. Everything we needed, in fact, for the Atlantic voyage.

We could never have reasonably expected the level of hospitality and enthusiasm for the project that the Tunisians showed to us. Given the uncertainty of when, or even if, we were going to arrive, it was incredible the speed with which the whole thing had been put together. They had been waiting for at least a couple of years to be given the green light. At first they thought we would be arriving in 2018, before it was postponed until 2019.

They had been able to follow us on our website as we had a satellite tracker, but we discovered later that another contact in the Lebanon had told them erroneously that the expedition was off, a mistake which could have derailed the whole project. So by the time we sailed into Tunis harbour, they would have been forgiven for thinking we were fake news. The fact that they did so much to welcome and support us was a huge tribute.

But perhaps the most fascinating aspect of our visit was learning so much more than we knew already about the history of ancient Carthage.

History comes alive when you see it with your own eyes. Tunis has three layers of antiquity built on top of one another. It all begins with the ancient Phoenician city, originally a colony of the city of Tyre, which was founded in the 9th century BC. On top of this is the Roman imperial city built after Punic Carthage was sacked in 146 BC. Then there is medieval, Islamic Tunis which lies beneath the modern city of today.

The shoreline has actually changed dramatically since those ancient times. The city was built in the south-east of an arrow-shaped promontory which sticks out into the Gulf of Tunis and which back then was a lot narrower than it is today. Its location gave the Carthaginians direct access to the sea, while at the same time was very easy to defend from the land, as the promontory was protected by a triple-wall which was built across the width of the isthmus.[18]

We were taken to see the remains of the huge ancient harbour complex which was divided between a section where the civilian cargo ships were moored and the inner port where the warships were moored. It was originally built as a defence against the Romans after the Second Punic War which the Carthaginians lost.

Beside the smaller outer section, there was a dock area which the archaeologists call 'Falbe's Quadrilateral' which was where all the cargo ships loaded and unloaded their goods. Adjacent to this was a large circular naval harbour called the 'Cothon' with a circular island in the middle which was the HQ of Carthage's top naval commander. At its centre was a huge tower from which he would have been able to scan the horizon for many miles out to sea and inland as well.

The feature that really brought the harbour alive for us was the model which demonstrates what it would have looked like 2500 years ago. In many ways it was like a modern football stadium with a double storey at the side of the harbour for hoisting the huge galleys out of the water. The mocked-up ships give a vivid idea of what it would have been like in ancient times.

The archaeology and the history of Tunis is quite overwhelming and much underplayed on the world stage. Thankfully, a real effort is now being made to promote the city as a major cultural centre. In the past, Tunisia has often been seen as a one-dimensional 'beach-and-sun-tan'

18. Saladin Christopher, 2020. *The Tale of a Mediterranean City Mapping. The History of Premodern Carthage and Tunis*. University of Minnesota

destination, especially by tourists from Eastern Europe. Sadly, very little of this tourist income actually permeates into the local economy as many tourists never fully engage with the culture of the country. This is a great pity, given that the city has so much to offer.

With its fledgling democracy, the country is slowly moving in the right direction and the Ministry of Tourism is making a real effort to build a new market in cultural tourism. The plan is to focus on tourists who are a bit older, have more to spend, and are really interested to know about ancient Carthaginian history. Visitors who will want to visit the sites where these incredible events of the ancient world took place. Huge numbers of cultural tourists visit Rome every year to see the ruins of ancient Rome, so why shouldn't the same be true of ancient Carthage?

Ancient Carthage is a classic example of the victors laying waste to the culture of those they have conquered. As well as sacking the city itself in 146 BC, the Romans did much to destroy the reputation of the Carthaginians, stereotyping them as thieves who were not to be trusted. However, even Cicero, the Roman statesman born 40 years after Carthage was sacked, admitted that: "Carthage would never have held an empire for six hundred years had it not been governed with wisdom and statesmanship."[19]

The Romans rebuilt Carthage in their own image and have left behind some astonishing artefacts themselves. The El Djem (ancient Thysdrus) Colosseum south of Tunis was built around 238 AD nearly four centuries after Carthage was destroyed. It is very well-preserved and in many parts better preserved than the Colosseum in Rome. It was the third largest amphitheatre in the Roman world after those in Rome and Capua and could hold about 35,000 people.

Like them, it was built for spectator set pieces like gladiatorial combat. It's constructed of honey-coloured stone and has a museum with hundreds of Roman mosaics on display. These come from both the amphitheatre itself and the surrounding Roman villas which were discovered when ancient Thysdrus was originally excavated.

It's easy to think of a city like Carthage as a very one-dimensional military machine, but it was also the centre of a highly developed civili-

19. Scullard H H 1990. *The Cambridge Ancient History, Carthage and Rome*, Ch 11, p. 486, Cambridge University Press.

sation. One very striking example of this was a statue we were taken to see of an ancient Carthaginian called Mago who has been largely lost to history. Mago was the 'Father of Agriculture' and wrote an extensive treatise on animal husbandry which, ironically perhaps, was revered by the Romans.

It extended to 28 books, and as well as advice on all aspects of farming, it included sections on vineyards, wine-growing, olive and fruit trees and bee-keeping. These were hugely sophisticated documents which, technical innovations aside, would have been as practical now as they were then.

Mago had absorbed all the farming knowledge not only of his own time, but also from the Phoenician farmers of Lebanon and the Berbers of North Africa. His texts actually survived the sack of Carthage itself and were taken to Rome where they were translated into both Greek and Latin with some fragments still surviving today.

It was also fascinating learning more from Mohammed Ghassen Nouira about how the Phoenicians produced the purple dye for which they were so famous. In the ancient world the dye was one of the most prized commodities in the world and worth more than its weight in gold. To this day it is associated with royalty and religious hierarchies. Even Prince's rock anthem *Purple Rain* owes a debt to the Phoenicians.

Mohammed had become fascinated not just on the theory of how this ancient dye was produced, but also on the practicalities. So much so that it almost cost him his marriage. He filled the kitchen of his house with molluscs trying to work out how to extract the dye while not really noticing that his experimentation was also producing some fairly intense anti-social odours.

What's more, he wasn't able to replicate the process of extracting the dye. He knew that it was produced from secretions that came from the glands of the snails, but the secretions he was producing were never purple. In the spirit of all famous scientific breakthroughs, he had arrived at the point when he was about to abandon the whole experiment.

However, one day, after he had left his workplace alone overnight, he returned to his 'lab' to find his workbench had turned purple. This was all that was needed to spur him on to experiment with different types of sea snail and how different shades of purple can be produced under different conditions.

It also revealed to me how this kind of knowledge was symptomatic of everything that made the Phoenicians such an advanced civilisation. Their cutting-edge seamanship with its possibilities of a trans-Atlantic crossing was not something that existed in isolation. So while Phoenician maritime expertise was the most advanced of its own time, so too their economy and culture developed in tandem.

Another feature of this was their coinage. The Carthaginians seem to have minted their first coins in about 410 or 409 BC, to pay for the expensive Second Sicilian War (410-404 BC).

The coins themselves were probably first minted in Sicily rather than Carthage, where mercenaries fighting on behalf of Carthage, needed to be paid. They were also a useful way of propagating cultural icons including their gods like Melqart, with his lionskin headdress, the goddesses Tanit, Astarte, and Isis, and famous generals including Hamilcar Barca and his son, Hannibal. The latter's astonishing feat of marching an army, including a contingent of elephants, over the Alps has reverberated down the millennia. Other designs included the prows of ships – used as battering rams on war galleys – palm trees, horses, lions, and, of course, war elephants; all potent symbols of ancient Carthage.[20]

While our visit to Carthage was a profoundly interesting experience, it was also a turning point and the start of the trans-Atlantic expedition that I had been planning for so long. It was very reassuring for me to be joined by the rest of the core crew at this point. Charlie and I were the only two members of the delivery crew to stay on board, although Sheimaa rejoined the expedition later in Tenerife.

As always with a new crew, it took a while for us all to get to know each other. As well as the core crew members, we were also joined by Boyd Tuttle along with Doug Petty and his son, Carson, who was just 19 at the time. Both Doug and Boyd are committed Mormons and there had been some speculation about how we would all gel, especially with the different religious traditions of the crew. As it turned out, the chemistry worked exceptionally well, and anyway for me it was important to have a multi-cultural, multi-ethnic crew representing the different countries who have an historical connection to the Phoenicians.

In the case of Doug and Boyd, this connection was their religious

20. Website: https://en.wikipedia.org/wiki/Carthaginian_coinage

belief derived from the Book of Mormon itself. The Book of Mormon records that around 600 BC, two groups migrated from Jerusalem, across the Atlantic Ocean to North America. One group, led by the prophet Lehi, departed from the southeastern Arabian Peninsula, probably Oman; and sailed around the continent of Africa. The second group, protecting Mulek, a son of King Zedekiah, from the Babylonian conquest of Jerusalem, likely sailed from a Phoenician port city in the eastern Mediterranean. The Book of Mormon records that some of the Native Americans are Lamanite descendants of the North American civilization that grew out of this ancient migration from Jerusalem. From their perspective, there was a likelihood that Mulek's people sailed in a Phoenician ship, hence their intense interest in the expedition.

While it was an interesting dynamic of the voyage that we all came from different cultural and religious backgrounds, there was never any friction between us. We all had our different responsibilities, duties, habits and rituals. The Muslim crew observed their prayers every day undisturbed and we also had some very stimulating discussions. We all understood that religious belief is personal. The only problem arises when someone demands that you believe what they believe on pain of death. Happily, there was nothing of that sort aboard *Phoenicia*.

I remember Steinar telling me that when he was a child, he had first read his fellow Norwegian, Thor Heyerdahl's book about the Kon-Tiki expedition and had dreamed his whole life of joining an expedition like the one on which we were embarking. He had also been incredibly patient with all the delays and had left his job to make it possible. "Ok, Philip. I'm with you," I remember him telling me.

And that was it. Three years after I had first made the decision to attempt a voyage across the Atlantic in *Phoenicia*, the expedition was finally about to begin.

***

Crew Member Story – Charlie Mannix Beale

Lisbon Port Entry

Everything was going well. We were sailing south down the coast of Portugal into Cascais, which is a very affluent part of Lisbon on the western edge of the Tagus estuary. It's a marina surrounded by beautiful beaches, the kind of place where glamorous people hang out. The marina is quite famous and has hosted the America's Cup in the past.

We were about five miles north of the harbour and the wind was pretty strong, so we decided the most sensible decision was to take the sail down and use the motor for a controlled entrance. However, when we attempted to drop the sail, it just wouldn't budge. The problem was that the halyard, which is the rope you use to haul up the yard, had become trapped at the top of the mast. We later discovered that the bolts holding the metal band at the top of the mast had sheered, causing it to slip down over the halyard, which then became jammed, making it impossible to release the yard. This meant that with such a strong wind, we came flying in towards the bay. It was like being on a bike that's going flat out down a steep hill when the brakes fail. By this stage we were really panicking and the only thing we could do was to try and reef the sail and pull it up towards the yard. So we threw some ropes attached to mallets, which we hoped would give them some weight, over the top of the yard.

I had been on the helm for hours at this point and just as the rest of the crew managed to get the ropes ready, I backed the sail. This meant that I had accidentally managed to bring the ship round on the wrong side of the wind. Instantly, there was pandemonium. The sail started flapping violently, sending all the ropes flying in all directions. The only option open at this point was to pull the yard around so that it was vertical rather than at right angles to the mast.

It was getting dark now and the sail was flapping wildly with all these wooden blocks attached to it. Eventually, we did manage to get the ship under control with the help of the engine and put the anchor down. But we still couldn't release the yard and the sail was still flapping and whipping around. It was also horribly loud and very embarrassing because Cascais is usually a very quiet, secluded place. There were some very fancy yachts moored nearby and there we were with this huge sail whipping around smacking itself against the mast.

The anchor watch that night was quite an unnerving experience which we all took in shifts, and the noise was unbelievable. So, the next morning the skipper had us all out of bed at sunrise to deal with the situation. The wind was still really strong and the sun was coming up over this very quiet, idyllic, little bay and we had this giant piece of canvas flapping around. It was also quite dangerous because all the wooden blocks were still being blown around attached to the ropes.

Fortunately, one of the young crew members was very athletic and a free runner back home in Belgium. The skipper managed to persuade him to climb up to the top of the mast and we all formed a piggyback stack and hoisted him up and he managed to cut the sail free with his knife. Then we flipped the yard around so it was horizontal again and finally managed to get the sail free.

So, there we were at 6 a.m. in the morning before people started arriving at the beach en masse, and at last peace and tranquillity had returned. One of the scariest moments for me of the whole trip was when I thought we were just going to plough straight into that bay!

The Pillars of Hercules

We set sail from Tunis, the site of the ancient city of Carthage, on Saturday 28th September 2019. After years of preparation and a challenging voyage to the start line from the UK, this was the first day of our long-awaited expedition to prove that a Phoenician crossing of the Atlantic 2000 years before Columbus was, at the very least, a realistic possibility.

Our departure from Tunis was incredibly uplifting. We had been treated like royalty from the day we arrived, and our departure was in many ways the climax of the whole stay. The team that had looked after us so well were all there, as was a huge crowd of well-wishers who came to cheer us off. There was much singing and dancing as we slowly left the harbour and made our way into the Bay of Tunis. It was a moment of huge relief and excitement for the whole crew. All our anxieties about what lay ahead fell away, and we were swept up in the excitement of the moment.

Just before we set sail, some of the city's theatre students, part of the team that had put on such a stirring performance when we arrived, came on board and gave us some parting gifts. Mine turned out to be a Phoenician-style costume which I immediately thought would be wonderful to wear when we arrived on the other side of the Atlantic. But it soon became clear that they wanted me to put it on right away, as we were leaving. Rather reluctantly, I donned the costume they had given me which, rather flatteringly, was of Yamm, the Phoenician god of the sea. At least, that's who I think it was meant to be.

As I made my way along the deck in front of the crowd, I realised I needed to play the part, especially when everyone on the harbour walls started cheering. As anyone who knows me will testify, I'm not a theatrical prima donna by nature. This, however, was different. I produced my best impression of a deity acknowledging his adoring followers, smiled benignly, and dispensed some regal waves as I took a bow.

When I look at the pictures now, I fear most people would think I look a bit ridiculous, but it felt good at the time, and seemed to be quite a crowd pleaser, so I was more than happy to oblige. It was certainly very uplifting to be given such a rousing send-off.

However, the realities of life at sea in a ten year-old replica of a 2500 year-old ship hit us very quickly. Almost immediately we encountered some strong winds as we sailed out into the Gulf of Tunis and the sea was very rough. We left in the late afternoon, but at about 2 a.m., when most of the crew were asleep, I received a message from our friend, Mohammed Ghassen. We were still in mobile phone range from the shore, but Mohammed's voice sounded strange and disembodied, and also clearly very concerned.

"Captain Philip, Captain Philip, is the Phoenicia in trouble? I've had a message from the wife of one of your crew members saying she has received a Mayday from her husband. Please confirm if emergency assistance is required?"

While things out in the bay were certainly challenging, and with new crew members aboard we were all taking a bit of time adapting to the rhythms of life back at sea, but they were certainly not that challenging. Far from it. The *Phoenicia* and her crew had experienced considerably worse conditions than this on many occasions. In addition, now I had by far the most experienced and competent crew sailing the ship since the finish of the *Around Africa expedition* nine years before.

Very taken aback by this message from Mohammed, I immediately confirmed that all was well. Nonetheless, when you're the captain of a ship at sea and you are asked if your ship is in trouble, it's very much like being accused of some wicked act during your schooldays. You immediately start believing you must be guilty as charged. Within 12 hours of leaving port, were we really in danger of sinking?

Happily, as a past master in controlling my 'Flight or Fight' response, I calmed down before the crew had a chance to sense my confusion. I immediately set about analysing how this Mayday could have been sent. After extracting some more information from Mohammed and think-ing the chain of events through logically, I realised the signal could only have come from one of the American crew members.

This conjecture turned out to be correct. The Mayday had been sent by accident from a tracker beacon that Doug Petty had brought with him. My next task was to wake Doug, who was understandably groggy and very confused. It turned out he had attempted to send a message to his wife saying that the ship had left Tunis, and all was well. Instead, the device had malfunctioned and sent a distress signal.

Doug was very embarrassed and apologetic, and we continued on our way. In these circumstances it's always best to look on the bright side and we were actually very lucky to be still in mobile range of land. If we had been marginally further out to sea and relying solely on radio communications, we would probably not have been able to get in touch with them again for another 24 hours. In which case, the coastguard would probably have felt there was no option but to launch a rescue mission.

Anyway, our Mediterranean adventures were not yet over. On the third day after leaving Tunis we were once again sailing parallel to the coast of Algeria, although this time from east to west when, suddenly and unexpectedly the wind turned against us. This was just plain bad luck because normally in September, the prevailing wind is from the east which would have blown us nicely in the direction of Gibraltar, our next destination.

After the Mayday incident, it had all been very exhilarating. This was the first time we had been able to hoist the sail to its full impressive height with a following wind. It was a very memorable moment and all of the crew were cheering and enjoying a real sense of elation.

The *Phoenicia* is like no other ship I know. It's by no means an easy ship to sail, but when the elements are with you, it has a grandeur that I have never experienced in another sailing vessel. When it's in tune with the elements, accompanied by just the sounds of the wind and the waves and the gentle creaking of the beams, it feels like the ultimate expression of everything that makes sailing a wooden ship so special.

Our euphoria was not to last long. Suddenly, everyone was looking up at the mast and I could hear Yuri yelling at me from the bows. "Captain, Captain, the mast is twisting badly. I think it's about to snap." As my heart sank, I couldn't help thinking this was turning into a rather badly-written TV melodrama. One moment we were cruising along nicely on Cloud Nine, the next on the verge of becoming a latter-day Mary Celeste.

Back in the real world, I found myself anxiously looking up at the mast. It was indeed bending alarmingly, and I think all the crew were worried. Since leaving the UK, the mast had never been under this amount of pressure. The yard was hoisted to its maximum height and had about half a ton of canvas weighing down on it, making the total weight, including the massive yard, the best part of a ton.

Phoenicia's mast is made of saroo, the Arabic name for a type of cypress fir. One of its qualities is its flexibility which, under the strain of about a ton of weight and the strong force of the wind on the sail, can make it appear and sound like it's about to break in two. We discovered later that the risk of it breaking was probably minimal, but theoretical likelihood is a difficult concept to hold on to when the mast is bending this way and that, looking as if it might snap like a matchstick at any moment.

In Tunis, we had examined it at close quarters and reinforced it with metal bands. But now we came to the conclusion that it was simply too dangerous to try to sail all the way to Gibraltar without further repairs. Much as I dreaded the prospect and had assiduously avoided it when we were sailing east, now I quickly realised the only answer was to take refuge in Algiers for a day or two. This would allow us to reduce the height of the mast and attach the yard lower down where there was more bulk and strength.

Weighing heavily on my mind was the safety of the crew. I would never have forgiven myself if the mast had broken and caused a life-threatening injury. The consequences could have been very serious indeed. The issue of the condition of the mast had now become something of a running sore. It needed to be sorted out once and for all, and the earlier the better. Waiting until we reached Gibraltar was no longer an option.

Even so, my reservations about our likely reception in Algiers had not gone away. The Algerian government is known to be suspicious of Westerners. They don't like private yachts or encourage tourism, so I knew it was bound to be a bureaucratic nightmare and, in all likelihood, an expensive waste of money extricating ourselves from greedy officialdom. As before, on the voyage sailing towards Carthage, I was very reluctant.

The sudden change in the direction of the wind also resulted in another incident that could have ended the expedition before it had really started. Around 6 p.m. on the evening of October 1st, I realised we were heading into some turbulent seas with some ominous skies. When you are only making 3 to 5 knots per hour, the loss of any of those hard-won nautical miles is a hard pill to swallow. After some discussion with the crew, I decided that the best option was to deploy a sea anchor. The latter can best be described as a type of underwater brake that slows the ship when it is being blown in the wrong direction.

To do this, we tied ropes to the four corners of the storm sail and attached them to the end of the anchor chain which we dropped into the water to arrest our backward motion. As the sun set in the west, I think some of the crew were becoming alarmed by the gathering clouds. We could see lightning strikes in the distance with the thunder reaching us a few moments after each strike as the wind became ever more gusty.

As this point I gave instructions to furl the remainder of the sail by gathering up and retying all the brailing lines. With all hands on deck, we lowered the yard arm and sail completely. This made sure that any forces acting on the mast would not be magnified by the weight of the yard arm. By 9 p.m., all of the preparations had been made to secure the vessel for some severe weather, but I know some of the more inexperienced crew members were beginning to worry that we might be in trouble.

By this stage, all of the crew had changed into their rain gear and were wearing life-jackets as we were hit by some strong south-easterlies. As we let out the sea anchor from the bow, the force of the water was so strong that the chain rapidly reached the end of its length about 200 feet forward of the bow. It soon became obvious from the tension on the chain that it was doing what we had hoped, and the ship realigned itself pointing into the wind. Exactly how much the sea anchor would arrest our backward motion was still unclear.

By the time the ship entered the heaviest cloud bank at around 11 p.m. Boyd had positioned himself near the bows intently watching the horizon to try and ward off the seasickness which was beginning to creep over him. At this stage the wind was whipping the waves into 15ft monsters. At times the ship would plunge into a gaping trough before being lifted up onto the top of a colossal wave and then thrown down into the next watery crevasse.

The weather conditions were deteriorating rapidly, and Boyd was feeling distinctly unwell when his turn for cleaning duty arrived. Making his way gingerly toward the galley with his headlamp set to red to keep his night vision intact, he staggered along the deck clinging tightly to anything he could find that would stop him being lifted off his feet.

Every now and then, a rogue wave would splash high enough to send a jet of water cascading across the deck. Once in the galley, Boyd realised that most of the work had been done and anyway no-one was thinking about washing dishes or cooking in these conditions. The rest of the crew were laughing and chatting as though it were a typical night at sea as Boyd sat resting his head on the table trying desperately to make the world stop rolling around inside his head. When you're feeling sea-sick every sound seems to be magnified and with the mast creaking and grinding, the teapot sliding back and forth across the stove top, and the steady pounding of waves, Boyd told me later it was like an 'orchestra of misery'. All he wanted was for it to end.

Still not feeling any better, Boyd soon realised that his turn at the helm was coming up next. Staggering to his feet, he pulled his raingear tighter round his face and climbed out of the galley by sliding up one of the weather boards and stepped over the threshold on to the deck. "The Phoenicians obviously didn't know about hinges," he joked later.

Once outside, he realised how much the temperature had dropped and how cold the rain felt. Moving carefully around the starboard side of the galley, he prepared to head toward the aft deck as he had done dozens of times before in calmer seas. Steinar and I always used to remind the crew about how important it is to keep a tight grip on the safety rope in rough seas. Boyd had never forgotten Steinar's warning that if a man falls overboard in a storm the chance of being rescued is about 1 in 100 with visibility reduced to just a few yards even with a searchlight.

But this time, just as Boyd reached for the safety rope, a huge wave struck the starboard side of the ship just as he was about to grab it. This sudden shock knocked him sideways off his feet. His memory of the whole incident is the classic slow-motion sequence of a near-death experience. First, he found himself grabbing desperately at the air as he lurched to the left. Then the two-and-a-half-foot high rail caught him just above the knee, the only object between him and the mile-deep ocean below.

With the ship rolling violently, the rail jammed into his lower thigh, throwing him even farther off-balance as all his do-or-die and fight-or-flight systems went into overdrive. But for Boyd, none of these seemed like a good option at that moment. Instead, his survival instinct took over and he literally willed his body to drop to the deck as fast as possible. Somehow he had to get his centre of gravity lower and avoid what at that moment seemed inevitable: "Man Overboard!"

Boyd estimated later that all this must have taken no more than two seconds, but as others have recorded when facing imminent death, this was all that was needed for his life to flash before his eyes. He found himself confronting all his successes and failures and everything that had led up to that moment. How would his beloved wife ever explain to his children and loved ones how she had agreed to let him take part in this voyage? To let him step out into the unknown with people he didn't know sailing an experimental craft based on a 2600 year-old design. He even started to grieve over the fact that he had placed her in that position with his 'crazy new idea for an adventure.'

Newton's First Law of Motion states that an object in motion stays in motion unless an external force acts upon it. Suddenly Newton became more important to Boyd than he ever realised was possible as he willed himself to bring his gravitational centre down. After crashing onto the railing, he teetered there for a split-second as the ship miraculously – at least as far as Boyd was concerned – rolled back towards the starboard side after cresting the wave. In some senses it was indeed a miracle because had the wave been any bigger, or lasted any longer at its peak, Newton's Law dictates that this object in motion, namely Boyd's body, would have continued along the same trajectory into the churning waves.

As his upper-half teetered on the rail, the ship rolled back beneath him. This allowed him to drop down to the safety of the deck as, with a massive sense of relief, he slowly crawled on all fours along the side of the galley. Finally, he reached the back window and pulled himself up to the standing position. At the same time, it began to dawn on him just how close he had come to experiencing the one thing that Steinar and I had warned the crew repeatedly *not* to let happen.

Then came an explosion of involuntary images as his brain came to terms with what had so nearly taken place. First, he saw himself grasping in panic for anything, a rail, a rope, a handhold, while at the same time, knowing he was clawing at thin air. The next sound would have been his impact as he hit the water, but with the engine running, the wind whipping, the rain pounding and the waves slapping the side of the boat, his screams would never have been heard. Or, if they were, they would probably have been mistaken for a shout or laughter coming from the galley. No one else was on deck at the time, and it might have been several minutes before anyone discovered he was gone.

Boyd and the rest of the crew had all been trained in the use of Emergency Position-Indicating Radio Beacons (EPIRBs). But he soon realised that without one in the storm-tossed sea, no-one would have had any idea when or where he went over. Even though his life-jacket would have inflated, nobody was in a position to see his fall – or even to hear his screams – and then to throw out an EPIRB to mark where he went in. And although we had the sea anchor deployed we were still moving at between 1 and 2 knots per hour due to the strong winds and within a few minutes Boyd would have been more than 100 yards away, far out of shouting or visible range.

Even if someone had noticed Boyd fall overboard or heard his shouts, it would have taken at least 20 minutes to haul up the sea anchor and turn the ship about. This would mean that by the time the search began, he would have been bobbing about in the open sea at least half a mile away, dooming it to failure before it had even begun. Boyd told me later that as these thoughts raged through his mind he uttered a silent prayer of gratitude for the voyage that almost wasn't. "Dear God in heaven, I'm just a lowly wannabe sailor in a wooden boat. Thank you! Thank you!"

While Boyd was still struggling with the aftermath of this terrifying experience, I was still wrestling with the decision about what to do concerning the mast. In the end, I reluctantly realised that we had no choice and that we would have to make for Algiers for repairs. Once the decision was made, we sailed into Algerian waters and made our way along its seemingly endless coastline. As we did so, we were taken by surprise one night when we were confronted by what looked like a small armada of lights coming towards us. We couldn't understand what these were or where they were coming from. It was only when we saw some fishing boats that we realised we had sailed into a maze of fishing nets.

By this stage we were in contact with the Algerian navy and they wanted to know if we were in trouble. We reassured them that we didn't need help, but that we needed to put into Algiers and get some repairs done for a day or two. As we sailed closer to our destination, we were soon surrounded by a phalanx of police and customs boats. They came alongside and asked us again what we were doing before providing us with a compulsory escort as we sailed closer to port.

Thus far, the reaction of officialdom was relatively reassuring. But we were concerned that their amused curiosity at this strange apparition of a wooden ship that was clearly no threat to their national security would be undermined by the fact that we had three Americans on board. Americans, in particular, are treated with suspicion, but much to our relief the coastguard that had been assigned to us was very friendly and gave us all the permissions we needed. He even radioed us to say that we had dolphins swimming alongside the bows of the ship, and would we like him to take some photos?

By coincidence, one of the Americans on board knew someone who worked at the American Embassy in Algiers, so we contacted him as soon as we were able to find mobile signal. His advice tallied with everything we had been doing thus far, basically to be very diplomatic and polite. The best strategy was to explain what we were doing, and try not to raise any suspicion of nefarious activities. Even so, the presence of Western spies aboard a replica of a 2500 year-old Phoenician ship did seem an unlikely scenario outside the confines of a Hollywood B movie.

Along with this eminently sensible advice, came the unexpected warning that under no circumstances should we fly the British flag, in case it should be seen as disrespectful. Even though this contradicted international maritime law, when we questioned it, their reply was the same: "Just don't fly it." This was their advice and so we took them at their word.

When we sailed into port, at the first location we tied up, we were battered by a bruising swell which felt very unpredictable and dangerous. Responding to our concerns, the coastguard then guided us into a bleak industrial area where we moored up alongside a giant harbour wall where some old tyres were found for us to use as fenders. Here there appeared to be no shops; no facilities like toilets; no signs of commercial activity - always a disappointment after a voyage at sea, when for days beforehand the prospect of a clean loo, hot showers, and a fizzy drink can seem like the very definition of Nirvana.

To our delight, we were met by members of the team from the American Embassy bearing gifts in the form of McDonald's burgers and some of those heavenly fizzy drinks. Nonetheless, our overall situation felt very strange. We were surrounded by giant wooden fishing boats with, rather incongruously, one tiny yacht squeezed in between them. This was crewed by two Spaniards who looked like they had been here since the 1960s, but who were very friendly and seemed as glad to see us as we were to see them.

We immediately noticed a police station close to where we were moored, so it was hardly a surprise when, shortly after we arrived, a huge posse of about twenty people turned up, some in a variety of official uniforms with others in suits and hi-viz jackets.

To our dismay, the very first thing they asked us in their broken English was "Where's your flag?" We replied that we had been advised not to fly the flag as a sign of courtesy. This excuse, which now sounded ridiculous even to us, cut no ice whatsoever. "Well, you must pay a penalty for not flying your flag. All ships visiting the port must fly their national flag. You must pay a penalty. You've broken the law."

Feeling more than a little aggrieved that the first black mark against us was an own goal, the next hurdle was another bout of form-filling for which we had to hire an agent in order to avoid accidentally admitting to being a crew of international spies sent in covertly to help topple the government. All the while, I was trying to avoid looking like an easy squeeze for yet more cash hand-outs. Nonetheless, they must have been rubbing their hands together under their official froideur, no doubt thinking we were easy prey, which, I suppose, is exactly what we were.

To make matters even worse, it then became apparent that we weren't allowed to leave the confines of the harbour. We were basically under house-arrest aboard the *Phoenicia*. On a more mundane level, we also needed to buy some diesel. Every task turned into a bureaucratic marathon, it was also very disappointing to find that we wouldn't be able to see anything of the city of Algiers itself. Even though we weren't technically under arrest, there was a policeman standing on the harbour wall next to the boat at all times of the day and night. Happily, while official policy was one thing, the individuals tasked with making us jump through the hoops were all very friendly, including our policeman on the harbour wall.

Once we had adapted to this strange new world of surveillance and form-filling, it actually turned out to be a memorable stay. The only hygiene facilities we were allowed to use were some dock workers' washrooms opposite a container vessel near where we were moored that was importing vegetables and fresh fruits, mainly bananas. It was all very basic, but we rapidly became embedded in this strange new community of maritime eccentricity and all the dock workers and deck-hands were very kind.

Before we arrived, we had braced ourselves for a hostile reception, but I don't think the Algerians had ever seen anything remotely like the *Phoenicia* before, so happily we fell neatly into the exotic, rather than the suspicious, category. All the young guys who were working on the banana boat came over to examine this strange new arrival and were soon jumping on and off the ship taking selfies. In return, they were very generous in gifting us an unlimited supply of bananas and other food, while making sure we were kept properly entertained with games like dominoes, as well as offering to let us use the internet on their phones.

Having at first thought that we wouldn't be given the chance to look around the city, the official from the Port Authority finally came up with a pass to let both our crew and, separately, the two Spaniards from the neighbouring yacht, see some of the sights, escorted by a professional guide. Much to our amazement, this pass even included our American crew and it turned out to be a very enjoyable experience. In fact, it was so interesting and we were so curious that we spent around five hours touring the city, so that by the time we returned to the harbour, our guide had to go home and so wasn't able to take the two Spaniards. Despite our profuse apologies, I'm not sure we were entirely forgiven.

Of course, the real reason we had made our unscheduled visit to Algiers was to fix the mast. And, as ever in a crisis, it was Dirman who solved the problem. For the captain of a wooden sailing ship, Dirman is one in a million. I have never met anyone with his unique combination of knowledge, practical skills and an even temperament. Without exception, Dirman was the crew member I would always turn to first when the *Phoenicia* needed a repair.

The rest of us had all been thinking that the obvious course of action was to attach some more metal bands around the mast to make it stronger. But Dirman was having none of it. "We should just cut the mast off at the top and make it shorter," he advised. "It's only rotten down to about six or eight feet from the top. It doesn't need to be that tall and it will still easily be able to hold the weight of the yard and the sail."

We were soon hauling Dirman up to the top of the mast where he drilled into it with a massive drill bit at the most rotten point. The idea was to hollow it out so that the rest of us could snap off the top section of the mast. After this was completed, we attached ropes to the very top of the mast for maximum leverage and, with the burliest tug-of-war gang we could muster, tried to snap it off. But despite our best efforts, pulling and pulling until we were all exhausted, we just couldn't get it to break.

The ever-forgiving Dirman was then hauled up the mast once again where he drilled another set of holes. After he had completed this task, we could see quite clearly from the deck that there were just a few bits of wood keeping the mast together. Just to make sure we would succeed in breaking it off this time, we asked a few of our new friends from the container ship to come and help us. To anyone who didn't know what was going on, it must have looked a totally bizarre sight. A chain gang of bruisers apparently trying to pull down the mast of an historic wooden sailing ship as the whole boat rocked back and forth in the water.

But still it wouldn't budge. This time it was the turn of some of the team from the adjacent warehouse to come and help us as the boat rocked back and forth even more violently in the water. Finally, with an alarming crack, the top of the mast snapped off. If we'd had a case of champagne on hand, we would have made short shrift of it. Instead, and rather more wisely, we went about refitting the halyard.

The long and the short of it, I had by then realised, was that it would almost certainly have been fine anyway. The mast was naturally flexible and incredibly strong. Then again, it is easy to be wise in hindsight. The worry it would have caused mid-Atlantic, thinking that it *might* break, made it the correct decision at the time. Our task completed, paperwork filled out in triplicate, fines and bills paid, and after exchanging warm goodbyes with our new friends, we were soon on our way again.

To our relief, our voyage from Algiers to Gibraltar was one of the smoothest of the entire expedition and a welcome change from our recent storm-tossed experiences. We sailed on 8th October 2019 and this time the gods were on our side. With a following westerly we arrived in Gibraltar five days later, not long after midnight and in pitch darkness. Early the next morning, the winds changed direction again, but by this time we were safely in port. We had made it to Gibraltar just in time.

Despite the relative ease of the previous leg, the whole crew was exhausted. We had been instructed over the radio to anchor on the Spanish side of the harbour near the airport. But we had barely begun to sort ourselves out when the Spanish authorities appeared in person and informed us that we needed to move. The reason? Our mast was too high for this area of the harbour. This information was greeted with some stifled guffaws and a few mumbles about sending Dirman up the mast to sort things out. Instead, we duly hauled up the anchor and did as we were instructed.

We stayed in Gibraltar for the next four days, primarily to replenish our food stocks and other necessities, but also to make a few ongoing repairs which required spare parts. Even though we would be making landfall three more times in Cadiz, Essaouira in Morocco, and Tenerife in the Canary Islands, we were fine-tuning now and making final preparations for the all-important 3600-mile Atlantic crossing to wherever the fates decreed we should make land-fall.

When we reached Gibraltar, there was a lot of coming and going on the ship. The most important crew member to join us was Maran Fazzi, who was to be our doctor for the trans-Atlantic leg of the expedition. Maran had completed her training to be a doctor two years before and had always been interested in expedition medicine. She had taken an Advanced Wilderness Life Support (AWLS) course and was on her way to becoming an instructor. She had actually found out about the expedition from our social media outlets, but with all the complications of planning the expedition, I had never actually met her in person.

Maran was really looking forward to putting all her theoretical knowledge into practice, but her experience of sailing was very limited, so I think that finding her niche on board and making it her home must have been quite challenging at first. Whenever you join an expedition, it's always a bit of a shock to the system. Adapting to life in cramped conditions, working out who everyone is, making new relationships, carrying out your duties, and establishing a routine, is no easy matter. But, much to her credit, she adapted very quickly and became a key member of the crew. In fact, by the time we reached Tenerife a few weeks later, I could see she was professional and well organised, so I asked her to look after not just the medical side of the expedition but also the management of our supplies of food which would be critical for the voyage across the Atlantic.

***

Crew Story – Maran Fazzi

Maran remembers some of the many highlights from the voyage including watching dolphins, star watching, fishing for mahi mahi, and swimming with a pilot whale.

Not long after we left Tenerife, we started to see pods of dolphins swimming all around the ship. I've always really loved seeing animals in zoos and when I was young I wanted to be a dolphin trainer, so dolphins have always been very special for me. I would always ask whoever was on watch to call me if I was down below, or wake me if I was asleep. I think most of the crew were a bit surprised that I loved dolphins so much that I would want to be woken from my precious sleep to see them. "Are you really sure, you want us to wake you?" they would ask, as if I had lost leave of my senses.

As it turned out it was only the first time we saw them that I had to be woken. And it was certainly worth it as far as I was concerned. The other times I was either on watch myself or on the deck. We would often see them at night, which was even more special than during the day, especially under a full moon. I remember one time at night, it was so quiet and mysterious, all you could hear was the swish of the bows cutting through the waves and the air through the blowholes of the dolphins. Utterly magical.

Another unforgettable memory for me was watching the sun rise and set every day. In our everyday lives, we hardly ever have time to just sit and watch these daily miracles. Back home in the city where I live, I used to attend some planetarium shows, so I had some basic knowledge of astronomy. But now here I was in the middle of the Atlantic with zero light pollution and in probably the best place in the world to enjoy the stars. It really was very, very special with just the sound of the wind and the waves. I actually used to enjoy looking at the stars most when I was on the helm, feeling I was in control, guiding the ship on its voyage across the universe!

It was my first experience of the wide ocean and it was real elation. It wasn't so much a religious experience, more an intense feeling of euphoria. It felt like the most intense feeling of freedom I've ever experienced, even though in a technical sense, we were all confined together in this very small space. Obviously, you can't be feeling like that all the time for six weeks in a row and it was only really when I had time to think about where we were on the planet that I realised how incredible a thing it was that we were doing.

I enjoyed fishing a lot too, but it was really Dirman who was the fishing guru. I learned everything that I know from him. Even if you were just helping get the fish on board, it felt so nice to be providing this extra dimension to the meals in terms of taste and diversity, but also in nutritional value, it was a very good feeling. The fish we used to catch that I always remember were the huge mahi mahi. It's a very muscular, beautiful yellowy blue fish with not too many bones, so it really is the perfect meal for a hungry crew.

Swimming from the ship was also a wonderful experience. On the first occasion it was near the beginning of the voyage. There wasn't much wind, and we had to make some repairs to the sail, so the ship was just floating around and not really going anywhere, so I didn't feel like I was going to be left behind. It's a very strange feeling to see the boat floating around in the waves and you feel so small surrounded by this vast ocean. The second time was around Christmas, and was definitely a bit more scary. I suddenly saw this grey shadow further out, but coming towards

The building of *Phoenicia*

The keel is laid.

First two planks joined.

First twenty planks.

Shell-first construction of the hull.

At launch, May 2008.

Archaeology and history

Eratosthenes (c.276-194BC), first to correctly estimate the circumference of the world.

Ship rock drawings Laja Alta cave, Spain, c.9-7th century BC.

Ship rock drawings Laja Alta cave, Spain, c.9-7th century BC.

Atlantic B.C.

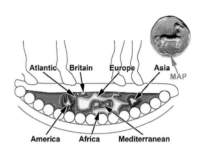

Carthaginian Gold Stater illustration (320-350BC) indicating Phoenician knowledge of the New World?

Marble sarcophagi in the Museum of Cadiz, Spain.

Phoenician exhibits at the Museum of Cadiz, Spain.

Christopher Columbus (1451-1506) after a painting, 1512, by Lorenzo Lotto.

Sculpture of a bearded man in caves at Samaná Bay, Dominican Republic.

An etching from The Destruction of the Indies by Bartolomé de las Casas.

Life on board

A good day's catch.

Barracuda for supper.

Christmas day at sea, 2019.

Dirman fixing a mast issue at sea.

Dirman with squid.

Phoenicia amonst the fishing boats at Essaouira, Morrocco.

Falcon.

Yuri and his rat catching trap.

Trimming the sail.

Sailing images of *Phoenicia*

Phoenicia with fresh winds.

Phoenicia by drone.

Phoenicia heading west.

Phoenicia's storm sail at full stretch.

Phoenicia at sunset.

Betty "Red Ant" and her husband Mike Lafontaine present her painted drum to Philip.

Phoenicia spilling the wind.

Phoenicia approaching Miami.

Crew in the USA.

us. For a moment it was quite frightening and I started swimming as fast as I could for the ship. Luckily it turned out to be a pilot whale and not a shark. What a relief that was!

While still in port, we tried to visit as many sites as we could with links to the ancient Phoenicians. The Rock of Gibraltar, that colossal limestone promontory that soars nearly 1400 feet above the swirling waters at the entrance to the Mediterranean, was one of the most fascinating of them all.

Gorham's Cave, on the eastern side of the Rock, is one of a complex of caves in cliffs just above the shoreline. In 2016, this hugely important archaeological site was designated as a UNESCO World Heritage Site. It burrows for more than 300 yards into the 200 million year-old Jurassic limestone reached via a colossal 100ft-high entrance. It was discovered in 1907 by a Captain Gorham of the 2nd Battalion, Royal Munster Fusiliers. You can still see his 'Kilroy Was Here' graffiti on the cave walls where he inscribed both his name and the date using the lamp-black from his lantern, a fine powder of left-over soot.

The site is world-famous for the evidence of habitation left behind both by the Neanderthals and later, early modern humans. This occurred over a staggering period of around 120,000 years up to around 32,000 years ago when the Neanderthals died out. Probably, many anthropologists believe, with a helpful shove from Homo sapiens.

Although today the caves are found in the cliffs above the beach, when they were first used they are thought to have been more than three miles inland, during a period when sea levels were much lower. Lines scored in the rock are thought to be abstract symbols suggesting that, until recently, Neanderthal cognitive abilities have been seriously underestimated.

Our focus of interest, however, was equivalent to yesterday in the long history of our species, even though it may seem ancient to us. It has now been shown that between the 8th and the 3rd centuries BC, the cave was in use again, this time by the Phoenicians. They used the cave as a shrine, making offerings to the gods before leaving the relative safety of the Mediterranean and braving the unknown waters of the Atlantic beyond. To do this, they were forced to sail through the Pillars of Hercules, the borders of the known world for the civilisations of the Eastern Mediterranean.

The caves, it is thought, were also a look-out point, defending the Phoenicians' lucrative trade routes around the coast of the Iberian peninsula and beyond. According to the historian, William Serfaty,[21] foreign ships that might be a threat – primarily the Greeks from the Eastern Mediterranean, the Etruscans from the Western Mediterranean, would be cut off by a force sent out to intercept them. This would be deployed from the nearby Phoenician city of Carteia, which had a powerful naval base.

Hundreds of items of Phoenician origin, left as offerings to the gods, have been found in the cave. These include incense burners in the form of small oil lamps, amulets, rings, ceramics, glassware, and scarabs. Scarabs were formalised engravings of dung beetles on rings and ornaments which represented immortality first in Egyptian, and later Phoenician, culture.

Archaeologists believe that most of the oldest items were made in Tyre, one of the founding city states of the Phoenician civilisation, but they also include a small blue and yellow glass amphoriskos which was brought to Gibraltar by ancient Carthaginian mariners and left as an offering for safe passage. Its creation has been traced to the island of Rhodes (5th century BC) and has become a symbol of the Gibraltar National Museum.

It was here that I reconnected with Museum Director, Professor Clive Finlayson, who had just been awarded the Gibraltar Medallion of Distinction by the Gibraltar Parliament, specifically for his work on Gorham's Cave. Clive had come down to meet *Phoenicia* when we came through in 2010 during the *Around Africa expedition*. It was his team of archaeologists who had conducted all the latest research in the caves, and it was amazing to hear from such an authority about the range of objects that had been discovered.

It was this research that first established that they were offerings to the gods from Phoenician sailors asking for safe passage before they

---

21. William Serfaty, dip.Arch.(Leics.) https://phoenicia.org/

ventured out through the Pillars of Hercules. One of Clive's discoveries that I found particularly fascinating was that many of the engravings on the rings and ornaments are almost impossible to see with the naked eye, with the help of a microscope can be seen in intricate detail.

In the museum, Clive and his team have enlarged these engravings so they can be seen in detail. And they are astonishing. Especially in light of the fact that the engravers were chosen because they had a rare form of astigmatism. This allowed them to work on a minute scale, engraving details which a highly-skilled craftsman would only be able to replicate today using a high-powered microscope.

There was, however, a slight disappointment connected to our second visit to Gorham's Cave aboard the *Phoenicia*. When I first met Professor Finlayson in 2010, he had suggested to me that on any future expedition, I should anchor the ship near the cave and make an offering as the ancient Phoenicians had done 2500 years ago. If anything was likely to ensure the success of the expedition, I felt sure this was it. Unfortunately, however, when it came to the crunch it proved impossible to organise. I put a proposal together and sent it to him, but I think a combination of work pressures and a recent illness meant that the event never took place. Happily, by and large, the gods proved to be on our side anyway.

As the offerings found at Gorham's Cave suggest, religious and mythological beliefs played a very powerful role in the lives of the people of the ancient world, and especially the mariners whose lives were played out at the frequently capricious whim of the waves and the weather. This was nowhere more evident than in the myths surrounding the creation of the Pillars of Hercules which marked the border of the known world. One Pillar is on the northern (European) side of what are now known as the Straits of Gibraltar, and the other on the southern (African) side.

The Rock of Gibraltar itself, the location of Gorham's Cave, is easily identified as the northern Pillar, with the identity of the other split between two possibilities. The most likely candidate is Jebel Musa, a high mountain on the coast of Morocco, while another less likely contender is Monte Hacho, a relative minnow by comparison, overlooking Ceuta, a city governed by Spain, about 15 miles further east.

The psychological significance of the Pillars in the ancient world cannot be overstated and was later absorbed into the collective psyche of both the Greeks and the Romans. During the later Carthaginian era of Phoenician history, the Pillars became associated with Melqart, the Tyrian god of regeneration and fertility, who as the offspring of Baal, was the son of the Lord of the Universe.

In the Greek version, Herakles was the offspring of Zeus, also the king of the gods, and a mortal woman, Alcmene. Both Melqart and Herakles are depicted in ancient statues wearing lion skins. Zeus' jealous wife, Hera, tried to kill Herakles at birth by placing two snakes in his cradle, a fate which he avoided by quickly strangling them. The unforgiving Hera, however, later put Herakles under a spell which made him kill his wife and two children, believing them to be his enemies.

His penance for this act, as decreed by Zeus, was to become the servant of the Mycenean king, Eurystheus, who was also consumed by envy of Herakles. The king's plan was to set Herakles twelve seemingly impossible tasks, the famous 'Twelve Labours', assuming he would die in the process. In the unlikely event that he survived, Herakles would be absolved of his sins and made immortal.

One of these tasks was to steal the red cattle of the three-headed monster, Geryon, who lived on the island of Erytheia beyond the western edge of the world. To find Erytheia, Herakles had to reach the Atlantic Ocean. In his way stood the mountain range which the ancients believed once separated the Mediterranean from the Atlantic. Undeterred, Herakles used his colossal strength to split the mountain in two, which he succeeded in doing with a single blow from his sword.

After reaching Erytheia and seeing off a two-headed dog called Orthus, Herakles killed the monster with his bow and arrow, captured the cattle, and returned east where, after many more adventures, he delivered the cattle to Eurystheus who promptly sacrificed them to, you guessed it, Hera.

The interesting part of the story from our point of view was that the island of Erytheia was thought to be based on the Phoenician colony of Gadeira (Cadiz), which we were shortly to visit. Other versions of the myth (and there are many) were recorded by the historian, Diodorus Siculus, who suggested that Herakles either created the Pillars as a monument to himself, or narrowed an already existing channel to prevent sea monsters invading the Mediterranean from the ocean beyond. Helpfully, Diodorus also suggested that readers should make up their own minds as to which version was true.

The underlying message of this complicated set of Chinese whispers is that, for mariners in the ancient world, sailing beyond the Pillars was the equivalent of blasting off into space in our own time. Those that did return, and many did not, related terrifying tales of near-death experiences and multi-headed sea monsters. The Romans believed the words 'Non Plus Ultra', translating as 'Nothing Beyond', were inscribed on the Pillars. They are words that have echoed down the centuries. Inspired by the voyages of Columbus, 'Plus Ultra' meaning 'Further Beyond' is today the national motto of Spain.

The Pillars were – in reality as well as mythology – on the western borders of the known world. Even for those prepared to risk their lives and sail beyond, the tides, combined with unpredictable currents, made them very difficult to navigate. However, if you did have the right knowledge, which over time the Phoenicians traders certainly gained, it made them easier to blockade and stop non-Phoenician ships, particularly the Greeks, from sailing out into the Atlantic.

Keeping the terrifying reputation of the Pillars alive, and magnifying it whenever possible, was another weapon in the Phoenicians' armoury. During the 5th century BC, the Carthaginian sailors Hanno and Himilco had sailed way beyond the Pillars. The former around the coast of west Africa and the latter around northern Europe.

In doing so they founded colonies and created lucrative trade routes, bringing back valuable commodities whose source they wanted to protect from their enemies, including the Greeks and the Romans. For this reason, they were notoriously secretive and probably deliberately created an ancient version of 'fake news', while at the same time ensuring that none of their sea charts or documents fell into the hands of their competitors.

According to the distinguished Phoenician scholar, Sanford Holst, Hanno the Navigator's report on his voyage sailing around the northwest coast of Africa beyond the Pillars of Hercules has innumerable references to hellish landscapes which may well be deliberate disinformation.[22] The following passage is typical:

22. Holst, Sanford. 2005. *Phoenicians: Lebanon's Epic Heritage* (Sierra Sunrise Publishing) p. 279.

...we passed a country burning with fires and perfumes; and streams of fire supplied from it fell into the sea. The country was impassable on account of the heat...and passing on for four days, we discovered at night a country full of fire. In the middle was a lofty fire, larger than the rest, which seemed to touch the stars.

"While many acknowledged that the Phoenicians sailed by the stars and went to distant lands, no one ever reported seeing their charts and maps," Holst concludes. "As a result, many who wished to compete with these sea traders were compelled to sail only within sight of land and feared to go beyond the Straits of Gibraltar."[23]

Holst also notes that the geographer and historian, Strabo, recorded that a Roman ship tailed a Phoenician vessel on its way to collect tin from Cornwall, trying to find the source of the trade. In response, the Phoenician ship lured the Roman ship onto some rocks, but in doing so found itself in trouble and both ships were wrecked. A potent sign of how determined the Phoenicians were to protect their secrets. Letting them fall into enemy hands would have been akin to a cowardly surrender.

It also vividly demonstrates the mindset of a people who realised that information, rather than raw military strength, was the underlying source of their power. During their frequent wars, whenever a town was in danger of falling to the enemy, any information that might be of use to the enemy was often destroyed. This, as well as the sack of Carthage and the burning of its libraries by the Roman general, Scipio, at the end of the Third Punic War in 146 BC, probably account for the almost complete absence of first-hand Phoenician accounts of their sea journeys.

23. Ibid, p. 327.

Beyond the Pillars of Hercules

S ailing through the narrow 14-mile stretch of water between the legendary Pillars of Hercules and leaving the Rock of Gibraltar behind us, was a powerful experience for all the crew. Especially for those who had just joined us.

As we made our way through the famous Strait of Gibraltar, I couldn't help thinking about the rock paintings at Laja Alta cave, which, although many miles away to our north, overlook the bay surrounding Gibraltar. The rock paintings clearly show sophisticated ships with sails and oars[24] and until recently had been dated to between 700 and 1000 BC when the first Phoenician ships would have made their presence known. A more recent study by Dr. Eduardo García Alfonso from the University of Granada has suggested the possibility that the rock drawings are even earlier, to 4000 BC.[25] Whatever the exact dates are, it is clear that these drawings demonstrate that ancient sailing ships have been in the area of the Strait of Gibraltar with access to the Atlantic for two or three thousand years at a minimum. And there was no doubt in my mind that we were following in the wake of these ancient sailors.

Our destination was Cadiz, ancient Gadir, just 70 nautical miles around the west coast of Spain. It was a relatively easy leg that took just 36 hours. This proved to be an excellent opportunity for the new crew members to bond with the old hands and get used to the routines of being at sea without any serious stress. As well as enjoying the significant symbolism of passing through the Pillars once more, I was also looking forward to visiting Cadiz, founded by the Phoenicians in around 1100 BC, making it one of the oldest cities in Western Europe. Probably *the* oldest.

Pandemic aside, the city is currently experiencing one of its periodic revivals in fortune after a time at the end of the last century when it had

24. See the photos of the rock drawings at Laja Alta in the colour section.
25. Source: Documentary, "The Neolithic: door of civilization" (June, 2016)

gained a reputation for seediness. Prosperous, and surrounded almost entirely by the sea on a narrow isthmus of land jutting out into the Atlantic, the city is the capital of the province of Andalusia in the deep south-west of Spain. It has been the principal port of the Spanish navy since the 18th century.

Cadiz slots nicely into that old travel writer's cliché of being a 'City of Contrasts.' At one end of the spectrum are the medieval cobbled streets of the *Casco Antiguo* (Old Town) with its elegant plazas and Roman theatre, one of the largest ever built in the Roman world. At the other is the modern town with its wide avenues, hi-tech buildings, and 500 foot-high 'Towers of Cadiz', an intricate lattice-work made of steel which carries the city's power lines over the bay.

Happily, both seem to rub along side by side, with tourists coming to enjoy its ancient sights, as well as the sandy beaches on the Cadiz peninsula lined with ritzy restaurants, bars and boutique hotels. The most popular beach with tourists and locals alike is La Playa de la Victoria with its epic two miles of golden sands which easily swallow the crowds in the height of summer.

But it was the Playa de la Caleta at the heart of the historic Old Town which we found the most fascinating. As well as being the smallest and the most beautiful, it has a castle at either end and has been used as a medieval backdrop in many films. Looking out over its own small bay on the projecting spit of land that borders the Atlantic, it is in all likelihood where the ancient Phoenicians first landed three millennia ago.

Those first settlers were from Tyre and the colony was first recorded, in documents written centuries later, as Gadir. This translates as 'Walled Compound' or 'Stronghold'. Judging by the sparsity of its early archaeological remains, historians believe it wasn't settled on a permanent basis until the 9th century BC, and it was only after serving as a trading station for several centuries that it first became a heavily defended fortress.

Trade was again the initial motivation. The Phoenicians were stretching the tentacles of their trading empire ever-westwards, first creating colonies across the Mediterranean, and later beyond the Pillars of Hercules. On the Iberian peninsula, they struck gold. Literally. Trading with the local Tartessian people, they had now found a lucrative source of mineral wealth that included gold, silver and, perhaps most significantly, tin.

The fact that for the first few centuries of settlement at Gadir there are very limited archaeological remains is consistent with what is known about the Phoenician's trade strategy. At the beginning of the first millennium BC, the Phoenician city states in the Eastern Mediterranean were still recovering from attacks by the surrounding Hittites, Mycenaeans, and Egyptians.

This recovery led to the second phase of expansion. At this point in their history, the Phoenicians were not trying to establish an empire in the later Roman sense of military conquest. Their efforts went into boat building and maritime exploration, so that they could trade further afield than any of their neighbours in the Mediterranean basin and build wealth and power accordingly.

As we know from Herodotus, their initial trading strategy was to build up a relationship with the local inhabitants based on mutual trust:

> *"They no sooner arrive but forthwith they unlade their wares and having disposed them after an orderly fashion along the beach, leave them, and, returning aboard their ships, raise a great smoke. The natives, when they see the smoke, come down to the shore and laying out to view so much gold as they think the worth of the wares withdraw to a distance. The [Phoenicians] upon this come ashore and look. If they think the gold enough, they take it and go their way."* [26]

This approach meant that the building of warehouses and infrastructure that would need to be protected was unnecessary. In truth, so far from home, they wouldn't have stood a chance anyway had the locals wanted to evict them. Their presence was allowed on the basis that this was a mutually beneficial exchange. They kept their cargoes and the secrets of their boat building skills safe by anchoring their ships out at sea. Later, when mutual trust had been established, they would mix with the local inhabitants on land and develop deep trading and cultural relationships.

That said, they were also canny traders. Very much like Columbus after his arrival in the Americas, the Phoenicians were looking for commodities that were rare and considerably more valuable back home. Just

26. Holst, Sanford. 2005. *Phoenicians: Lebanon's Epic Heritage* (Sierra Sunrise Publishing) p. 279.

as gold was to be for the conquistadors looking for El Dorado, so too was gold and silver for the Phoenicians in Iberia. According to the Greek historian, Diodorus Siculus, they found copious quantities. He writes:

> *"Much silver trickled away from the fiery ground and as they melted, the silver bearing ores formed countless rivulets of pure silver. The natives (of Iberia) did not know how to exploit it but once the Phoenicians heard of the affair they bought the silver in exchange for objects of negligible value. The Phoenicians took the silver to Greece, to Asia and to all other countries then known, thus obtaining great riches. It is said that such was the cupidity of the traders that they replaced the lead anchors of their ships with silver ones after there was no more room for silver in the vessels and there was still a great quantity of the metal left over."* [27]

His comment that when their ships were full they threw away their anchors and substituted new ones made of silver, is probably an exaggeration but we understand the sentiment that the Phoenicians were dealing with industrial quantities of silver and would later manage the mining process as well as the exports from Iberia.

However, the goal of the Phoenicians was always long-term and trade orientated. Evidence suggests that as well as their famous dyes, the Phoenicians traded fresh and preserved fish as well as fabrics, wood, glass, metals, incense, papyrus and carved ivory. During its long history as a Phoenician colony, Gadir's huge protected harbour also made it the perfect jumping-off point for voyages of exploration which, in time, would lead to yet more lucrative trade routes.

It was from Gadir that the explorers, Hanno and Himilco, set sail. Once again, this suggests that the level of trade between the eastern and western ends of the Mediterranean and into the Atlantic beyond was far greater than is usually realised. Hanno's voyage, as recorded by Herodotus, explored the west coast of Africa, while Himilco sailed north, around what is now Portugal, to the coast of Brittany.

---

27. Aubet, Maria Eugenia, 2001, *The Phoenicians and the West: Politics, Colonies and Trade*, 2nd Edition, Translation: Mary Turton (Cambridge, TAS, Australia: Cambridge University Press) p. 280.

The latter was searching for sources of a mineral that to modern ears sounds considerably less alluring than gold. That mineral was tin. Although from a 21st century perspective, tin would not seem to have anything like the same value as precious metals, to the ancients it was in many ways even more valuable.

Historians name epochs by their defining discoveries or events - the 'industrial' and 'digital' revolutions, for example. Much further back, and lasting for millennia, not just centuries and decades, were the Stone, Bronze, and Iron Ages. The voyages of Hanno and Himilco were made during the era known as the Bronze Age, when tin was exported from the Iberian peninsula, and even from Cornwall, to the Eastern Mediterranean.[28] The discovery that tin, when combined with copper, was both much stronger and easier to mould than copper alone, spread from the Near East across the Mediterranean and Europe.

This led to a technological revolution that could not be ignored by any civilisation intent on growing or maintaining its power. As well as driving a boom in ornamentation, bronze was critical to the development of stronger and more lethal weaponry. But the constituents of this metal were in short supply, and for the Phoenicians the tin trade was highly lucrative.

There is no evidence that Himilco reached Britain, but he was almost certainly following a route that had already been established by the native tribes of Spain and may well have returned with tin from Brittany, that had in turn been imported from Cornwall in the far south-west of Britain.

As time went on, however, and the power shifted from the founding city states in the eastern Mediterranean to Carthage on the north African coast, the Phoenician strategy gradually evolved into an imperial mentality, involving the subjugation of the local people rather than the mutual trust of previous centuries. Perhaps this was inevitable, given the course of events in the eastern Mediterranean.

As the power of the founding city states like Tyre waned in the face of Persian expansion, the one-time colony of Carthage took over as the Phoenician powerhouse and asserted its control over Gadir. The ever-expanding Roman Empire was also a threat to Phoenician hegemony,

28. Ibid.

culminating in the First Punic War between Rome and Carthage in the 3rd century BC. This led directly to competition between Rome and Carthage for influence on the Iberian peninsula.

After peaceful beginnings, the one-time friendly traders eventually enslaved their trading partners as the increasing value of their trading routes gradually became essential for keeping their own enemies at bay. At the height of their power, it is estimated the Phoenicians had as many as 30,000 slaves working for them in the mines on the Iberian Peninsula.[29]

In this duel to the death, as it turned out to be, between the Phoenicians and the Romans, Carthage was at first dominant under their general, Hamilcar, who used Gadir as his military base. But after his death in battle, they were forced into a policy of appeasement.

Nonetheless, tensions simmered and eventually led to the outbreak of the Second Punic War. It was from Gadir that Hannibal led his troops and elephants over the Alps, famously defeating the Romans in a series of battles in Italy itself. In the long run, however, the Romans proved to be an unstoppable force. The Third Punic War ended with the sack of Carthage in 146 BC and with it the collapse of the Phoenician civilisation.

For Gadir, however, albeit under a long succession of new rulers, the story was only just beginning. Nearly 1500 years later Cadiz, as it had become known, was where Columbus began his second and fourth voyages to the New World. These expeditions led to the most dramatic of the city's periods of wealth and expansion when, in 1493, it became the headquarters of the Spanish treasure fleets.

The multi-faceted history of Cadiz and the pivotal role it played in the story of the Phoenicians was highlighted still further when our wonderful guide, Fernando Pineiro, showed us around the town and the museum. This introduction had come about by a modern day Lebanese-Mexican academic, Dr Habib Chamoun-Nicolas who I had met on my earlier travels to promote the expedition in New York. Dr Habib had studied the Phoenicians trading and negotiating tactics and wrote the book "How to negotiate like a Phoenician",[30] which describes

29. Ibid.
30. Chamoun-Nicolás,Habib, 2007.*How to negotiate like a Phoenician*. Key negotiations Llc.

how Phoenician principles can be applied in modern business negotiations and sales. When I asked him if he could introduce me to some of his wide network of friends in Cadiz and our other ports of call, he was only too happy to help. Indeed, behind the scenes Dr Habib went on to make a number of other important introductions as the expedition progressed, for which I will be forever grateful.

One of the museum's most important archaeological treasures is a marble sarcophagus carved into the shape of a human that was discovered at a site called the Necropolis de la Punta de la Vaca in 1887.

It was discovered by accident when three Phoenician tombs were uncovered during land-clearing in advance of an International Maritime Exhibition. The sarcophagus was by far the most significant find and led to the creation of the museum itself. The discoveries in the three tombs demonstrated the importance of Gadir as a Phoenician colony, a fact which up until that time had not been fully appreciated. This resulted in a gold-rush of archaeologists visiting the city.

"One of the archaeologists was Pelayo Quintero Atauri," Fernando told us. "He was convinced of the existence of a female sarcophagus similar to the male one found in the necropolis. He searched throughout the city, excavating various Phoenician and Roman sites, but just could not find what he was looking for. Pelayo Quintero was so intrigued by the elusive 'Lady of Cádiz' that he even dreamt about her at night."

Sadly, his dreams were never realised and he never discovered her whereabouts. Then in 1980, more than forty years after his death, an excavator bumped into something large and made of marble. "It was a sarcophagus in the shape of a human and very similar to the one found almost a hundred years previously," Fernando continued. "But this time it was carved in the shape of a female. Amazingly, the artefact was unearthed near the very spot where Pelayo Quintero had so often slept and dreamt of the 'Lady of Cadiz'."

Inspired by our time-traveller's journey along the highways and byways of the ancient Phoenician world, hidden beneath the colourful streets of modern Cadiz, the next leg of our journey followed in the wake of Hanno the Navigator. According to Pliny the Elder, Hanno sailed from Cadiz around the west coast of Africa. Our destination was another Phoenician colony, the port city of Essaouira, south of Casablanca on the Atlantic coast of Morocco.

Sailing south-west down the Iberian peninsula into the Atlantic, this time we crossed the Straits of Gibraltar while keeping to the west of the Pillars of Hercules and sailed down the coast of Morocco in north Africa. This was a leg of about 350 miles, but in contrast to the benign conditions on our short hop to Cadiz from Gibraltar, the weather had now turned against us and we were confronted with rough seas and ferocious thunder and lightning.

Although it may seem counter-intuitive to readers who have not spent much time at sea, sailing a ship in a storm is in some ways simpler than sailing it with a benign, following wind. In a storm, the top priority is to make everything safe in terms of furling the sails and making sure there is no loose rigging, ropes, or random items rolling around on deck. The crew must all be wearing life-jackets and all safety measures must be in place.

But once you're in the eye of the storm, the main objective is simply to keep the ship on a consistent bearing without crashing your head against a beam or falling on someone else. As the skipper, staying calm is very important, as this gives confidence to the crew and helps avoid panic setting in. Especially for crew members like Maran, for example, who had never experienced a storm at sea before.

Beyond all that, it was really a matter of making sure that we were still heading south and not out into the Atlantic or, worse still, towards the rocky cliffs on the Moroccan coast. But even with the best-laid plans of mice and men, accidents can still happen; and on this occasion, they did.

Aziz, like Dirman, a hugely experienced and reliable veteran of the *Around Africa expedition*, was carrying out essential tasks on deck. Although he is not exactly sure what happened, somehow he tripped and fell head-first down one of the hatches. It was one of those accidents that can happen to anyone in high seas when you are braced against the lurching of the ship.

One moment the constant buffeting seems to have settled into a pattern, the next a more powerful wave, or one ripping in from the side, throws the boat in an unexpected direction. If you happen to be mid-step, you can sometimes take the power of it away by bending the legs, but when it's a wave that lifts the boat right out of the water, it can be impossible to judge. Especially if the unexpected comes just as you are negotiating a stairwell to go below decks.

We all heard Aziz scream, followed seconds later by the sound of his shouts above the deafening roar of the storm. The noise certainly made my heart skip a beat. Quite a few beats, if I'm honest. Thankfully, apart from the obvious shock and pain from such an awkward fall, he was actually shouting to tell us he was not badly hurt. We all came to the rescue, but when I saw where and how he had fallen, I was amazed he wasn't seriously injured. He could have easily broken his neck by falling head-first down the hatch and landing some seven or eight feet below. Although he turned the colour of a ghost, he hadn't broken a bone or knocked out his brains, which could so easily have happened.

Stairwells on sailing ships are always very steep for reasons of space, and even slipping in wet shoes can result in a nasty bruise on your behind or the back of your head. Had he been seriously hurt or killed, it would have almost certainly meant the end of the entire expedition. His apparent 'luck' was probably because he is such an experienced sailor, and he had instinctively managed to relax his body and roll with the lurching of the boat. Either that or it was some miraculous intervention from Yamm, the Phoenician god of the sea who had given us his blessings when we left Tunis.

The Cadiz to Essaouira leg took us about a week. This was much longer than we had expected, but for much of the voyage we had a headwind blowing against us and we were very worried at times that we were being blown too close to the coast and might strike some off-lying rocks. Happily, this ignominious and dangerous fate was avoided. In fact, as we sailed closer to Morocco, we began to make up time and actually recorded our fastest speed of the expedition at about eight or nine knots with the current in our favour and a following wind in our sail.

A significant problem that did arise unexpectedly was the increasing number of fishing boats we encountered the closer we came to Essaouira. Avoiding their fishing nets was difficult enough during the day, but at night it was even more of an issue and the last thing we wanted to do was to get caught up in them. Understandably, given that fishing is their livelihood, the fishermen were not happy to see us and if we had inadvertently interfered with their nets, it could have turned ugly, even if it wasn't intentional.

By this stage the weather had calmed down a bit and we were about ten miles offshore. Even so, there were still fishing boats everywhere and, to make matters even more difficult, there were also FADs (Fish Aggregation Devices), which are used to catch deep-sea fish like tuna and marlin. They are tethered to the sea-floor with concrete blocks, but you can spot them from the groups of buoys on the surface. Getting caught up in one of those could have been a real problem.

Avoiding any serious snagging, we managed to navigate our way successfully to Essaouira. We arrived in pitch darkness, sailing between the spit of land at the north end of the town's half-moon shaped bay and the Isle of Mogador, the largest of the off-lying 'Purple Islands'. Mogador protects the port against the full force of the Atlantic trade winds and the swirling currents. It is due to this accident of geography that Essaouira is known as one of the best anchorages in Morocco and also, no doubt, why Hanno landed here.

But our trials were not yet over. It was only now that we discovered that the harbour entrance itself is alarmingly narrow. To make matters worse, the system of harbour lights was incredibly confusing and very difficult to distinguish from the lights in the town. At the entrance to most harbours around the world, where leisure boats frequently visit, the navigation lights are generally very consistent and well-positioned so you can easily interpret not just port from starboard, but also the correct channel to follow when entering and exiting.

Sadly for us, Essaouira did not fall into this category. There was also still quite a swell and the winds, while not as bad as they had been, continued to blow fiercely. To make matters worse, many of the fishing boats which were leaving port early in the morning didn't have any lights. There were also rocks on either side of the channel looming out of the darkness that looked far too close for comfort.

While equipped with the basics, one piece of modern technology the *Phoenicia* did not have was a depth-sounder and if ever we felt its absence, it was now. Running aground at night in the harbour entrance in the weather conditions we found ourselves in would have been both very dangerous and profoundly embarrassing. This scary experience was a situation when all hands really were needed on deck if we were to successfully navigate our way to wherever it was we were meant to be going. The location of a safe place to anchor wasn't at all clear either. We wanted to be in shallow water but not so shallow that we were grounded on the beach.

In the cabin, I had Charlie looking at the GPS position on the chart and trying to match it up with what the crew were seeing with their eyes. As far as we could make out from their contradictory shouts and hand-signals, this was clearly a confusing kaleidoscope of different coloured lights. It was virtually impossible to see where we were going with so many other boats at anchor in the bay which we were desperately trying to avoid.

It was only when dawn finally broke that we could really make an assessment of how successful we had been. As it turned out, and given the problems we had encountered, we hadn't done too badly. We were all in one piece and so was the ship. This counted as a major success whichever way you looked at it, and we were all relieved to have anchored and arrived safely.

Our first task was to call up the Port Authority, as we'd been told we would be allowed into the main harbour, which is not usually possible for visiting boats. It proved to be a frustrating morning because we were unable to get a response. Happily, after repeated calls, we eventually made contact and were told it would be no problem to relocate.

We immediately pulled up the anchor and motored around to the main harbour where we were told we would see a large orange boat which we were to moor up alongside. Acting as instructed, we made our way deeper into the harbour looking around everywhere for what we assumed would be a boat that would be very easy to find. But as always seems to be the case with anything you simply can't miss, we couldn't see it anywhere.

This turned out to be hardly surprising as it was tucked in behind a harbour wall and was impossible to see until we were right on top of it. A small detail the Port Authority had neglected to mention. Fitting ourselves into this tiny space required another miracle of helmsmanship from Dirman, but once we had moored up, we started to take stock of our surroundings.

The orange boat turned out to be a Search and Rescue vessel that was on 24-hour call for emergency deployment by the coastguard. We thought it was a bit odd, but that's where we had been instructed to go by the Port Authority and the boat's crew seemed very happy for us to moor alongside, so that's what we did.

Over its long history, during which it has been both a Portuguese colony and a French protectorate (French is still widely spoken),

Essaouira has had a bewildering series of names, the most enduring being Mogador, after the off-lying island, and this was how it was known during the French protectorate from 1912 until independence in 1956.

Pottery inscribed with the Phoenician name Magon has been found, evidence of a Carthaginian presence around the city in the 5th century BC. As on the Iberian peninsula, Phoenician interest in processing and trading metals was the prime motive for establishing a colony on Mogador.[31] Archaeologists have found that the Phoenicians traded iron and iron implements made from a deposit a few miles from Essaouira, along with copper and gold from the Atlas Mountains and frankincense from the Sahara.[32]

Up until this point our first impressions of Essaouira Harbour had been defined by one thing, and one thing only. The smell. Essaouira would make Billingsgate fish market on a sweltering day in June smell like the perfume counter at Harrods in comparison. It stank, it really did. Throw in hundreds of boat-shaped swarms of flies and dive-bombing gangs of screeching seagulls and you get the picture.

Having said all this, it wasn't long before we fell in love with the place. Fish, after all, is what Essaouira lives by. It's one of the most productive fishing ports in the country because of the huge shoals of sardines carried into Moroccan waters by the Canaries current. Alongside the all-conquering sardine, other favourites including sea bass, shrimp, swordfish, bream, mullet and mackerel all feature on the menus of the fish restaurants lining the harbour, cooked fresh on outdoor griddles. Mussels are also harvested from the adjacent rocky coast and served up in tajines cooked with onions and lemons.

The city is massively colourful and atmospheric, so that once our olfactory glands had acclimatised to what Essaouira's fishermen evidently hardly noticed, we were more and more charmed by what we saw. If you hold your nose and open your eyes, it's really a very enchanting, laid-back place and a lot more relaxed than the more famous, but frenetic, tourist destination of Marrakesh about 100 miles inland.

The port was full of trawlers made of teak and eucalyptus. It was amazing to watch the fishermen bringing in their daily catch and the

---

31. Pappa, E. (2010). *Reflections on the earliest Phoenician presence in north-west Africa.* Talanta, XL-XLI, pp. 53-72.
32. Ibid.

routines they would go through, throwing the baskets of fish from the deck up onto the quayside. Sometimes, depending on the tide, the boats would be really low down, but the fishermen would still manage to throw the fish baskets high above them onto the harbour wall. The result of this daily routine was that the surface of the harbour wall was caked in fish-scales like a layer of slushy ice and snow.

As soon as we could, we took the opportunity to look around and enjoy the hustle and bustle of the medieval fort area surrounding the port, as well as the Old Medina with its pavement traders, souks, colourful local clothes, carpets and tapestries temptingly displayed against the background of the peeling medieval walls. Although it felt like it would be easy to get completely lost in this maze of streets, we soon realised that there was a simple logic to the layout, with all the streets linking into a central walkway that ran from the main square by the waterfront to the northern gate.

Apart from the smell of fish, one of the first things that strikes you about Essaouira is its trademark colour. The rule is generally quite simple. If it's not white-washed Moroccan white, the ubiquitous colour of heat-reflecting buildings in any desert landscape, then it will be painted blue. Everything from the fishing boats in the harbour to the shutters and doors on the houses and the walls and gateways of the narrow streets.

While it would be easy to conclude that blue reflects the colour of the sea, which is so central to the city's existence, its millennia-old use can be traced right back to the arrival of the first Phoenicians and our old friend the murex snail, which the Phoenicians used as the source for their famous purple dye. Indeed, the colour of the fishing boats we had passed in the waters surrounding the islands outside the harbour was the very same as the dye produced on those islands when the Phoenicians first arrived here 2500 years ago. But this colour is blue, rather than purple.

The original murex shells that were used to produce the dye in the city of Tyre, known as Tyrian Purple, was a reddish purple that was to become the colour of royalty, both in the ancient and modern world. However, this original dye was made from a species of marine snail called *Murex Brandaris* rather than the *Murex Trunculus* found in the islands off Essaouira. The pigment from the latter starts off as purple, but rapidly degrades into a spectrum from bluish-purple through indigo to royal blue.

The distinguishing architectural feature of this city, with the ocean on its west flank and the desert to the east, is its combination of Moroccan and European styles. The layout of the modern city dates back to Sultan Sidi Mohammed Ben Abdallah who in the 18th century commissioned a French architect, Théodore Cornut, to fortify the city and launch attacks against rebels from the south.

Under orders from the sultan, Cornut copied the format of the famous French military engineer, Sébastien Vauban, who built groups of fortified buildings around the borders of France in the 17th century. Put simply, his fortresses were designed to make a siege so difficult and drawn out that they would absorb much of the energy of an attacking force, enabling the defenders to easily keep them at bay. This feature has been described by architectural historians as similar to the use of crumple zones in modern cars.[33]

Essaouira's Sqala du Port is formed of two massive artillery platforms at right-angles to each other. Each is lined with cannons and built in the style of a Vauban fortification in the beautiful honey-coloured desert stone which protects the inner harbour. The square tower where they meet has panoramic views back over the harbour and towards the Medina further north.

These massive platforms have also become very popular with film location finders. *Game of Thrones* fans would instantly recognise the slavers' city of Astapor where it is known as the 'Walk of Punishment'. Slaves who have committed crimes or disobeyed their masters are tortured and put on display in chains along the harbour as a warning to others. Luckily, we all avoided this fate.

We also heard of other more recent connections to Tyrian Purple, most of them almost certainly apocryphal, but which we rather liked anyway. The first was that Jimmy Hendrix, who visited the town in the 1960s, used to write his songs on the beach near a village just along the coast called Diabat. Apparently *Purple Haze* was inspired by the humble murex shell. Whether he imbibed some of the pigment powder for inspiration, history doesn't relate.

33. McGlynn S, 2012. *How Fighting Ends: A History of Surrender.* Edited by Holger Afflerbach and Hew Strachan. Oxford University Press.

Other rumours suggest that Hendrix wanted to buy Mogador Island, the original 'Purple Island', where he planned to establish a commune with Bob Marley and Timothy Leary, both also visitors from the 1960s, where they would grow another of Morocco's more infamous exports. In reality, so far as we could establish, Marley only visited for a few days and stayed in a luxury hotel. He never made it to Diabat either. In this case it appears fiction was stranger than fact.

As we had discovered from painful experience, Essaouira is known as Morocco's 'windy city'. But far from being a deterrent, the winds which we had encountered out at sea are today one of the main attractions for tourists. Those powerful eastern trade winds, known locally as *charki*, have turned the three miles of wide, sandy beaches that stretch around the bay to the south of the city into a windsurfing and kiteboarding Mecca. The reason the bay works so well is that Mogador Island protects it from the full force of the easterly wind coming in from the Atlantic and funnels it cross-shore across the bay from the north.

As we felt was bound to happen at some stage, on a day when most of the crew were in town and there were just four of us on board, a distress call came in to the coastguard. Inevitably, it was one of the more blustery days of our stay as we frantically started releasing the ropes, with the crew of the Search and Rescue boat trying to push us off and shouting at us to get a move on.

We finally managed to push ourselves free and out into the middle of the harbour as their boat made a speedy exit. Unfortunately, we were left drifting fast towards the harbour wall and for a moment it looked like the horse's head was going to be knocked into the water for the second time on the voyage. Luckily Charlie managed to save the day by jumping onto the harbour wall and fending us off just in time before we retied our mooring lines.

Before setting sail once more, we were honoured to be hosted at a reception given by André Azoulay, President and founder of the *Association Essaouira Mogador*, where I was delighted to talk about the significance of *Phoenicia* stopping in Essaouira and our adventures on the journey so far. It was an extremely kind gesture because André and his team were at the time working flat out on the preparations for the 16th Atlantic Andalusia Festival which is held every year at the end of October.

Atlantic B.C.

Essaouira is famous for its many music festivals and by extraordinary serendipity, we had timed our visit to coincide with a festival celebrating the city's connections to Andalusia. A connection that can be traced back 2500 years to Hanno, who had himself also set sail from Cadiz. And what an inspiring way to end our stay it turned out to be. Three days of Andalusian music and dance, including heel-clacking flamenco shows, classical orchestras, and artists from all over Morocco, Spain and beyond.

The Fortunate Islands

On the days before we left Essaouira, the north-east wind that had been fanning out across the Atlantic increased to a Force 8 gale. At its strongest, it was gusting at around 40 knots. This meant that even the fishing boats were forced to remain in port and the red light on the harbour master's office remained obstinately on red. All boats were forbidden to sail. If we were to make the short hop to Tenerife and then cross the Atlantic before Christmas, as we were still hoping, the light would need to very quickly turn green.

Much to my relief, in the early hours of 2nd November, a yellow light shone out over the harbour. This, at least, meant that the wind speed had dropped by 10 knots or so to a borderline Force 6-7 on the Beaufort Scale. In the harbour, it was nothing like as strong as we knew it would be out at sea, protected as we were from the full force by Mogador Island and the harbour walls themselves. Through binoculars we could easily see the 'white foam from breaking waves blowing in streaks' predicted by the Beaufort definition of a Force 7.

The yellow light meant that, as skipper, I was allowed to make my own judgement about whether or not it was safe to set sail. At our own risk, of course. Our next port of call was Tenerife in the Canary Islands, 500 nautical miles south-west of Essaouira, the final stepping-stone before our much-anticipated Atlantic crossing. After lunch, and after watching England's defeat by South Africa in the final of the Rugby World Cup – a result which I was determined not to take as a bad omen – I decided that there was nothing to be gained by delay.

The make-up of the crew had changed once more, something that had become the norm during our visits to port. This time we had bid a fond farewell to two of our crew members, Ian Bond and Ray Korpan, who had sailed with us from Gibraltar. Ian is an old friend of mine from back home in Wiltshire in the UK, and Ray was from Saskatchewan in Canada. Both had been with me aboard *Phoenicia* before, and they had clearly enjoyed the experience as much as the rest of us had enjoyed having them on board.

As some departed, others arrived. Our three new crew members were Habiba Machichi, a Tunisian who had been a point of contact in Carthage and had helped arrange the memorable events we enjoyed there, along with Max Cattini, a young zoologist and musician, and David Hosking, both from London.

David described himself as an 'old man of the sea' but, as a tough-as-nails 65 year-old, he had certainly earned his stripes. An ex-Royal Navy officer like myself and a veteran of the Falklands War, he won a gold medal at the 1980 World Rowing Championships and is the father of London 2012 Olympic rowing gold medallist, Sophie Hosking. In 2011, he also rowed the Atlantic (Canaries to Barbados) in just under 32 days as leader of a six-man crew, breaking the record by more than 24 hours, which was sadly broken just a day later!

This was followed by his attempt to break the world record for circumnavigating Britain in the world's toughest rowing challenge, the Row Around Great Britain race, a non-stop, unsupported 2000 mile epic. At the time, 27 days (minus a few hours) was the record, and his team were one of the favourites. Sadly, the fates were against David on this occasion and a steering equipment failure meant they had to drop out after seven days as they were rounding Land's End.

Bidding the crew of the orange coastguard ship a final farewell, we let slip our mooring just after lunch and headed out into the bay. As always with a potentially difficult navigation, I had Dirman, my most trusted lieutenant, at the helm. Our brush with catastrophe coming into port, albeit in pitch darkness, was fresh in everybody's minds. While confusing lights were not a problem in broad daylight, the shallowness of the water and the narrowness of the harbour exit channel most certainly were.

The trick to a successful exit from a harbour like this is not to dawdle, but to keep up enough speed to keep the ship steady. It's a skill that needs both manual dexterity and an instinct honed by a lifetime at sea, talents that Dirman had demonstrated time and again.

The issue for us was that while most boats steered a course halfway between the rocks on the port side and the harbour wall on the starboard side, I wanted to remain upwind as much as possible in case the engine failed and we were blown onto the rocks to port. While I concentrated on the engine, Dirman and I performed our delicate double-act once more. It is not one the Phoenicians, using oars in their harbours, would have recognised. Happily, this tricky manoeuvre passed off without incident.

Our journey to Tenerife was one of the less comfortable legs of the expedition. The tone was set within a few miles of passing Mogador Island as we made our way out into the Atlantic once more. We were confronted with five-foot waves and a strong wind. The harbourmaster's yellow light had been yellow for a reason.

For most of the crew, the conditions were nothing to be too worried about, but seasickness, like altitude sickness, can take anyone down whatever their state of health. Our new recruit, Habiba, was the victim on this occasion. Within a couple of hours of leaving port, she was feeling both dizzy and sick, as well as being barely able to talk, as all the colour drained from her face.

Seasickness isn't a direct result of the see-sawing movement of the sea. Rather, it is caused by the contradictory messages sent to the brain by the vestibular canals of the inner ear and the eyes. The former sense movement, while the latter move with the boat in an attempt to keep the scene in front of them static. This conflict triggers a release of hormones that results in the symptoms that we all know and hate, including nausea and vomiting. The word 'nausea' itself is derived the word 'naus' which is an ancient Greek word for ship.

As well as the rough seas, another factor that may have triggered Habiba's seasickness was more prosaic. Even after we had left Essaouira harbour, the ship still stank of fish. True, the flies and the seagulls had dispersed, but it had been impossible for the crew to avoid bringing the fish scales which were plastered all over the harbour walls onto the boat. To make matters worse, as we left the harbour and fresh air gradually surrounded us once again, we realised that many of the ropes were still soaked in fish-saturated water from the harbour itself.

We tried dragging as many of these that weren't in use behind the ship to see if the seawater would gradually wash away the smell, while also sweeping the deck and washing down all the woodwork. Unfortunately, the smell was so ingrained that nothing we did seemed to make much difference. Even weeks later, after we had crossed the Atlantic, the odour of fish never entirely left us.

Dirman had a suggestion for Habiba which was less conventional than the usual advice of keeping your eyes on the horizon. "Tie your scarf around your stomach as tight as you can," he advised, while singing her an improvised sea shanty. "Canary...Canary...Canary... tomorrow Canary," he crooned. This may have gone down well with hardened Indonesian sailors, but judging by Habiba's expression, she was unimpressed.

As we were soon to discover, Habiba's affliction was not the usual 'here today, gone tomorrow' variety of seasickness. For the entire leg to Tenerife, she was virtually unable to stand and we all became very concerned for her. I also seriously doubted whether she would recover enough for the Atlantic crossing, which I knew might take anything up to six or seven weeks without sight of land.

Habiba had initially intended to join the ship in Tunis and had arrived at the harbour with her extended family in tow to wave her off. Sadly, officialdom was having none of it. Our next destination, the British Overseas Territory of Gibraltar, was at that time still in the EU. This meant that under Tunisian law, Habiba needed a visa and she was barred from joining the ship. Undeterred, and underlining her determination to join the expedition, following our departure from Tunis she applied for a U.S. visa – our final destination – and travelled to Morocco so she could join the ship in Essaouira.

We were all a little uncertain as to how she would adapt to life at sea, even before the seasickness struck. "Please look after her," one of her friends had begged us in Tunis, "she's never been to sea before and she can't swim." Also, although we were a multi-lingual crew, everyone apart from Habiba had at least an understanding of English, which was the language we used to communicate. She spoke both her native Arabic and French, but no English, which made communication difficult. Luckily Maran spoke French which, given her role as the ship's doctor, was a godsend, especially when Habiba became so ill. Nonetheless, the crew's initial sense of optimism descended into a more subdued state, especially when Habiba refused to eat or drink.

Back at the helm, I was also concerned that the currents and the wind might blow us south of Tenerife to a point where it would be very difficult to sail north again against the winds and the current. It wasn't until our third day, when we were about 70 nautical miles west of

Morocco, and sailing nearer to Tenerife, that the wind finally responded to our prayers.

We approached the island from the north and sailed down the east coast, much as I had originally planned. As soon as we rounded the north-eastern promontory in the early morning, the peak of Mount Teide came into view. Tenerife is the largest of the seven main Canary Islands and is volcanic, like all the others. Mount Teide's volcanic cone rises more than 12,000 feet above sea level, the highest point of all the islands in the Atlantic.

Seen from the deck of the *Phoenicia* early in the morning it was an awe-inspiring sight, soaring above a massive outcrop of eroded lava with the surrounding peaks of the caldera covered in a thin layer of cloud. Due to its proximity to the sea, Mount Teide has the longest sea-shadow of any mountain or volcano in the world. As dawn broke, and the sun rose behind us in the east, we could see its shadow stretching out towards its island neighbours in the west, La Palma and La Gomera.

Happily, for us – and the islanders themselves – there was no sign of the flares that were recorded bursting out of the sides of the volcano when Columbus and his fleet sailed past in 1492. These were followed by 'a great fire in the Orotava Valley'.[34] Even though the most recent volcanic activity on Teide was in 1909, debate continues as to its current level of danger. Not that anyone seems too worried. The surrounding National Park is the most popular in Europe, receiving up to four million visitors a year.

It was during this period of calm sailing that David recounted some of his experiences serving in the Falklands war. "We were adrift at sea for five days after HMS Glamorgan was hit by an Argentine Exocet missile," he recalled. "During that time, we only drank a sip of water every four hours, and survival biscuits from a rescue raft. In fact, our first meal was corned beef from an Argentine warship which had itself been hit."

As it happened, the crew of the *Phoenicia* were lucky not to experience a similar fate. Ferries are often a law unto themselves and don't pay much attention to sailing ships even if, according to the rules of the sea, it should be the ferry that gives way. They also travel across the water at

---

34. Colón, F., Pané, R. and Serrano y Sanz, M., 1932. *Historia del almirante don Cristóbal Colón*. Madrid: V. Suárez.

very high speeds and the sensation of one bearing down on our ancient wooden sailing ship felt very similar to riding a bicycle towards a tank approaching head-on.

As we made our way down the eastern side of Tenerife adjacent to the main port of Santa Cruz de Tenerife, we were sailing at the relatively high speed of six or seven knots, with the sail fully unfurled. At first, I thought the ferry emerging from the port was going to change course and give us a wide berth by sailing astern of us, but gradually, as we got nearer, I could see that it was steadfastly maintaining its bearing on our starboard bow. The problem was exacerbated by the fact that once *Phoenicia's* sail is up, it's only possible to reduce the speed relatively slowly.

At one point I really thought we were on a collision course, but the ferry finally crossed in front of us, missing us by about a hundred or so metres. This may sound like a wide margin, but when you are watching it converging at the speed it was going, it can definitely be classified as a near-miss. We actually had the right of way, but we would have been smashed to pieces if we had collided. Ferries can reach 25 knots (around 30 mph) which is probably why they were so confident they could avoid us. But it was a scary moment.

As we edged around the south of the island, we could see clusters of settlements spread along the coastline, surrounding a collection of huge plastic domes. After anchoring off the San Miguel Marina early in the morning, it wasn't until midday that a space was found for us. When we eventually moored up, it was alongside a bright yellow-and-red submarine taking tourists on reef safaris. It felt like the start of an unlikely comedy partnership.

"Welcome to Banana Island," said the owner of one of the cafés, as we gratefully disembarked for a warming cup of coffee, his greeting instantly solving the riddle of the huge plastic domes. It was the morning of Thursday, 6th November 2019. We had arrived in Tenerife.

It was primarily because of the islands' historic connections with the Phoenician voyages of exploration, and as a launch-pad for the voyages of Columbus, that we had decided to visit the Canaries in the first place. Tenerife itself was almost certainly visited by Hanno who, according to Pliny the Elder, visited the island in the 5th century BC. Back then, as today, Mount Teide would sometimes have been visible from the coast of Morocco. It is also widely accepted by historians that the Phoenicians, the Greeks, and the Romans traded with these islands over many centuries.

The Canaries also featured in multiple ancient texts. Pliny the Elder called them the 'Fortunate Islands', and Marinus of Tyre gave them a prominent place in his calculations while placing his zero meridian of longitude through them. As with the tiny islands off Essaouira, the Canary Islands were also known as the 'Purple Isles' because they were a source of the murex sea snail which the Phoenicians used to make their signature purple dye.

The first inhabitants of the islands were the Guanches people, who are today mostly associated with the Silbo whistling language still alive on the island of La Gomera. It is thought likely that the Phoenicians first brought the Guanches to the islands from the African mainland where their ancestors had inter-married with the Berbers. Supporting this theory is the fact that their language and religious beliefs were a combination of Phoenician and Berber.

A connection to the Tartessians of Andalusia, who the Phoenicians traded with from Cadiz, has also recently been established on the neighbouring island of Lanzarote. The archaeologist, Pablo Atoche Peña, professor at the University of Las Palmas de Gran Canaria, has unearthed what appears to be a warehouse that dates back to the 10th century BC. The warehouse was about 1000 square feet in size with several different rooms holding the remains of ceramics and a stone stela with engravings.

Although the remains suggest the builders were definitely either Tartessian or Phoenician, Professor Atoche believes it is much more likely that they were Phoenician. The latter had a more advanced maritime technology and a huge sphere of influence which, by the 10th century BC, dominated much of the Mediterranean.[35] All of these discoveries point to an early Phoenician presence in the Canary Islands. As the wind blows to the south and south-west for around 80% of the year, it seems highly likely that some of the Phoenician visitors to the Canary Islands ended up, intentionally or otherwise, in the Americas.

35. Mederos, M., Sánchez, T. and Atoche Peña, p. 2013. *De Oriente a Occidente*. Las Palmas de Gran Canaria: Fundación Canaria Mapfre Guanarteme.

Another archaeological site on the island that we were keen to see, this time suggesting a possible trans-Atlantic link, was enthusiastically endorsed by Thor Heyerdahl of Kon-Tiki fame. Heyerdahl had long believed that there was a connection between the ancient Egyptians and the civilisations of Central America. Halfway up the east coast of Tenerife are the Pyramids of Güímar, six pyramid-shaped structures built from lava stone which appear to support this theory.

Heyerdahl had himself come up with a theory suggesting a transatlantic link between Egypt and Central America in which Tenerife was a potential stopping-off point. When he later heard about the Güímar pyramids, he became so intrigued that he went to live on Tenerife for twelve years at the end of his life, researching possible parallels between the terrace structures, the pyramids of Egypt and the pre-Columbian Mesoamerican ceremonial sites.

The huge Heyerdahl museum on the island has a display of all the photos, models and replicas from his expeditions. These include both the original Kon-Tiki expedition across the Pacific and his Ra and Ra II expeditions on boats made of papyrus reeds across the Atlantic in 1969 and 1970. While the first of the Ra expeditions narrowly failed to reach Barbados, the second crossed the 3800 miles of water between Morocco and Barbados in 57 days. The belief that contact between the ancient Egyptians and the central Americans was physically impossible had been comprehensively disproved.

After the Güímar site was discovered by Emiliano Bethencourt in 1990, he and other researchers[36] demonstrated that parts of the structures are aligned with the solstices and have stairs facing the direction of the rising sun on the winter solstice. By standing on the highest pyramid on the summer solstice, the viewer can also watch the sun setting behind one mountain peak before emerging again and setting behind a second. Heyerdahl believed that the temples were built for sun worship and in a video in the museum's auditorium explains that the stepped pyramids were not just farming terraces, but have angles and curves similar to those in Egypt.

Before Bethencourt brought them to Heyerdahl's attention, it was thought that the most likely explanation for the existence of these stone

36. J. A. Belmonte, A. Aparicio and C. Esteban,1993. *A solstitial marker in Tenerife: the Majanos de Chacona. Archaeoastronomy* No. 18, p. 65.

terraces is that they were built by local farmers. In the 1800s the land had been cleared to exploit the cochineal (woodlouse) which had accidentally been brought to the Canaries by the Spanish, but had proved to be an excellent source of carmine, another potent dye, later famously used by the British army for their bright red tunics. The discarded lava rocks were used for building pyramidal structures, of which there are still many other examples around the island today.

For this reason, many archaeologists believe that the pyramids were built in the 19th century and that a more likely theory for their orientation was the importance of solar symbolism in Freemasonry.[37] The owner of the Güímar site from the 1850s was Antonio Díaz Flores, a Freemason who had also studied the Egyptians and the construction techniques of the pyramids. Given that there were no recorded pyramids on the site before Flores' purchase of the land, and given his interests, it seems most likely that he was responsible for building the pyramids. Like many architectural and historical mysteries, speculation will no doubt continue.

Our stay in Tenerife was a little frustrating and longer than we had intended, mainly due to problems with Habiba's passport. Unfortunately, she had not managed to get herself an EU visa before leaving Morocco and the Spanish authorities in Tenerife decided to make it very difficult for us, even though her intention at the time was to stay with the expedition until we reached the U.S.

The other problem we had to contend with was Habiba's health. I was extremely concerned that she would not be physically capable of making the voyage across the Atlantic after her serious bout of seasickness. I know Maran was very worried about her as well. In the end I decided it was too much of a risk to take, not just for her, but also for the rest of the crew. If she had succumbed once again and been unable to eat or drink, it could have been very dangerous. Everyone felt disappointed. We were sad for Habiba missing out on the Atlantic crossing, and I know she was embarrassed at being the cause of so many problems.

On the other side of the coin, the crew were all delighted to welcome Sheimaa back on board. After leaving us in Tunis, Sheimaa's life had been turned upside down back in Beirut. First there were the dis-

---

37. Antonio Aparicio Juan/César Esteban López, 2005. *Las Pirámides de Güímar: mito y realidad.* Centro de la Cultura Popular Canaria, La Laguna pp. 30-31.

turbances on the streets in the wake of the 2019 October Revolution, before she then decided that her job in fundraising was going nowhere due to the ever-worsening economy. If that wasn't enough, she had also split with her fiancé.

I think that by the time she arrived in Tenerife, she was probably very relieved to have left her old life behind and to be joining us on a mad expedition crossing the Atlantic. Even so, it was a decision that brought with it many uncertainties, as she had no idea what she was going to do when she finally returned home. But we were all very happy to have her back on board. She had been hoping to join us again in Essaouira but had been obliged to give a month's notice on leaving her job, so joined us in Tenerife instead.

The island was also our last opportunity to prepare the ship for the long voyage across the Atlantic. We were determined to put the time to good use, cleaning, refilling the water and diesel containers, restocking provisions, and most importantly inspecting the ship and making any repairs necessary to make her as seaworthy as possible for the trials ahead.

In the process, we strengthened the steering oars, recorked the decks to prevent water leaking into the cabin below, and reinforced the side stanchions, some of which were showing signs of rot. Finally, we did some more work on the sail, repainting the stripes purple and white.

I also asked Yuri to put on his wetsuit to examine the hull, which he gave a clean bill of health, much to my relief. However, David had a particular issue with a section of planking towards the stern on the starboard side. He was worried that with the prevailing winds and currents it was vulnerable to wave damage in the Atlantic. The impact of waves varies, depending on your location. In the Bay of Biscay and the Mediterranean, where the water is relatively shallow, the waves are closer together and hit with a sharper impact than in the Atlantic, where the distance between the waves is generally longer and the wave cycles slower.

To my eyes, and most notably to Dirman's, noted for his expertise at ship repairs, it didn't seem to be too much of a problem. Nonetheless, David's concerns were spreading unease among the rest of the crew and I knew Sheimaa was worried. David had apparently said to her, "Sheimaa, this ship isn't just a replica of an ancient ship. It is an ancient ship. It was built in 2007, is made entirely of wood, has sailed around Africa, and has been sitting in a freezing and damp English harbour for most of its life. I know the Atlantic and the waves are going to be smashing into the boat right around these rotten planks."

"I've lived my life," he went on. "If I die on this trip, that's fine. But you are young and have no idea what you're getting yourself into. This is serious. We're talking about the Atlantic Ocean here and the seas can be very treacherous." David was certainly insistent. Even so, we weren't prepared for what happened next.

Arriving back at the marina one evening, we were confronted by a huge hole in the side of the ship. David had removed a section of the hull about four feet square, only about a foot above the waterline. I was shocked. Were it not for the fact that our departure had been delayed anyway due to the problems we were having with Habiba's visa, I would also have been quite angry.

David is a very experienced sailor, but he has no real qualifications as a boat-builder, and he knew that Dirman was the member of the crew I had instructed to oversee any repairs. I think Dirman himself was a little confused and angry and was wondering why he hadn't been consulted. It was a situation that was made worse by the fact that when we first arrived in Tenerife, Dirman had discovered that a great friend of his, a fisherman, had been lost at sea. Understandably, it was a loss that had hit him hard.

Steinar was also concerned and contacted some of the boatbuilders who had constructed the Viking ships that he had skippered. He told me that on seeing pictures of the hull, they were unsure about David's handiwork. Not that it was necessarily unsafe, just that it wasn't the way they would have done it themselves. As it turned out, David was able to carry out the repairs, whether they were necessary or not, without delaying us any further.

In the end David decided not to join us on the voyage across the Atlantic. He told us that his wife, Louise, had been ill. Due to the delay in Tenerife, he thought that we would probably not reach the other side of the pond until after Christmas and he wanted to be with his family. Whether it was also anything to do with how he perceived the state of the ship, I am not sure. Either way, it was sad to see him go.

Who Shrunk the World?

As we left Tenerife, I knew I would have some spare time to think hard about the historical context of our mission. After all, there would be days and days of nothing but ocean ahead of us. Of course, there was still a constant supply of work. A sailor's job is never done, as there are always repairs and maintenance to be completed. Every sailing vessel has many moving parts: ropes fray, sails wear thin and tear, while leaks develop below decks and need repairing.

In spite of these challenges, while also keeping the watch system running and ensuring everyone was physically and mentally strong, I now had time to think through once again what the ancients knew about the Atlantic. In particular, why Christopher Columbus wrongly came to be credited with the discovery of the Americas from a European perspective.

It is widely accepted that by the time of Columbus, indigenous communities had been living in the Americas for at least 30,000 years, having first arrived there via the land bridge that once existed between Asia and Alaska. Other theories exist, but it is generally accepted that most – although probably not all – indigenous Americans arrived in the north west and gradually spread throughout the Americas. Others, such as the Clovis people, arrived from Europe by literally walking across the frozen Atlantic during the last Ice Age, around 10,000 BC.

I had brought with me a number of reference books and had loaded my laptop with a large number of relevant articles, some of which were good, while others were poorly argued and documented. One of the latter recounted how early Atlantic sailors from Iberia in about 1000 AD had used the sextant, even though it wasn't invented until the 18th century. Sensibly, I was sceptical of that particular article. Another author had misunderstood an ancient description of gybing in a square-rigged vessel, claiming it was a description of tacking when the wind comes from in front of the ship. He also inaccurately claimed that square-riggers were capable of sailing into the wind.

I have loved history from my early school days, when I relished being able to recall historical facts and dates in our weekly tests. I was delighted to be in the top two in my class for history, something which I sadly was unable to replicate in any other subject. I also had a passion and admiration for Elizabethan sailors like Sir Francis Drake and Sir Walter Raleigh. So perhaps it's little wonder that I ended up rewriting history by sailing thousands of miles across the world's oceans in replicas of ancient sailing ships.

My first task was to put the relevant ancient scholars in chronological order and to understand their contribution to the understanding of the world in ancient times. These scholars were variously described as writers, mathematicians and cosmographers. Today we would probably classify them as geographers, philosophers, astrologers and historians, with many of them covering multiple disciplines.

The scholars I was most interested in were Pythagoras (c 570-c 495 BC), Aristotle (384-322 BC), Strabo (63 BC-c.AD 24), Marinus of Tyre (AD 70-130), and Ptolemy (AD 100-170). Last, but certainly not least, was Eratosthenes (276-c194 BC), the Greek/Egyptian polymath and chief librarian at the library of Alexandria who was the first to correctly estimate the circumference of the world.

What all these intellectuals knew was that the world was round, and not a flat spinning disc as some earlier Persian academics had believed. However, Eratosthenes had gone further and had carried out an ingenious experiment. By knowing the distance between two points and recording the sun's position above them from reflections in well water, he was able to calculate the circumference of the world.

Eratosthenes knew about a well in Syene, now Aswan, Egypt, where at noon on the summer solstice (21st June), the sun illuminated the entire bottom of the well without casting any shadows. This indicated that the sun was directly overhead. Eratosthenes then measured the angle of a shadow cast by a stick at noon on the summer solstice in Alexandria. He realised that if he knew the distance between Alexandria and Syene, he could calculate the circumference of the Earth using basic mathematics.

In those days it was extremely difficult to determine distance with any accuracy. Some distances between cities were measured by the time it took a camel caravan to travel from one city to the other. But camels have a tendency to walk at varying speeds and wander off the track. So Eratosthenes hired bematists, professional surveyors trained to walk with equal-length steps.[38]

They found that Syene was just over 5000 stadia from Alexandria. Eratosthenes therefore measured the angle of the shadow cast by a stick at noon on the summer solstice in Alexandria. He found it made an angle of about 7.2 degrees, (about one fiftieth) of a complete circle. From these measurements, he calculated the circumference of the world to be around 252,000 stadia, approximately 24,000 miles.[39] His estimate, compared to the actual distance of 24,900 miles, was only 3% out.

Following this discovery, a number of later scholars erroneously managed to shrink the circumference of the world. It is believed this mistake occurred through incorrectly translating Egyptian miles into Roman miles.

Decades after Eratosthenes' measurement, Posidonius (c135-52 BC) used the star, Canopus, as his light source alongside Rhodes and Alexandria for distance. He calculated the Earth's circumference to be 18,000 miles, some 7000 miles short of the correct figure. This is thought to be down to a mistake in his calculation of the distance between Rhodes and Alexandria. Ptolemy in his 2nd century AD treatise on geography used this smaller value of 18,000 miles for the circumference of the world. This was later translated from Greek into Latin in the 15th century, a copy of which was owned by Columbus.

Marinus of Tyre (Tyre, being the birthplace of the Phoenician civilisation) was the first geographer to propose what we now understand to be a system of degrees of longitude. He believed the known world, from China in the east to the Fortunate Islands in the west, covered

---

38. Website: https://www.aps.org/publications/apsnews/200606/history.cfm
39. There is some debate about the length of the stadium used in Eratosthene's calculation. The Greek stadium was about 606ft and if that was used then Eratosthenes was in error. However, Pliny in his "Naturalis Historia" claims Eratosthenes made 40 stadia equal to the Egyptian schoinus, and therefore taking the schoinus as 12,000 royal cubits of 0.525 metres each, the length of the stadium was 516 ft. If we accept the account of Strabo that Eratosthenes measured the circumference of the earth as 252,000 stadia and multiply it by 516 that equals 130,032 feet. And if divided by 5280 (the number of feet in a mile) Eratosthenes circumference would be just over 24,600 miles, very close to the actual 24,900 miles circumference of the earth.

about 180 degrees,[40] with the other half being an ocean stretching from Iberia to Cathay (or Asia as we now know it). Commentators still debate the exact location of the Fortunate islands, but many assume (but probably wrongly) that the ancient texts were referring to the Canary Islands.

However, if the known world according to Marinus and Plutarch was 28% smaller than it was in reality (24,900-18,000 = 6900 miles/24,900 x 100 = 28%), this would add an extra 3486 miles (28% of half the world at 12,450 miles) to the length of the known world. This would make the known world extend from the capital of China to beyond the Canary Islands to the outlying Antilles Islands of the Caribbean. And not to put too fine a point on it – we are in the Americas.

Professsor Lucio Russo summarises the position in this way:

> "It is plain that the only possibility is that the difference in longitude transmitted by Hipparchus was not referring to the same places Ptolemy referred to. Since it would not have been possible to move the position of the capital of China (to generate the error we are dealing with, it would have been located outside of China!) there is only one alternative left: with the name "Fortunate Isles" Hipparchus was not referring to the same islands Ptolemy was referring to. We shall thus believe that in Hipparchus times the "Fortunate Isles" were not the Canary Islands, but islands that were located further away and that subsequent scholars did generate the error by identifying them with the Canary Islands, thus shrinking the known world." [41]

It appears that Ptolemy incorrectly identified the Blessed Islands with the Canaries and since it was known that the Blessed Islands were at the antipodes to the capital of China, Ptolemy made ends meet by erroneously enlarging the longitude of all known places, and shrinking the width of a degree of longitude to 500 instead of 700 stadia. He had successfully managed to shrink the world and thereby confuse Columbus and geographers ever since.

---

40. Website: https://www.jstor.org/stable/1149831 is the reference.
41. Russo, L., 2013. *L'America dimenticata (Forgotten America)*. Milano: Mondadori. Translated for the author p. 166.

Another related issue is the location of Thule. Thule was visited by Pytheas of Massalia (Marseille), a Greek who in about 325 BC sailed from Marseille to northern Europe. Although his original writings have been lost, we know from later writers such as Strabo and Pliny, that Pytheas visited much of modern-day Britain and Ireland. He accurately described the Arctic, indigenous people, the polar ice, while also observing the midnight sun.

For more than 2000 years, historians and geographers have been trying to understand where Thule was located. The description by Pytheas doesn't fit Scotland and the Shetland Islands where many commentators, from Plutarch to the present day, have placed it. However, if we adjust Thule's location to the correct longitudinal scale, it would be located on the east coast of Greenland. This fits the description of the topography perfectly. As I believe, Plutarch misrepresented Scotland as extending to the east across the North Sea, it follows that in ancient times the known world really stretched from China, in the east, to Greenland (Thule) in the north west and the Caribbean in the west.[42]

I thought too about the ancients' knowledge of the Caribbean. What precisely did they know? Plutarch, in his *Life of Sertorius*, explicitly refers to the 'Isles of the Blessed', which he states were much further away from the Canary Islands:

> *"Having sailed from there and crossed the Cadiz strait, Sertorius sailed keeping the coast of Iberia on his right, landing just above the mouth of the river Beti, which throwing itself into the Atlantic Ocean gives the name to that part of Iberia. He was met there by some seamen that had just returned from the Atlantic islands, two of them separated by a small strait, which are ten thousand stadia away from Libya* (the ancient name for Africa) *and are called 'of the Blessed.'*
>
> *They have sparse amounts of mild rain and moderate winds that carry with them dew, not only being provided with good and fatty land, fit to be ploughed and planted, but also producing spontaneous fruits that are sufficient to nourish the inhabitants abundantly and pleasantly with no efforts or works required, leaving them a lot*

42. Ibid.

of leisure. Due to the small difference between the seasons and the mildness of the season changes, on these islands predominates good weather. In fact nothern and eastern winds that come from that side of the world, transported through an immense space get dispersed and dampened, while the southern and western sea winds that wrap them at times bring with them sparse moderate rains, but for the most part nourish the land refreshing it with humid and terse air, so even among the barbarians has spread the belief that the Champs Elysees[43] are located there as well as the base of the blessed as Homer wrote.

Having heard all this, Sertorius felt an extraordinary desire to settle on those islands and live there in peace, free from tyranny and unending wars.

Given that Setorius was ultimately betrayed by his own soldiers and stabbed to death, his understanding of the precarious nature of being a rebel Roman general (of which he was through leading a rebellion from Iberia against Rome) was well founded." This testimony is very interesting. According to Russo it seems to suggest that in Roman times some ships were sailing from the Atlantic ports of the Iberian peninsula, and in particular from Cadiz, towards places unknown at the highest levels of the State. Some later authors, although being aware that the 'Fortunate Isles' had long been identified with the Canary Islands, had not forgotten the accounts of other islands much further away in the ocean. These were known as the Hesperides (the Western ones).

For instance Solinus, writing in around AD 200, wrote:

> *"Beyond the Grorgades, forty days of navigation away, in the most intimate recesses of the sea, are located the Hesperides Islands, as stated by Sebosus."* [44]

---

43. Means the Elysian fields – i.e heaven, the final resting place of the souls of the heroic and virtuous in Greek mythology and religion.
44. Russo, L., 2013. L'*America dimenticata (Forgotten America)*. Milano: Mondadori. Translated for the author.

Statius Sebosus was an author of geographical works of which little is known. He is also referenced by Pliny who likewise points out that Sebosus claims that the Hesperides islands are located beyond the Gorgades, forty days of navigation away.[45] It is thought that Sebosus' source could have been the highly educated and well connected Moroccan king, Juba II, who may have sponsored an expedition to the Canary Islands during his reign.

In the 5th century AD, Martianus Capella wrote a postscript to the usual information on the Fortunate Isles (Canaries) providing an excerpt which is similar to the Solinus quote above:

> *"There also are the Gorgades Islands, in front of a promontory called Western Horn; it is said the Gorgades lived there; they are two days of navigation away from the continent. Beyond that are located the Hesperides Islands, that are in the inner depths of the sea."*

These accounts leave little doubt that the ancient writers associated the name of the Fortunate Isles with a place far away across the oceans referred to as the 'Hesperides', with connotations of tropical islands.

It therefore seems reasonable to conclude that as the winds and currents from Iberia and Morocco consistently blow south-westwards across the Atlantic, the 40 days sailing mentioned by Solinus would put a ship in the Caribbean. It was true too for Columbus and, as we shall see, for my own expedition, both achieving the feat in 39 days. We can therefore deduce from this, that in all probability, the ancients were in the New World before Columbus.

It follows that the next important question is which of the ancient seafaring cultures were the most likely to have reached the Caribbean and the Americas? History is very clear about the most likely candidates, as the first recorded voyages in the Atlantic were those of the Phoenicians

---

45. Ibid: Ultra Gorgadas Ilesperidum insulse. sicut Sebosus adfirmat, dierum quadraginta navigazione in intimos maris sinus recesserunt Collec-tanea. Rerum MemorabiliUM, LVI, 13 ss.). Statius Sebosus was an author of geographical works of which very little is known. Pliny mentions him a couple of times and says Sebosus asserted that the Hesperides islands are located beyond the Gorgades, forty days of navigation away (Naturalis Historia. VI, 201).

and Carthaginians. The first long-distance ocean voyage ever recorded was the circumnavigation of Africa, as described by Herodotus. Writing in 450 BC, Herodotus records that this event took place in around 600 BC. Most academics now believe that this voyage really happened, owing to the detail of the account. Between 2008 and 2010, I also conclusively demonstrated that a Phoenician vessel was capable of such a voyage as recorded in my book, *Sailing Close to the Wind*.[46]

The voyage that Herodotus records is not the only evidence we have for the pre-eminence of the Phoenicians in all areas of maritime and seafaring in the ancient world. The voyage of the Carthaginian, Hanno, who sailed down the West coast of Africa around 350 BC, illustrates their dominance. Hanno sailed at least as far as modern-day Senegal and possibly as far as Cameroon.

In addition, we should take into account the voyage of Himilco who sailed from the Mediterranean to northern Europe in about 600 BC. Himilco was not the first to sail to northern Europe, at least according to Rufius Festus Avienius in a poetical piece dated to the 4th century AD. Avienius records that Himilco followed the route of the Tartessian sailors of southern Iberia to trade for tin and other metals, most likely to Cornwall, but possibly to Britanny. Strabo, writing in the 1st century BC, also records that the Phoenicians had some 300 trading settlements down the eastern Atlantic coastline from Iberia to Morocco.[47]

Indeed recent archaelogical analysis of tin ingots found from a Phoenician wreck in Israel have been traced to Cornwall through the tin's unique metallic signature.[48] Proof, if it were needed, of the incredible distances that the Phoenicians would go to in search of, and to trade in, valuable commodities such as tin. Himilco described his voyage north as challenging, taking four months, while becoming becalmed and having to escape the clutches of both seaweed and sea monsters.

46. Beale, Philip and Taylor, Sarah, 2012. *Sailing Close to the Wind*. Lulworth Cove Press and available on Amazon.
47. Markoe Glenn, E. 2000. *Peoples of the Past Phoenicians*, British Museum Press, London, p. 88.
48. Website: https://www.cornwalllive.com/news/cornwall-news/scientists-find-tin-found-israel-3341918. Further evidence of Phoenician contact with southwest England is provided by the Saltford coin found in 2012. www.saltfordenvironmentgroup.org.uk/history/history002.html

The latter observation was probably added to deter the Greeks from venturing into the Atlantic.

All this information suggests that the Phoenicians were not only the first recorded sailors of any note to sail in the Atlantic, but they were also very active along the eastern Atlantic seaboard. They had knowledge of the North American continent from Pytheas who reached Thule (almost certainly Greenland) and the Hesperides Islands (Caribbean) from the other accounts mentioned above. Simple logic dictates that of all the dominant civilisations in the Ancient world, the Phoenicians were the most likely to have made voyages to the New World.

Atlantic Before Columbus

*"Man cannot discover new oceans unless he has the
courage to lose sight of the shore."*

André Gide

The final leg of our journey to prove that the ancient Phoenicians were capable of sailing across the Atlantic two thousand years before Columbus was set to be the longest and most important part of our journey. After a busy two hours making final checks, we set sail at 9 a.m. on Saturday, 22nd November, 2019, from Marina San Miguel on the south coast of Tenerife.

It is impossible to be sure whether or not a Phoenician ship crossing the Atlantic in 500 BC would have visited Tenerife, nonetheless, we were soon passing the island of La Gomera from where Christopher Columbus set sail on his first voyage of discovery in September, 1492. Either way, we were following in the wake of history.

There were twelve of us on board. The crew was made up of four Brits (myself, Charlie, Max and David), two Norwegians (Steinar and Diderik), two Lebanese (Sheimaa and Remi), one Brazilian (Yuri), one Dutch (Maran) and last, but probably most important of all, our two Indonesians (Dirman and Aziz).

Our new recruits were Remi Kahwaji, a Canadian of Lebanese descent who worked as an engineer in the aircraft industry; 23-year-old David Smith, a computer scientist from Scotland; and Diderik Cappelen, who had sailed with Steinar on one of his Viking ship expeditions. Each had heard about the expedition independently and through their sheer interest and enthusiasm for the project persuaded me they would be valuable additions to the crew, a decision that was well vindicated.

Progress was relatively slow for the first few hours as we were still in the lee of Mount Teide, which was blocking the wind blowing in behind us from the north-east. But five hours after leaving Marina San

Miguel, we caught a wind blowing steadily from the north and were able to hoist the mainsail.

As the crew adapted to life back at sea, we were greeted by a pod of whales which came within a few feet of the boat, lifting our spirits still further. My hope was that after catching the North Atlantic winds that were blowing us more south than west, we would eventually catch the trade winds from the Western Sahara. These would blow us somewhere in the region of the 20th parallel which runs across the northern Caribbean. At this stage we had no idea where we would make landfall on the other side of the Atlantic. Once again, our fate was in the hands of Yamm, the Phoenician god of the sea.

As night fell, the lights of La Palma island were still visible from our position around 20 miles from the mainland. "Enjoy the last city lights," I told the crew. "After this we won't see civilisation again for the next 30 days." Overall, we averaged about 2.5 knots during the first 48 hours, putting more than 120 miles between us and Tenerife.

As anyone who has ever crewed overnight on a sailing ship will know, the normal rhythms of life on land are turned upside down on a sea voyage of any length. On land, everyone adapts their biorhythms to the changing hours of night and day, depending on the seasons and their location on the planet, usually sleeping for around eight hours at a time in any 24-hour period.

At sea, these rhythms are necessarily disrupted. At all hours of day and night, a watch team is responsible for sailing the ship with one or two of the group at the helm steering the ship and navigating. Meanwhile the other members of the watch keep a look-out for passing shipping, make sail adjustments, carry out routine checks below decks and prepare meals for the rest of the crew. The basic requirements, in fact, of life at sea.

It can take a few days to adapt to these new routines, especially for the new crew members when everyone is still getting to know one another. On a long voyage like the one on which we were embarking, however, it soon becomes second nature. While initial fatigue can feel overwhelming, especially after a night watch, the body soon adapts accordingly.

The watch system we used on *Phoenicia* for the Atlantic crossing is known as a 'Swedish watch' system. Before we set sail, I had divided the crew into three four-man watch teams with each 24-hour period made up of three four-hour shifts (day-time) and two six-hour shifts (night-time).

Watch One ran from 8 a.m. until midday; Watch Two from midday until 4 p.m.; and Watch Three from 4 p.m. until 8 p.m. During night-time, the Sunset Watch started at 8 p.m. continuing until 2 a.m., followed by the Graveyard/Sunrise Watch ending at 8 a.m. Members of the latter would be woken at about 1.30 a.m. with some hot drinks and biscuits. I knew this would be the time when some of the new crew members would wonder what they had signed up for. You're in a deep sleep and suddenly you are being shaken into consciousness. It can be very disorientating and just getting out of bed requires all the energy you can muster.

The benefit of having three teams and five shifts is that each day everyone is on watch at a different time from the day before. Also, every three days, each watch team gets a full eight-hour overnight sleep. Everyone gets their fair share of the benefits, namely sunsets, sunrises, and lie-ins; but also their fair share of the less popular duties, namely being woken in the dead of night… and washing up. On top of this we also had a 'Happy Hour', a weekly get-together for the whole crew when we would gather around the helm at 4p.m. on a Wednesday. This was a chance for everyone to enjoy some sweet treats, soft drinks and even an occasional can of beer.

Each watch was soon given an appropriate nick-name, derived from a defining characteristic. My team were the Phoenicians with Maran, David and Remi; Steinar led the Vikings with Yuri, Sheimaa and Diderik; while Charlie's team were dubbed the Chess team alongside Dirman, Max and Aziz.

The Chess team were so-called because of their expertise at moving strangely shaped objects around a board made up of 64 alternate black and white squares. Charlie had been given a chess set as a leaving present when he left his work. Its defining feature was not so much its design, but the fact that it was magnetic, a critical design feature in choppy waters. Although chess isn't recorded until about the 7th century AD, games like draughts, backgammon, and go date back to several millennia BC, so it's perfectly possible that Phoenician sailors played board games at sea. Just not in a storm.

During the voyage from the UK to the Mediterranean, Charlie had been the chess champion, but when Dirman came aboard, all this changed. Dirman's down-to-earth, logical, mind was a match for everyone. I've always believed that had Dirman been born in America, he would have ended up working for N.A.S.A. He always has such a friendly, smiling, demeanour – a true reflection of his character – but he also has the practical intelligence of a genius, and the work ethic of a human dynamo.

Each of the crew had their preferences for different watch times. "The ideal time for me is 8 a.m. to 2 p.m. because you can rest soundly without worrying about being woken up," Maran told me. "The most difficult is 2 a.m. to 8 a.m. because in addition to being very sleepy when the sun comes up, your eyes feel sore and then you have to serve breakfast for the whole crew."

There was a little bit of cheerful banter between the watch teams as to which was best at cooking up meals. Even within teams, some enjoyed cooking and others didn't. Yuri is a great cook, so he was our champion chef, and he would serve up some delicious dishes, whereas the Vikings were the complete opposite and found it challenging even preparing some porridge. They frequently came to an arrangement where Yuri would cook, and the Vikings would do all the washing-up because they couldn't cook! An excellent exchange, in my book.

Everyone had their individual skills. 'Scottish' Dave was acknowledged as the crew's overall champion tea-maker; Maran baked delicious creamy tuna and sweet potato pies; Yuri made his trademark apple pies; while Max made a tasty Italian/Asian fusion of pineapple and coconut risotto with red curry paste.

However, by our fifth day on the water one ingredient had been noticeably absent from the menu: fresh fish. We were beginning to worry that we had entered another fishing drought or that Atlantic fish stocks were worse than we had been led to believe. It was now that we discovered that our lures were no longer attached to our fishing lines. On examination, it was clear they had been swallowed, Jonah-like, by much bigger fish than we had expected to encounter which was both encouraging, and disappointing, in equal measure.

At this stage, we were sailing comfortably before some easterlies which were driving us towards the Caribbean. The winds were generally light, and the rain clouds kept away, although on occasion we felt some keen breezes. By noon on Thursday, 5th December, we had covered around

330 miles. The main event of the day was the hooking of three large dorado. But once again, we were to be disappointed. Their sheer size had caught us by surprise, and the lines weren't strong enough to hold them.

In our hour of need, Dirman once again came to our rescue. By far the most accomplished fisherman of us all, he knew everything there was to know about which tackle and lures to use, and at what depth they should be deployed. Dirman persuaded us that sometimes traditional equipment works much better than the new-fangled, modern tackle we had been using. Under his instruction, we replaced our modern fishing lures and started trailing two traditional Indonesian lures, made of two pieces of frayed coloured rope. These were equipped with bigger and stronger hooks which had been fashioned on-board by Dirman himself.

According to our fishing guru, we needed to reach a minimum speed of 3.5 knots in order to persuade the fish to chase our lures. This was a speed that, until recently, we had been struggling to achieve. Dirman being Dirman, however, was soon strolling over to the stern with a big grin on his face and pulling out a large dorado. Dorado are strange looking fish with a yellow underbelly, also known as mahi mahi. They always went down well with the crew as they are very nutritious and rich in vitamins and selenium. When prepared well, they also taste great, often quite strong but with a slightly sweet taste.

Our first catch was big enough to provide lunch for the whole crew and within two hours of hauling in our prize, we each had a sizeable portion of fried fish, rice, and salad. A good fishing day always went down well with the crew. It added diversity to our diet and much-needed novelty to our jaded taste buds, along with a welcome boost in nutritional value and fat-free proteins.

Flying fish would also land on the deck, often in the middle of the night, which we would collect in the morning and eat for breakfast. Flying fish taste a bit like sardines. Nothing special, many would say, but again a change of diet and taste was always welcome. One gave Steinar quite a surprise when he was on the helm during a night watch and it suddenly catapulted out of the water. He said he felt like someone had kicked him in the behind. Much to everyone's amusement, the same thing happened to Remi the following night.

On another occasion, a flying fish flew through the cabin window, and narrowly missed landing in the frying pan. That, we decided, would be the ultimate sign that the gods were on our side. Overall, however, we were not as fortunate with our haul of fish as we had been during the *Around Africa expedition*. For some reason, the plentiful tuna which we harvested then were not to be found in any quantity or size in the Atlantic.

Towards the end of the voyage, in more tropical waters, we did manage to haul in a balloonfish. But this was definitely a novelty catch, rather than a gourmet addition to the menu. We were actually quite scared of it when we saw it wriggling around on the deck. This strange creature can blow itself up to three times its normal size and has long spines sticking out like a sea urchin. It both looks, and is, poisonous. A feast for the eyes, but not for the stomach.

The word 'remote' takes on an entirely different meaning when you are at sea. On land, it often denotes a sensation of loneliness. At sea, the sights, sounds and smells are very different, and the experience of remoteness is more of a womb-like sensation, especially at night when the weather is calm, and the temperature is warm. As on land, with the vast canopy of stars above, it made us viscerally aware of our insignificance in the great scheme of things, protected from the vast ocean only by this wooden cradle called a ship.

At sea, the sailor also has an uninterrupted view of the horizon. The first and last glimpses of the sun, as it came and went on its daily round, were always very special moments. I still find it mesmerising, however many times I see it. The colours and the patterns of light flashing across the sky are different every day depending on the formations of the clouds. But on a clear day it is the anticipation of that tiny ember of orange light, which signals its last goodbye or first hello, which takes the breath away.

On nights with a full moon, there would often be bioluminescence in the water. This creates the surreal sensation that the stars are both above and below, and that you are floating along in a celestial bubble. On the many nights when there were shooting stars the feeling was even more intense. We were sailing during the season of the Leonids when there would sometimes be many hundreds over the course of a single night.

I think the crew were all really appreciative of how different being at sea is to everyday life. We felt much more connected to the natural rhythms of life. It wasn't a religious experience or a mad euphoria. There's no way you would survive anyway if you were in a state like that for six weeks solid. But when you are at the helm and in control of the ship, it can be a very moving experience nonetheless. An intense feeling of freedom and adventure.

It was also inevitable, given the objective of the expedition, that we would try to imagine what it would have been like for a Phoenician sailor in the 5th century BC. In our own time, we carry a map in our head that we hardly realise is there, but which tells us where we are on the planet. This helps us feel far safer than we would without it. We stand on the shoulders of many centuries of scientists and explorers who have gone before. But for the ancient Phoenicians, this really was the unknown, the final frontier.

The Phoenicians knew the points of the compass, using the stars to steer a course. If they were sailing from, say, Carthage to the Pillars of Hercules, they would steer a certain angle checking their position by the stars. Maran and David enjoyed picking out the constellations and we would all track the Pole Star which was easy to find in the northern sky. Using the night sky, we could also deduce our approximate latitude.

One story we had heard about the Phoenicians was that they used doves to find the direction of land. Apparently, they often took half a dozen doves with them and if they became disorientated, they would release a dove. It would circle the boat a few times and then in whichever direction it flew off would be the way to land. Not that this method would have worked very well in the middle of the Atlantic.

Some aspects of everyday life, often ones we all take for granted on land, soon lose their meaning after being at sea for a while. Money is one of them. We were sailing from Tenerife which uses euros, while our destination at this stage could have been any one of a number of different countries. We were also an international crew without a common currency. We very quickly discovered that the value of a coin or note, of whatever denomination or nationality, drops to zero in a closed system, especially when shortages begin to make themselves felt.

Spurred on by Sheimaa, instead of money we started to use the oldest currency of them all. Barter was the primary currency of trade in the ancient world, so it is perhaps appropriate that a bartering economy began to develop on the *Phoenicia*. The Phoenicians were known as great traders and barterers, so it was entirely appropriate that Sheimaa continued the tradition.

She began by exchanging a piece of sponge or loofah she had brought with her from Lebanon, but both goods and services were up for auction. Sheimaa, for example, really hated washing-up. Especially after a long night shift. But being an excellent forward planner, she had stocked up before we left Tenerife with an impressive store of chocolate, sweets, and various toiletries whose value index increased rapidly the further we sailed from land. But toilet rolls were soon to become the new international currency.

It was on only our tenth day at sea when Maran, who was in charge of stocktaking, reported that the supply of toilet paper was running low, leaving only thirty rolls to last us the rest of the journey. If we kept using it at the rate that we had been doing, we would certainly run out. The problem occurred because we had all been leaving the rolls of toilet tissue next to the heads on the deck. If it rained during the night these would get wet. Before we knew it we were running low. "We will ration, one person, one roll of tissue for the next 20 days," Maran suggested. So, we decided we had to divvy up the rolls that remained, and if some people used more than others or let it get wet, then that was their problem.

"Let's trade," Sheimaa might say. "I have chocolate. What do you have to exchange, Dirman? How about your toilet tissue? I'll exchange it for chocolate." Dirman immediately agreed. For Dirman this was a valuable exchange, as neither he nor Aziz usually used toilet paper for their ablutions, preferring to wash in the Asian way instead. Sheimaa's plentiful supply of chocolate also turned out to be a good bartering tool for not doing washing-up duties, while David's all-consuming desire for chocolate meant he was forever doing the dishes.

By this stage, some of the crew started amassing debts of owed toilet paper. Before we knew it, the whole ship was in need of the type of quantitative easing that was used after the 2008 financial crisis. But then halfway through the voyage another stash of toilet paper was discovered, an event that caused a mass inflation of the currency. Anyone who had been hoarding toilet paper, suddenly found their bargaining power reduced, and anyone who had debts in toilet paper could get off lightly. All in, it was like an experiment in applied economics, except that instead of gold being the standard against which the currency was valued, we had toilet paper.

Those who have never been on a sailing ship for any length of time often think of life at sea as a constant struggle against the wind and the waves, especially in the middle of a wide ocean. This certainly can be true, but most of the time it is to do with the practicalities of living in a confined space and how smoothly the routines of everyday life are operating. However, despite my many years' experience on the world's oceans, I had never before realised how disruptive the presence of an uninvited guest can be.

We made the discovery soon after leaving Tenerife. This was the unwelcome revelation that we had a stowaway on board. Not human it must be said – although in many ways it would have been far less problematic if it had been.

Our stowaway was, in fact, a mouse. At least, that's what we assumed it was, after discovering that our precious supplies of food had come under attack. Our invisible friend started by showing a particular liking for milk and hot-chocolate powder, apples, rice and sweet potatoes. Not thinking too much about it, other than as a minor irritation, we put down some mouse traps which we thankfully had the foresight to buy in Tenerife, thinking that this would soon solve the problem.

Sadly, our optimism proved to be unjustified. The mouse traps remained stubbornly empty and our food supplies diminished still further. Five days after leaving Tenerife, we were beginning to find excrement liberally scattered around the ship in the most unexpected places. Two plastic drums made of thick plastic and filled with pasta had also been punctured. There was only one conclusion to be drawn. This was certainly not a timid, sweet-natured, Mickey Mouse, but a seriously hungry rat looking for trouble.

Defence, rather than attack, immediately became our first priority. We started by re-organising our food supplies and putting the more vulnerable items in rat-proof boxes. By this stage two kilograms of apples had been bitten into and thirty packets of biscuits. The quiet aft of the ship below the helm became a safe haven with hanging bags and a hammock full of vulnerable food out of reach of the rat. All the other barrels and boxes of food that remained untouched, we covered in grease which, according to Dirman and Aziz, would be a potent deterrent.

It was only now that we began to think in a more offensive way. To this end, we deployed some home-made traps that we hoped would be more effective than the ones we had already tried. Dirman designed a particularly ingenious one made from a cardboard box, a bucket of water, and a trapdoor. Another contained a piece of card with sticky plastic on the top surface that was supposed to disable the rat if it came into close contact. But this lethal contraption was barely noticed by our wily adversary. The next time we saw it, it had been torn in two with the missing half found next to a well-chewed pack of wet-wipes.

Nonetheless, things went quiet for a day or two and a wave of optimism swept over us. Perhaps the creature had died from eating the wet-wipes? This theory seemed to have some credence, when we detected a strong odour of rotting flesh coming from the ballast area. Unfortunately, however, our optimistic assessment turned out to be wishful thinking.

Our first sighting of the rat came one night when Max saw it scurrying across the deck. Later, when he was sleeping, he said he felt it walking over his chest and on his hair. This was news that no-one wanted to hear. Then the next morning at about 3.30 a.m. while on watch, Max again spotted it at the bow of the ship running along one of the railings. He called over to Charlie and the rest of the Chess team who were on watch with him and they all tried to corner it. Unfortunately, it darted off and completely vanished before the rest of the team had a chance to see it. The next morning there was some speculation that it may have fallen into the sea, but once again this proved to be wishful thinking.

At this stage, the rest of us started to interrogate Max, asking him where it went, what colour it was, and most importantly, how big it was. "About this big," he replied, holding his hands about ten or eleven inches apart. "Is that with or without the tail?" His hands moved slightly closer together.

Being the only person to have seen the rat, Max soon found himself the butt of jokes from the rest of the crew who wondered if it was a pet rat that he had befriended in Tenerife and brought on board. Either that, or he was imagining it. The latter possibility seemed highly unlikely given the chewed fruit, the holes in more food packets, and the ever-more-pungent odour beneath the floorboards. Also, this was a rat which didn't finish what he'd started. More and more apples were being nibbled before having to be thrown out.

A situation that in a domestic setting on land would have been a mere nuisance, on an expedition like ours had potentially more devastating consequences. Nobody needs an in-depth knowledge of the history of the Black Death to know that rats carry disease. We wanted to be remembered for crossing the Atlantic in a replica of a Phoenician ship, not for dying of bubonic plague, or more probably Weil's Disease, in the process. It was imperative that we caught the rat quickly.

Beneath the decking, in the bowels of the ship, there were 20 tons of steel sheets acting as ballast. It was clear the rat was living underneath these boards and that it could travel from one end of the ship to the other with impunity. Its droppings were also beginning to smell to high heaven.

The crew reacted to the situation in different ways. I knew Sheimaa was secretly very scared although, as always, she put a good face on it. Being the ship's doctor, Maran wasn't so scared of the rat itself, but more about the health implications. It was leaving faeces everywhere and possibly even in the food, potentially infecting everyone on board in the process. In such a confined area, I knew some of the crew were petrified at the thought of it crawling over them in the night or getting stuck in their hair. I know I was. Unsurprisingly, hammocks became the favoured option for sleeping at night.

Any lingering hopes that the rat may have jumped overboard were dispelled the night I saw it myself. It was scuttling over some food boxes in the hold during a routine check while I was on watch. After talking tactics for a few minutes with the rest of the team, we sat in silence for the rest of the watch, trying to think of ways we could outsmart the creature. I went back to bed, but found it difficult to sleep thinking of ways we could outwit this cunning adversary. But finally, I came up with a plan.

The next morning, I shared my idea with the rest of the crew: we would fumigate it with exhaust from the engine. As we discussed this option over breakfast, it was obvious not everyone was convinced. For a start, it was pointed out, everything in the main cabin would stink of diesel. "Well, we have to do something," I countered, with a resigned expression.

A short time later, we discovered another hole which our friend had chewed through the side of a barrel of nuts. Now there was unanimous agreement that we had no choice but to give it a go. In preparation, we brought all the fresh food, bread and biscuits that had not been touched up on deck, battened down the hatches, and by 3 p.m. we were ready to suffocate the rat. We then started the engine, the diesel generator, and the water pump and all the exhaust ducts were funnelled into the cabin and below the deck.

It was a baking hot day, so all we could do was lie out on deck for three hours with all our gear piled up around us hoping this latest ruse would finally put an end to the rat. We thought that if it didn't actually kill the rat, it would certainly wake up with a serious headache and would be easier to dispatch. As if to taunt us still further, the carbon monoxide alarm was soon ringing loudly below decks.

How much of a headache the rat woke up with, or even if it had one at all, is an open question. Suffice it to say, the next night in the same place as before, at nearly the same time, Max again spotted the rat. Much to his frustration, he was again the only one to see it. But after our attempt to trap it in some upturned buckets, the rat escaped once more and, we concluded with grudging respect, it probably didn't end up jumping into the sea. Our fumigation attempt had ended in failure.

Defeat is not a word that the crew of an ancient Phoenician ship would have recognised. So, true to their memory, we were soon hard at work creating ingenious traps out of anything we could cobble together. Dirman designed another trap, again using a bucket filled with water, but this time with a beer can suspended over it baited with peanut butter. The idea was that when the rat fell off the beer can, it would drown. Apparently, he had once managed to lure two mice back home in Indonesia with a similar device. Two days later, all the bait had been polished off. But once again, there was no sign of a drowned rat.

Now it was Charlie's turn. His creation was simpler in concept, namely an upside-down steel box with a block of wood under it attached to a piece of string. Inside the box he had left bait including slices of cheese, apples and biscuits. The only problem with this was that someone had to sit in silence staring at the box at all hours of the day and night ready to pull the string. On my watch, Maran told me she almost started to hallucinate after staring at it for so long. Then a group of flying fish landed on the deck right next to her, making her jump out of her skin.

Not to be outdone, Yuri was soon hard at work building another trap. We couldn't really work out what he was trying to do, but after cobbling away for a morning with a metal basket, some wood, wire and a piece of metal he had extracted from the anchor, he came up with what looked like an impressive feat of engineering.

It all centred around a see-saw mechanism which triggered a metal door. He loaded the wooden ramp at one end with some of the rat's favourite foods, namely nuts, apples and peanut paste. The idea was that its weight would upend the ramp and release a metal door which would slam down behind it. We dubbed it the Mickey Mouse Night Club. We put it next to the food down below and waited. Yuri also set up an infra-red camera so we could monitor whether or not the rat was checking it out, but all we saw was the crew going back and forth. Now we had three traps, I noted. One Indonesian, one British, and one Brazilian.

By now, all of us had admitted to becoming obsessed by the rat. Max said he thought he had felt it again in his hair, as did Sheimaa. Others had dreams about rats and it inevitably dominated many of our conversations, becoming the source of a gnawing sense of unease among the crew – along with some bad puns! A sense of paranoia, sleepless nights, lack of appetite, and strange smells were becoming more pronounced with every day that went by.

Much to our initial frustration, the first time the rat took some food from Yuri's trap, the mechanism failed to activate. Undeterred, Yuri made a few adjustments. The rat had managed to eat some of the food without triggering the trap door, so he adjusted the trigger mechanism to make it more finely balanced. He also moved the trap nearer to where the rat had attacked some apples earlier in the voyage and covered the area with a black plastic sheet. This blocked out the light and made the rat's navigation more dependent on smell.

Then one morning when I was in the cabin, I heard some loud shouting. Usually when this happens at sea, my unconscious reactions immediately prepare for the worst. Had someone fallen overboard? Was there some serious damage to the ship? Were we on a collision course with another boat? Alternatively, the racket sometimes turns out to be a reaction to one of nature's unpredictable interventions, like dolphins leaping around the bows of the ship, a fish on the line, or some unwanted spice in Yuri's lunch.

But this morning, it was different. The shouting was like nothing I'd heard before on the ship. A mixture of bewilderment and celebration, something on a par with scoring a world-cup winning goal or winning the lottery. I knew at once it could only mean one thing. We had finally caught the rat.

Apparently one of the crew had noticed the door to the trap was closed and a repetitive squeaking noise and vibrations were coming from inside. Yuri was quickly on the scene and looked through one of the small holes in the trap. Sure enough, the rat was inside. Pandemonium soon broke out with everyone screaming and shouting with the intensity you would expect if someone had fallen overboard.

By the time Yuri had brought it up on deck, it was chewing vigorously away at the wood trying to get out. "What did I say? Once again I saved you!" Yuri shouted happily and we all applauded. Immediately, there was a loud debate about what to do with it. "Chop off its head!", "Burn him!", "Put him on a raft and send him out to sea for a year!" were some not-so-helpful suggestions. The crew were clearly looking forward to seeing the back of our unwelcome stowaway. Finally, the almost unanimous verdict became clear: death by drowning was the only sensible option.

We were worried that if we just threw the rat over the side it would use its claws to climb up the planks of the hull and back onto the ship. In the end, we decided that the only solution was to throw the trap over the stern attached to a rope with another rope attached to the door. Once the trap had been in the water for five minutes and safely out of reach of the ship, we would open the door and bid farewell to Mr Ratty.

In the process, we lost part of the door of the trap which was made of a piece of equipment from the anchor, which was a nuisance. But at least the rat was gone. 'Ratgate', as we had come to know it, was finally over. In honour of his brilliant invention, and because he also plays the flute, Yuri was now dubbed the 'Pied Piper of the Caribbean.'

During the long saga of Ratgate, it had become something of a sensation on our social media channels, and over the following days voices were raised objecting to the rat's fate, with some clearly feeling that our actions were barbaric. Along with the many problems the rat had made for us, my priority was the crew's safety. With it still on board, we might also have had to jettison huge quantities of contaminated food, so quite what the alternative option would have been, I am still at a loss to know. Indeed, one of Steinar's Norwegian friends suggested we should eat it.

What mattered most, of course, was the morale of the crew, and we were all ecstatic. We had been caught in a web of anxiety as to where we were going to find the rat next and nobody could sleep well at night, so we had all been very tense. On the flip side, while we were very happy to see it go, it had given us a sense of unity and this now fed into our determination to safely complete our crossing.

One amusing event had certainly lightened the mood during our stand-off with the rat. We had been sailing for about ten days when we found ourselves in the middle of a flotilla of boats which kept passing us at all hours of the day and night. We soon discovered they were taking part in the annual Atlantic Rally for Cruisers (ARC). It's an event that has been running since the mid-1980s which gives yacht owners the chance to make an Atlantic crossing from the Canaries to St. Lucia in the Caribbean in the company of other boats.

It's not officially a race, more an opportunity for crossing the Atlantic with the knowledge that there's a support network in place. Everyone gets to know each other in the weeks leading up to the event when participants congregate in Las Palmas in Gran Canaria. Around 200 yachts take part every year. We had seen a number of boats passing us the previous night and it was a Tuesday afternoon on a clear, sunny, day with a moderate wind. The crew were gathered around the helm enjoying some sun as a handful of catamarans sailed slowly past. Suddenly, there was a crackle over the VHF radio.

"Wooden boat, wooden boat!" came the voice over the radio. It was such a comical salutation that I was barely able to contain my laughter. I decided a suitable riposte was in order. "Plastic boat, plastic boat. This is wooden boat, do you copy?" I replied, much to the amusement of the crew.

The boat turned out to be an Italian catamaran and we enjoyed a friendly exchange of wit and repartee. Our new friends were interested in knowing where such an unlikely looking vessel was heading. Or, they wondered, had they sailed through some sort of time warp? I reassured them that they were still in the 21st century and that we had an international crew on board. And one 'mouse'. "Is this a pet or clandestine mouse?" they wanted to know. I emphasised it was the latter and that it was in the process of being hunted down.

We also had some helpful discussions about the likely direction of the wind in the near future. Our progress had been continuing steadily with the ship covering about a hundred miles per day. The wind was now mainly from the east accompanied by overcast skies, rain showers and strong gusts of wind. We agreed that it would probably be best to change course slightly and head further south where we would hopefully catch the best of the West Sahara winds before heading west once again.

In contrast to our rodent visitation, halfway through our ordeal we were visited by an altogether more welcome stranger. Around this time Charlie, Steinar, and Yuri had all had birthdays which we celebrated with cakes baked by Maran, David and Max. Steinar, like many Norwegians, is a big coffee drinker, so it was only right that his cake had coffee flavoured icing and we also flew the Norwegian flag. For Yuri's birthday, Maran baked a delicious chocolate cake with coconut icing during the night watch, but Mother Nature came up with the biggest surprise.

At midday, to everyone's amazement, a peregrine falcon swooped down and perched on the cabin window looking straight in at us. He – we just presumed he was male – really was a stunning creature, and very striking to look at in such close proximity. During the time he was with us, he alternated his perch between where we first saw him outside the cabin, to the top of the mast, and then near the horse's head on the bows of the ship.

Sheimaa dubbed him 'Baalito', meaning 'Little God' in ancient Phoenician. Baalito was a beautiful bird whose navigation systems must have gone badly awry. We decided he must have been surviving by hopping around between container ships. We were around 300 miles from the African coast when he first landed on the ship, so he had most probably come from Cape Verde which was the nearest landmass at this stage in our voyage.

Peregrines have penetrating eyes, jerky head movements, and fearsomely sharp talons like all birds of prey. Baalito's real splendour was revealed when he opened his wings and we could see the amazing patterns on his chest feathers, like raindrops on a white background merging into butterfly shapes further down. His huge tail feathers would spread out like a fan as he took off. Seeing Baalito at close quarters was mesmerising enough, and it was easy to see how prey would be instantly hypnotised by his approach.

When he was circling, Baalito had a beautiful outline. When his wings were folded against his body, his sleek, streamlined, shape looked like a jet fighter or, more accurately in design terms, the other way round. According to Guinness World Records, the peregrine falcon is the fastest animal on the planet. Its dive, or 'stoop' as it is known, has been recorded at more than 230 mph.

Although you would be forgiven for thinking that the incredible speed at which they dive would make it more difficult to target moving prey accurately, in fact the opposite is true. But it requires finely-tuned steering in order for the falcon to come away with its prize. The g-forces it generates (up to 10g) would make a human instantly black out, but somehow falcons manage to keep their cognitive functions operating smoothly.

Baalito stayed with us for two days and two nights. We put out fresh water and threw pieces of fish into the air for him to eat. Sadly, he just wasn't interested, as if he was too proud to accept help from mere mortals like us. He was always on the hunt for his own live prey, particularly flying fish. We spent so long admiring him that at one stage we began to believe that he might hold the answer to our own little problem, and kill the rat.

On the final morning of his stay, we saw him circling around the boat as if he was about to fly off. But then, much to our surprise, he suddenly made a head-long dive into the water. Presumably he had seen a fish near to the surface, and we were all eagerly waiting for him to reappear. But he never did. It was one of the saddest moments of the entire trip. When you're surrounded by nature, and at the mercy of the elements yourself, you feel more of an affinity with the natural world, however red in tooth and claw. A harsh reminder indeed.

Back in our own world of twelve crew members living life in cramped conditions in the middle of the Atlantic Ocean, one unfortunate incident that did cause frustration was when a drum of our precious flour became contaminated. It became an issue when some of the crew started tasting a bitter flavour in the food. We had stored a lot of flour for the voyage in Tunisia and we had been very careful about it.

Flour is very vulnerable to water and we had previously had to throw some overboard which had somehow become damp. But we now had so much flour that everything we were eating seemed to have elements of bread in the recipe.

The drums in which it was stored were big 250-litre plastic containers which had at one time contained diesel, but had been empty for a while and were just getting in the way. Before being used for food storage, they had been cleaned and scrubbed many times with washing powder. As I knew we would get storms with water leaking into the storage area down below, they seemed like the perfect receptacles to store food.

The problems started during one of our Wednesday Happy Hours when Yuri had made an apple pudding using flour from a new barrel. Charlie mentioned that he had noticed a funny taste. I didn't think much of it except that maybe the apples were a bit off. We all forgot about it for a while until a few days later it occurred to Charlie that the barrel we had filled in Tunisia might have been the source of the problem. This created a divide among the crew between those who said anything made with the flour tasted awful and was making them sick, and those who didn't.

I tried to make a joke of it. "Diesel fuel should increase our body power to pump bilge water," I suggested. Not everyone was amused. Thankfully, we still had a considerable amount of rice, pasta, and noodles that were stored in different drums. Maran, in her capacity as ship's doctor, did some research on the issue but did not seem over-worried about it.

With our minds no longer absorbed by the rat, all our mental focus returned to the overall objective of sailing west. The latter had been made easier by strong following winds allowing us, on good days, to average more than five knots. This was much more than had been possible during the first week after we left Tenerife, when the winds had been very light, and we had made very slow progress. The problem seemed to have been that the 'Azores High', an area of high pressure which often has high winds from the Western Sahara associated with it, was much further south than it usually is at this time of year. Due to this, we had to sail a lot further south than we had expected. This had slowed our progress considerably.

However, now that we had connected with a high pressure area, the strong winds were causing their own problems. I gave the order that if we reached the speed of six knots, we should reduce the sail area, a process known as furling or reefing. The Phoenicians were probably the first to use a sophisticated system for furling or reefing sails. Eight brailing lines run from the foot of the sail and over the boom to the aft of the ship where they are secured by wooden belaying pins. This reduces the pressure on the mast and protects it from breaking.

The ingenuity of the Phoenician system was that the sailors did not have to climb the rigging to adjust the sails. Instead, they could do it from the comfort of the aft deck by pulling on the brailing lines – a process very similar to pulling up a venetian blind. The winds had by now strengthened to Force 5, with ten-foot waves breaking over the bows. With both the wind and the current in the same direction, and our mainsail fully deployed, we were covering up to 120 nautical miles in a day.

I woke one morning to the news that two rips had appeared in the sail, one about a foot long and the other almost double that. Given all the stresses and strains on the cotton sail, it was relatively easy for it to tear. This would also have been the case in ancient times. Like the Phoenicians, we had no modern sailcloth materials which use polyester or nylon and can withstand extreme sailing conditions.

We also had problems with the stays, the highly-tensioned ropes that support the mast. The latter were always very noisy and made a terrible creaking noise at the best of times, a sound that was amplified below decks. Then one day, for no immediately obvious reason, the sound abruptly stopped. As it turned out, Sheimaa had been brushing her teeth on deck when one of the stays had broken and a heavy wooden block had come crashing down in front of her face. As ever, it was Dirman who came to the rescue and he was soon being hauled up to the top of the mast to fix it.

Meanwhile, I had all hands on deck to bring down the yard so we could make some repairs to the sail. We also took the opportunity to replace some of the wooden brailing hoops that guide the brailing lines along the face of the sail and which had snapped off the previous week. All this work took about four hours before we could raise the sail once more. While this was going on, we took turns to go for a swim. Without the sail, the ship was only moving slowly through the water and the sea was at this stage very calm.

It's a very strange sensation swimming in the middle of the Atlantic Ocean. There are literally thousands of miles of sea in every direction and perhaps 10,000 feet of water, and who knows what else, beneath you. It's a strange mixture of complete exhilaration and intense vulnerability. At the same time there is the surreal sensation of watching a Phoenician ship from the 5th century BC floating past in front of you.

There's also the terrifying possibility that a shark might suddenly appear from nowhere. So we were all keeping an eye out for a dorsal fin while listening to the Jaws theme tune playing inside our heads. On one occasion when we went swimming, actually on Christmas Day itself, Charlie saw a grey shadow appear underneath him which, understandably enough, nearly stopped his heart. Happily, it turned out to be a pilot whale.

We also had to be very careful, because even though the sea was very calm, the current can be much faster than you think. We would sometimes leap off the side of the boat and find ourselves bobbing around in the water, looking down into the endless blue beneath. Then, in a flash, you would lift your head and realise the boat was speeding away from you and if you didn't make a quick sprint to safety you would be in trouble.

All in all, our voyage was remarkably free of incident. But not entirely so. One of the challenges of sailing at night is that it's sometimes very difficult to interpret the lights on another boat. Distance is notoriously hard to judge, as is the size of an approaching ship. Is that a huge ship that's a long way off, or a small sailing yacht that's relatively close? If it's a container ship or a cruise ship that is miles away, it can still be on top of you in minutes. It might not even notice, if it did hit you.

One particularly scary moment was caused by a yacht overtaking us one evening in the early hours of darkness. It was sailing far too close, causing us to change course and nearly back the sail, which with the wind on the wrong side would have caused all sorts of problems. On this occasion, Steinar was on the helm. He thought at first that it was a big ship on our starboard side on the same bearing and that it would simply overtake us. But then he realised that it was a smaller boat that was crossing right in front of us.

We were on a starboard tack and when two sailboats are on an opposite tack, the boat on the starboard tack has the right of way. We suspect it was on auto-pilot and not keeping a look-out, because the boat just resolutely kept to the same course. In the end, it came within metres of hitting us and we almost backed the sail trying to avoid it. But given the thousands of square miles of ocean around us, it would have been nice if they could have kept to the rules of the sea and avoided us.

We had now been travelling at a speed of 4-5 knots for 15 days, with the Western Sahara winds blowing at speeds of 20-25 knots. Rain had also been following us and I warned everyone to be more alert about the build-up of rain-bearing cumulonimbus clouds which often increase wind speed. The wind can also sometimes suddenly change direction, which could have easily broken the mast.

On one particular night, the wind was quite fresh, and we had partially reefed the sail using the eight brailing lines. Unfortunately, one of the lines was rubbing on the main starboard stay and by morning the stay was badly frayed. A little later it suddenly gave way and a bemused Sheimaa let out a characteristic "Woa!" as it fell on the deck just in front of her. Luckily, we had another quarter stay rigged on the starboard side further aft, so there was still plenty of support for the mast.

But then the starboard brace, which is attached to the yard, suddenly snapped, leaving it hanging in thin air. Fortunately, the break occurred near deck-level and Steinar was able to join the two pieces of thick hemp rope together, so we were able to continue as if nothing had happened, except that there was now a large knot on the starboard brace.

Finally, the knots that tie the halyard to the yard began to chafe at the mast itself. With no time to lose and with all hands on deck, we brought down the yard and the sail, retied the knots and added a new temporary stay in place of the one that had broken. We also made a small repair to an emerging hole in the sail and within less than an hour we were on our way again.

The nearer we came to the Caribbean, the more concerned we became about the amount of water that was leaking into the hull of the ship. It was as good a cue as any to thoroughly check the ship for leaks and to patch them with putty or cement. Nonetheless, even after we had taken these precautions, water was still seeping into the ship. The leak was coming mainly from the stern of the ship in the keel area. It was getting worse and worse and we were pumping the bilges continuously.

The hull of the Phoenicia has an area of 40 cubic metres but now, especially in bad weather with big waves, the leaking was increasing. We agreed that on every watch each member of the crew should take it in turns on the hand pump which Dirman had constructed for us.

At times this was a concern, but we just about managed to keep the water levels under control with some much-needed plugging of holes below decks.

Luckily, the winds had by now begun to lose their power and to blow from a more southerly direction. We recorded our first sub 100-mile day for a couple of weeks, making just under 80 miles in 24 hours. By now we were beginning to enter the Caribbean region and the maritime traffic began to increase, with many more seabirds approaching the ship, a sure sign that land was getting nearer.

History has not recorded the mood of the crews of Columbus' three ships, the *Santa Maria*, the *Niña* and the *Pinta* just before they landed, in what is now the Bahamas, on 12th October 1492. But it is a fair bet that after their 36-day voyage, it electrified their mood. The specific island – called Guanahaní in the local language – is thought to be Watlings Island, modern-day San Salvador, although there is still some heated debate as to whether or not this is correct.

According to Columbus, after 36 days of sailing, it was Rodrigo de Triana, a sailor aboard *La Pinta*, who first spotted land, shouting out in the early morning hours, "Tierra! Tierra!" as a canon was fired in a pre-arranged signal. It was Charlie who took the honours of sighting land for the first time on the other side of the Atlantic, when he spotted the outline of La Désirade Island, part of Guadeloupe in the French West Indies. An ecstatic shout had to make do in place of a canon.

It was quite a surreal moment as we had not seen land for 35 days, just sea and more sea. And now suddenly we could smell the scent of vegetation being blown towards us and hear the sound of people partying in hotels. We also started to see a lot more boats and leisure craft in the Caribbean waters.

We had now been at sea for more than five weeks since leaving Tenerife, covering a distance of more than 2400 nautical miles as the crow flies, while following the prevailing winds and currents. When

Columbus arrived in Guanahaní, he was looking for a bigger prize. After visiting four small islands nearby, he sailed on to what is now Cuba, and then east again to the island he dubbed Hispaniola. Here he landed first in the west, in what is now Haiti, before heading back east again and landing on the north coast of what is today the Dominican Republic.

It was only as we came closer that we realised the Dominican Republic was likely to be our first port of call. The winds might have blown us towards the British Virgin Islands, Guadeloupe or even Puerto Rico, which we passed to the north. But it also made sense to land on the island that Columbus considered his most important discovery in 1492.

It was interesting to see the effect that our imminent arrival had on the crew. Everyone started sprucing themselves up a bit to look more presentable, even though we still had another four days' sailing until we arrived in Santo Domingo, the capital of the Dominican Republic, which was now only around 600 miles off. The sense of relief was palpable. We really were going to make it OK.

We next steered north into the Guadeloupe Passage between Guadeloupe itself and the island of Antigua and were soon entering the waters around Puerto Rico which comes under US jurisdiction. Here we found ourselves being checked out by a US reconnaissance plane and coastguard boats making sure we were not smugglers.

A few days later, the southern tip of the island of Hispaniola came into view. Hispaniola is the second largest island in the Caribbean after Cuba and is split between the Spanish-speaking Dominican Republic in the east and French/Haitian/Creole-speaking Haiti. It is also the location of the first European settlements in the Americas. These were founded successively during each of Christopher Columbus' first three voyages, namely La Navidad (1492), La Isabela (1493), and the first permanent settlement and current capital, Santo Domingo (1496).

At night, we could see the lights of the Dominican Republic twinkling ever brighter, and the crew's spirits began to rise still further as we sailed closer to Santo Domingo itself. Early in the morning of 31st December 2019, we were intercepted by a Dominican Republic naval ship which instructed us to follow it into port. At the same time, a speedboat carrying Yuri's wife, Vera, came out to meet us. With them they brought a welcome gift of cold drinks and fresh fruits, including apples, oranges and bananas, the first we had enjoyed for 25 days. A reminder, if one were needed, of how much we usually take such things for granted.

Before we arrived, we had managed to make contact with some Lebanese Americans who lived in Santo Domingo and knew staff in the Dominican Navy, but even so we had no real idea of what to expect by way of a welcome. I was certainly feeling the pressure as we came into port. After so long at sea, I wanted to be sure our arrival look dignified, and not like the arrival of a group of refugees, which at times is what it felt like.

As we came into the harbour at Santo Domingo, I couldn't help noticing out of the corner of my eye that Sheimaa was trying to talk to me. However, I was under maximum pressure and there were other priorities I needed to concentrate on. In the end, it was Charlie who shouted at me: "Skipper, you've got your shirt on inside out!" I'm glad he did because the rest of the crew were wearing the smartest clothes they could muster. Charlie even asked Sheimaa to shave his head to tidy up his untidy mop. This she succeeded in doing, only for Charlie to drop the electric razor into the harbour trying to clean it.

The female crew members all looked terrific, and after 39 days at sea I'm not sure how they managed it. I think Sheimaa, in particular, was very keen to look her best. This was partly because Lebanese women in general are very careful about their appearance, but it was also because she quite rightly saw herself as being a representative of the ancient Phoenicians in whose honour this voyage had been made.

I know that when I first set foot on the pier, I wasn't the only member of the crew who felt shaky. In fact, Aziz told me later it felt like an earthquake had hit him. It's something that quite often happens when you have been at sea continuously for a long time, on a relatively small ship. You feel unstable when you step back on land because for weeks your body has been making constant adjustments to the rolling motion of the boat.

Then, suddenly, you're standing on land that is completely still, while your brain continues to compensate for the rolling motion of the sea. It can make you feel very dizzy. So much so, that many sailors report waking up during their first night back on land and being unable to stand, as the room is moving around so much. Either that, or they've just been celebrating too much.

We were amazed to be greeted by a Navy marching band dressed in full immaculate white regalia and gold braid, led by the Deputy Commander of the Dominican Republic Navy, Admiral Hector Juan Martinez Roman. This was followed by a drinks reception where we were treated like royalty. The event was televised, and speeches were made, including one by me. We were even being compared with Columbus. All this on New Year's Eve. The ensuing party in the Officer's Club was certainly one none of us will ever forget.

Although feeling very euphoric, we were all exhausted and it felt very odd trying to get our bearings. We just had to fling ourselves into it and smile and shake hands with everyone. We were all bursting with emotion, and it was quite difficult going from an enclosed bubble with just twelve of us on the boat to suddenly being surrounded by people all wanting to talk to us and have their photograph taken with us.

I remember watching Sir Francis Chichester on TV arriving back in Plymouth after the first single-handed circumnavigation of the globe. Suddenly, he turned *Gypsy Moth* around and started sailing back out of the harbour again. Now I understand why. He had been completely on his own for months. But even with a crew of twelve and being at sea for a much shorter period of time, the contrast between these two different worlds of an empty ocean and an emotional crowd filling the harbour was very intense.

Our welcome was organised by the Lebanese community, so we wanted to underline the modern-day connection of the crew with the ancient Phoenicians. The Lebanon has very close historical connections with the Dominican Republic. Even the President is Lebanese. In the 19th century, many Lebanese emigrated to the Dominican Republic after the famine there, and now three generations on, many only speak Spanish and not their native Arabic. Nonetheless, their connection to Lebanon is felt very strongly.

To underline the Phoenician connection, Sheimaa had brought a Lebanese flag with its Cedar of Lebanon on a white background between two red stripes, and proudly held it high throughout the emotional proceedings of that never-to-be-forgotten New Year's Eve.

Hispaniola

"Gold is a treasure, and he who possesses it does all he wishes to in this world and succeeds in helping souls into paradise."

Christopher Columbus[49]

We arrived in Santo Domingo in the Dominican Republic on 31st December 2019 after 39 days at sea. Yuri's family cooked us an excellent meal, before we headed out on the town to enjoy one of the most memorable New Year's Eve celebrations any of us could remember. We then spent nearly three weeks in the Dominican Republic as the guests of the Dominican Republic Navy and the Club Libanes-Sirio-Palestino.

During this time, my attention turned to Christopher Columbus, or as he is known in the Spanish-speaking world, Cristóbal Colón. Columbus not only rediscovered this island for the Europeans and named it Hispaniola, but was arguably also the most destructive force ever to have made contact with it. Today, the island of Hispaniola is divided between Haiti in the west, which occupies about 36% of the landmass, and the Dominican Republic in the east.

I set myself the goal of trying to understand the enigma of Cristóbal Colón. I wanted to know who he really was, and what he really knew before he set sail across the 'Ocean Sea' when the Spanish monarchs, Isabella and Ferdinand, finally commissioned him to do so in 1492. How much knowledge had he borrowed from ancient sources? How

---

49. Letter to the King and Queen of Spain, 1503.
50. Although relatively little is known about the life of Marinus of Tyre, other than he originated from Tyre in the then Roman province of Syria. Nonetheless most biographers describe him as Greek. George Sarton (1936). *"The Unity and Diversity of the Mediterranean World"*, Osiris 2, pp. 406-463.

much did he rely on the works of the Phoenician[50] cosmographer and cartographer, Marinus of Tyre? What sort of character was he? How did he come to be largely responsible for the annihilation[51] of hundreds of thousands of Taíno and Arawak natives?

The more I investigated, the deeper the mystery, and the more conspiracy theories I found. These differing conclusions are perhaps not surprising when we understand how complex Columbus' character was, and how he deliberately intended to mislead his Spanish sponsors. The most detailed accounts of his voyages and his administration of Hispaniola were not written until decades later. The first was by his son, Ferdinand Columbus, in *The Life of the Admiral Christopher Columbus by his son Ferdinand*, and the second by Bartolomé de las Casas[52] in *A short account of the Destruction of the Indies*. The latter was a settler from Spain, a slave owner (initially), and later a monk and bishop who lobbied King Charles 1 of Spain[53] for the rights and respect of indigenous peoples.

So, who was Columbus? Almost certainly he was not the son of a peasant weaver from Italy as most textbooks would have us believe, although such a person did exist in Genoa and had trading links with Madeira. However, the stories that, at the age of 27, he survived a shipwreck off Portugal and swam ashore knowing nothing of sailing; and that he was uneducated, but yet a couple of years later married one of Portugal's leading noblewomen, are completely implausible.

Even by his own account, he had been sailing since the age of 14 and almost certainly grew up in a noble family. Otherwise, in the stratified society of medieval Portugal, he would never have been allowed to marry a noblewoman from the highest levels of the aristocracy. To take place at all, the marriage had to be blessed with the patronage of the King of Portugal.[54]

His brother Bartholomew Columbus, for example, was able to meet the English king, Henry VII, in 1489 and propose sponsorship for his brother's project, but this was declined. Bartholomew then called on

---

51. Bartolomé De Las Casas, Anthony Pagden 2004. *A Short Account of the Destruction of the Indies* (Penguin Classics). Casas estimated 250,000 natives were annihilated in Hispaniola.
52. Ibid.
53. Charles I, King of Spain was also Charles V, the Holy Roman Emperor.
54. Rosa Manuel 2016 *Columbus the Untold Story.* Outwater, New York. p. 88.

Charles VIII of France in Paris on his way back to Spain, and stayed with him for a considerable period, before returning to Spain and sailing in 1494 to meet Christopher in Hispaniola.

Such contacts and access to royal households were virtually impossible to come by in medieval times. The doors are not exactly open even today to such proposals. My own attempts to gain token patronage from the UK's royal family simply received a polite letter back from Buckingham Palace in London thanking me for my 'interest' and wishing me well.

We can be certain, therefore, that Christopher Columbus was a nobleman. Indeed, in one passage, he states that he was not the first admiral in his family.[55] He was an experienced sailor and had made several voyages down the west African coast and also sailed north, possibly reaching Ireland and Iceland in 1477.[56] His skills were easily the equal of Portugal's other leading adventurers of the day, Vasco da Gama and Bartholomeu Dias.

There is no doubt that the Portuguese were the pre-eminent sailing nation of the 15th century. Dias, a nobleman of the Portuguese royal household, rounded the southernmost tip of Africa in 1488, helped on his way by a somewhat fortunate storm. He anchored in Mossel Bay in what is now South Africa, thereby establishing the maritime route to India and Asia that the Portuguese King João I, had long wanted. His voyage was followed up by Vasco da Gama in 1497, a fellow Portuguese, and the first European to reach India by sea.

When Bartholomew Dias returned to Lisbon from rounding the Cape of Good Hope in South Africa, Columbus is recorded as being there when he arrived. In return, Dias was instrumental in arranging Columbus' welcome in Lisbon after his first voyage to the New World, following an attempted seizure of his ship and potential imprisonment at the hands of the Captain of Santa Maria Island in the Azores, where Columbus first made landfall on his first return voyage.[57]

---

55. "I am not the first Admiral in my Family. Let them give me whatever name they wish, for in the end, David, most knowledgeable King, was first a shepherd." Don Cristopher Columbus cited in Manuel Rosa, 2016. Columbus the Untold Story, p. 88.
56. Rosa Manuel 2016 *Columbus the Untold Story*. Outwater, New York.p. 29.
57. Christopher Columbus, The Four Voyages, 1969 Penguin Classics. Translated by J M Cohen.p. 104.

Did Columbus already know there was land to the west in the 'Outer Ocean'?

According to his son, Ferdinand, and Bartolomé de las Casas, Columbus paid particular attention to gathering evidence for the existence of lands to the west of Iberia. It was noted that the inhabitants of the Azores had observed that when the winds blew from the west for several days, it littered their shores with pine debris that they were not familiar with from their native shores.

On other occasions, the bodies of two men with unfamiliar foreign features were washed ashore, as well as small, covered boats known as 'almadias'. A sea captain named Martin Vicente had picked up a piece of curiously carved wood after days of westerly winds. Giant reeds (possibly bamboo) were also found with joints that could contain upwards of 4 quarts (8 pints), a feature not known amongst European vegetation at that time. It can be inferred, therefore, that Columbus knew there was a strong possibility of westerly winds at the latitude of the Azores and when these blew strongly, evidence of islands or a land mass to the west became evident.

A fellow sailor, Pedro Vázquez de la Frontera also talked to Columbus about the Western Sea. He told him that: "when they arrived among the grasses (hierbas), it would be necessary to follow a straight road because it was impossible not to find land but they would need to be brave to confront the obstacle of the grasses of the Sargasso Sea." This was from a sailor who had sailed through the region under the orders of the King of Portugual[58] in an attempt to find India via the route around Africa. Located about a thousand miles west of Madeira and the Canaries, the Sargasso is the belt of sea with no currents and becalmed water that gives rise to its infamous sea-grass.

It also seems very likely that Columbus met a pilot who had been cast adrift in a storm and landed somewhere in the modern-day Lesser Antilles on the eastern edge of the Caribbean, providing proof that there were other islands in the 'Ocean Sea'. The pilot was sailing near Madeira when a strong storm blew up from the east and, once offshore, he could only run with the winds as they were so strong.

58. Wadsworth, James E,2016. Columbus and His First Voyage: A History in Documents, Bloomsbury Publishing, p. 117.

The crew were so weak and malnourished it was all they could do to keep the ship afloat, when they eventually reached an island. The island was uninhabited, but they were able to make repairs and find food and eventually found a favourable westerly wind by which to return. It is believed that it was this story that ultimately convinced Columbus he would find land if he ventured further to the west in the central Atlantic than anyone of his generation had dared to do up to that point.

Columbus was, therefore, convinced that there were lands, riches and treasures to be discovered if he sailed west. And in this belief, he was aided by his trust in the ancient cosmographers and cartographers. They had significantly overestimated the size of the known world, while underestimating the size of the oceans separating Cathay (China, India and the Far East) from Europe. Through a further error in his own calculations, he had reduced the size of the oceans still further, convincing himself that it was perfectly practical to sail from Spain to Cathay in a relatively short voyage. The truth, of course, was very different. There were both islands and a giant continent prohibiting such a voyage reaching its intended destination.

The ancients who had most influence on Columbus, according to his younger son, Ferdinand, were Ptolemy and Marinus of Tyre. Marinus of Tyre – Tyre being a founding Phoenician city now in modern-day Lebanon – was a geographer, cartographer and mathematician and is credited with being the father of mathematical geography. Little is known about his life, other than what Ptolemy's influential *Geography* tells us, and what was corroborated later by the Arab historian, Al-Mas'udi (c. AD 896-956).

Marinus was a Phoenician who lived in Tyre at a time of rising Roman influence over the region. Ptolemy goes out of his way to praise the work of Marinus for his painstaking research, critical approach to his sources, and his willingness to correct his own work. He further confirms that both the broad concepts he adopted in the *Geography*, and also the detailed statistics, are taken from Marinus. Ptolemy states that Marinus said of the merchant class generally that: "they are only intent on their business, and have little interest in exploration, and that often through their love of boasting they magnify distances."[59]

59. Ptolemy, translated and edited by Edward Luther Stevenson,1932. The Geography; New York: The New York Public Library, p. 33.

Nonetheless, Marinus contributed the first theoretical structure for longitude and latitude in cartography with the invention of equi-rectangular projection. This is still used today and plots the lines of latitude and longitude as parallels on a rectangular world map for illustrative rather than navigational purposes. Using this approach, he was able to plot the location of some 8000 cities and towns. Marinus was the first geographer to propose the likelihood of the Antarctic, for which he coined the term, as a counter-balance to the Arctic Circle.

He believed that the 'Ocean Sea' was separated by the continents of Europe, Asia and Africa, and that Africa and Asia combined in the south to encapsulate the Indian Ocean. He underestimated its size and, although Ptolemy corrected this error to some extent, it was still a significant underestimate. It was, therefore, through the works of Marinus of Tyre that the idea of sailing west to reach the east was made a plausible possibility in the mind of Columbus.

In a letter, after his fourth voyage, Columbus specifically comments on Marinus' calculations, which he says were "very near the truth." It appears that he knowingly tried to mislead the Catholic monarchs into believing he had reached China, when in reality he had reached the eastern coasts of Costa Rica, Nicaragua and Panama.

In this letter, he states:

> *"In all these places where I have been, I found all that I had heard to be true. This convinced me that it is so in the case of the province of Ciguare, which, according to them, lies inland to the west nine days' journey. They say that there is in that land an infinite amount of gold, and that the people wear corals on their heads and very large bracelets of coral on their feet and arms; and that with coral they adorn and inlay chairs and chests and tables. They said also that the women there have necklaces hanging down from the head to the shoulders. All the people of these places agree in this that I have related, and they say so much that I should be content with the tenth of it. They also know of pepper.*
>
> *In Ciguare they are accustomed to trade in fairs and markets; so these people related, and they showed me the way and manner in which they carry on barter. Further they said that the ships carry*

cannon, bows and arrows, swords and shields, and that the people go clothed, and that in the land there are horses, and that the people are warlike and wear rich clothing and have good houses.

Also they say that the sea surrounds Ciguare, and that from there it is ten days' journey to the river Ganges. It appears that these lands lie in respect of Veragua as Tortosa does in respect of Fuenterabia; or Pisa in respect of Venice. When I left Carambaru and arrived at these places which I have mentioned, I found the same customs among the people, except that any, who had the mirrors of gold, bartered them at the rate of one for three hawks' bells, although they were ten or fifteen ducats in weight. In all their customs they are as those of Española. They collect gold by different methods, although these are all nothing in comparison with those of the Christians.

This which I have said is that which I have heard. That which I know is that in the year ninety-four I navigated twenty-four degrees to the westward in nine hours, and I cannot be in error because there was an eclipse; the sun was in Libra and the moon in Aries. That also which I heard by word of mouth, I knew in detail from the written word.

Ptolemy believed that he had well corrected Marinus, who is now found to have been very near the truth. Ptolemy places Catigara twelve lines from his west, which he fixed at two and one third degrees above Cape St. Vincent in Portugal. Marinus comprised the earth and its limits in fifteen lines. In Ethiopia Marinus draws beyond the equinoctial lines more than twenty-four degrees, and now that the Portuguese have sailed there, they find that this is true. Ptolemy says that the most southern land is the first place and that it does not lie more than fifteen and one-third degrees beyond. And the world is small. The dry land is six parts of it; the seventh only is covered with water.

Experience has already shown this, and I have written it in other letters and with illustration from Holy Scripture concerning the situation of the earthly paradise, as Holy Church approves. I say that the world is not so great as the vulgar believe, and that a degree from the equinoctial line is fifty-six and two-thirds miles; easily this may be proved exactly. I leave this subject, inasmuch as it is not my intention to speak of this matter, but only to give an account of my voyage, hard and toilsome, although it is the most noble and profitable." [60]

The influence of Ptolemy – and by deduction Marinus – is easy to understand, as from around 1477, Ptolemy's *Geography* was printed with maps attributed to Agathodaemon of Alexandria, a contemporary. These caused a sensation in European cartographic circles. It divided the known world of Eurasia into 180 degrees from Portugal to Catigara in China. This greatly exaggerated the size of the known world by some 80 degrees, as previously noted.

This error was then compounded further in two respects. First, Columbus preferred the smaller estimate of the circumference of the world calculated by Marinus of Tyre, who had estimated the 'oecumene', the area of the inhabited parts of the planet, to be 225 degrees.

Columbus then compounded the error himself, adding further degrees for additional islands in the east, which he claimed Marinus did not know about. Therefore, the distance of the 'Ocean Sea' as a percentage of the whole sphere was shrinking with every step of his calculations.

Adding fuel to the fire, were several important observations from other ancient writers like Pliny (*Natural History* AD 77), Strabo (*Geography* AD 17-23) and Seneca. The latter, writing in about AD 50 and living in what is now modern-day Spain, made some interesting observations in *Natural Questions*. Here he states that: "from the coast of Spain the Indies could be reached in a few days."[61]

Was he, one wonders, referring to the Hesperides, as previously discussed? Either way, Seneca's writings encouraged Columbus, who knew of the prophecy from his play, Medea:

"There will come a time in later years when the Ocean shall loosen the bonds by which we have been confined, when an immense land

60. The Voyages of Christopher Columbus, Being the Journals of his First and Third, and the Letters Concerning his First and Last Voyages, to which is added the account of his Second Voyage Written by Andres Bernaldez. Translated and edited with an introduction and notes by Cecil Jane. London: The Argonaut Press, 1930.
61. Helen Wallis OBE, "What Columbus Knew," from *History Today*, May 1992 (42): p. 19.

shall be revealed and Tiphys (the Piloys of the Argonauts) shall disclose new worlds, and Thule will no longer be the most remote of countries." [62]

Indeed, Columbus's son Ferdinand commented after his father's death "Now it is considered certain that this prophecy was fulfilled in the person of the admiral."[63]

The final piece of information that influenced Columbus was a letter sent to him by Paolo dai Pozzo Toscanelli, a Florentine physician, cosmographer and cartographer. Toscanelli first sent the letter in 1474 to an intermediary in Lisbon for the attention of King Afonso V of Portugal. Then later, in 1481, he sent a copy with a map to Columbus. Toscanelli had knowledge of the men of Cathay's visit to Rome in the reign of Pope Eugenius IV and described what he heard:

"The magnitude of their rivers in length and breadth, and on the multitude of cities on the banks of rivers. On one river there were near 200 cities with marble bridges great in length and breadth, and everywhere adorned with columns. This country is worth seeking by the Latins, not only because great wealth may be obtained from it, gold and silver, all sorts of gems, and spices, which never reach us; but on account of its learned men, philosophers, and expert astrologers, and by what skill and art so powerful and magnificent a province is governed, as well as how their wars are conducted." [64]

Extract from the First Letter of Paolo Toscanelli to Columbus

In his original letter to the intermediary in Lisbon, Toscanelli wrote:

"From the City of Lisbon due west there are 26 spaces marked on the map, each of which contains two hundred and fifty miles, as far as the very great and noble city of Quinsay (Hangchow)... and apart from the island of Antilla, which you call the island of

---

62. Ibid.
63. Ibid.
64. Columbus Christopher, Markam, Clements R., 1972 *Journal of Christopher Columbus (During His First Voyage, 1492–93) and Documents Relating to the Voyages of John Cabot and Gaspar Corte Real.*

the Seven cities, to the very noble island of Cipango, there are 10 spaces, which make 2500 miles, that is two hundred and twenty-five leagues. This land is most rich in gold, pearls and precious stones... but because the way is not known, all these things are hidden and covered, though one can travel thither as with all security." [65]

In a second letter, Toscanelli gives more detail of these men as extremely learned and willing to share their knowledge:

"They said voyage is not only possible, but it is true, and certain to be honourable and to yield incalculable profit, and very great fame among all Christians. But you cannot know this perfectly save through experience and practice, as I have had in the form of the most copious and good and true information from distinguished men of great learning who have come from the said parts, here in the court of Rome, and from others being merchants who have had business for a long time in those parts, men of high authority." [66]

Columbus – Character, Achievements and Faults

The most well-known portrait of Columbus, which was painted in Italy over ten years after his death in 1506, is almost certainly not a true resemblance. Columbus was not dark-haired but fair-haired, almost blond. Even the Metropolitan Museum of Art in New York, which owns the painting by the Italian painter, Sebastiano del Piombo, no longer describes the painting as a portrait of Columbus, but describes it as "Portrait of a Man."[67]

The most reliable likeness is the painting by Pedro Berruguete and Alejo Fernández, who were court painters to the Catholic Monarchs between 1504 and 1506, the period when Columbus returned to Spain for good and before his death in 1506. It shows him to have fair hair

65. Helen Wallis OBE, "What Columbus Knew," from *History Today*, May 1992 (42): p. 19.
66. Toscanelli. Helen Wallis OBE *What Columbus knew*.
67. Rosa Manuel, 2016. *Columbus the Untold Story*. Outwater, New York. p. 322.

and a somewhat ruddy complexion. He had bright eyes and was an imposing and well-built man.

He could be charming and polite in the appropriate company, but with subordinates and his officers he was less so. He argued with his captains, often keeping them in the dark about his calculations as to where they were. As a result, on several occasions, his crews were on the point of mutiny. He trusted virtually no-one except members of his own family. However, if he could maintain the interest and support of Queen Isabella, he would continue to receive the supplies and ships he needed. This, despite the fact that he was often at odds with Bishop Fonseca who ran the office in Seville that controlled these vital support functions.

After spending over a decade in seeking a sponsor for his plan from the royal courts of England, France, Portugal and Spain, his lucky break came when the Moors were finally expelled from Spain. Queen Isabella then turned her energies to other objectives and the Spanish court granted him his wish in April 1492. In the commissioning document, the *Capitulations of Sante Fe*, it was declared: "Whereas you, Christobal Colon, are setting forth… to discover and acquire certain islands and mainland in the Ocean Sea."

He left Spain on 3rd August 1492, with three ships – *Santa Maria, Niña* and *Pinta*. His first destination was the Spanish-controlled Canary Islands, where he stayed on the island of Gomera for five weeks, making repairs and stocking up with provisions. He left Gomera on 6th September. Five weeks later, on 12th October, he arrived in the Lucayan Islands (modern-day Bahamas), which he named San Salvador, meaning Holy Saviour.

His logbook recorded:

> "Many of the men I have seen have scars on their bodies, and when I made signs to them to find out how this happened, they indicated that people from other nearby islands come to San Salvador to capture them; they defend themselves the best they can. I believe that people from the mainland come here to take them as slaves. They ought to make good and skilled servants, for they repeat very quickly whatever we say to them. I think they can very easily be made Christians,

for they seem to have no religion. If it pleases our Lord, I will take six of them to Your Highnesses when I depart, in order that they may learn our language." [68]

On the second voyage, a letter written by Dr Chanca, a Spanish physician, confirmed the native people worshipped all kinds of idols in their houses, which they named 'Turey', translated as 'to the sky':

"They also say they want to be Christians, but they are actually idolaters but... they could be converted to Christianity if we had an interpreter for they imitate everything we do, they bend their knees at the altars and Ave Maria and cross themselves... I once made a show of wanting to throw these [idols] in the fire, which so upset them they were at the point of tears. They also think that whatever we bring them comes from the sky, for they call it Turey, that is to say sky." [69]

When Columbus came across Lucayan, Taíno and Arawak natives he referred to them as 'Indians' which has been adopted as a term for indigenous peoples across the Americas to this day. Initially he was careful to ensure that his crew treated them with respect to ensure he could return at a future date. He noted how primitive they were in terms of warfare and weapons writing: "these people are very simple in war-like matters ... I could conquer the whole of them with 50 men and govern them as I pleased."[70] He also noticed the gold earrings of some of the Arawak and took them prisoner, demanding that they show him the source of this gold.

Columbus then headed for the north-east coast of Cuba, before sailing east along the northern coast of Hispaniola. The *Pinta* went on an unauthorised excursion to look for the island of 'Babeque' or 'Baneque' which the natives said was rich in gold, but returned empty-

68. Robert H. Fuson, Ed., 1992. *The Log of Christopher Columbus*, Tab Books International Marine Publishing.
69. Columbus Ed and Trans, J M Cohen,1969. *The Four Voyages* Penguin Classics, p. 154.
70. Markham, Clements R. et al (Ed.) 1893. *The Journal of Christopher Columbus (During His First Voyage, 1492–93) and Documents Relating to the Voyages of John Cabot and Gaspar Corte Real.* Hakluyt Society, London.

handed. Meanwhile, Columbus landed at La Navida on the north coast of Hispaniola, modern-day Haiti, and befriended the local chief, Guacanagari, who allowed him to build a settlement and leave 39 men behind. The plan was that these men would later be re-united with Columbus on his return in a proposed second voyage.

On Christmas day, the *Santa Maria* ran aground at La Navida and was later used as target practice for Columbus' cannons in order to frighten the native population. He then headed east along the coast in the *Niña* and met up with the *Pinta*, before making one final stop at the Bay of Rincón. At the eastern end of the Samaná Peninsula, he encountered the warlike Ciguayos, the first hostile reception of the voyage. After an initial exchange, the Ciguayos declined to trade more bows and arrows and fighting broke out. A couple of the Ciguayos were wounded by arrows to the chest and a cut buttock from a Spanish sword. Columbus named it the Bay of Arrows.

When we ourselves arrived in the Dominican Republic aboard *Phoenicia*, we naturally attracted the attention of those who were interested in our thesis that the Phoenicians were the first to reach the Americas, and the island of Hispaniola in particular. As we got to know our hosts, it emerged that some of them also believed that the Phoenicians had reached the island of Hispaniola in the ancient period. Part of their thinking was based around the local place names for rivers and bays, which were not considered indigenous names. Furthermore, there were curious rock drawings and statues in caves in the Bay of Arrows that pointed to influences from the East.

One of our hosts, Elvis Alam, kindly agreed to take us to the caves on an excursion around the island. Once there, we climbed into a couple of motorised canoes and headed through the mangrove swamps and along the bay to the caves. There we found numerous rock drawings of ships and several statues, some clearly with beards. How old they are is not certain, but they are clearly of historic importance and suggest the recording of an important event. This may have been the arrival of Phoenician sailors.[71]

It soon became clear that many of the islanders themselves believe their home was visited by the ancient Phoenicians. We received many

71. See photos of these statues and rock drawings in the colour section.

visitors to the ship who believed that the Taíno people, who inhabited the island before the arrival of Columbus, were originally Phoenician.

One commonly-held belief is that the Samaná peninsula in the northeast of the island is named after the Phoenician word 'Zamana', meaning a ship's captain, and was given the name by the Taíno. This theory is impossible to prove, and the Taíno were later wiped out by the Spaniards. However, a cave in the region – now a popular tourist attraction in Los Haitises National Park – has large numbers of Taíno petroglyphs and pictographs. One face has distinctive 'Mediterranean' features, sporting a thick moustache completely unlike any of the other images.

Another piece of my research turned up an interesting book written in 1889 by a French Administrator of Haiti, Vicomte Onffroy de Thoron. He was an intellectual and linguist and had previously published a book on linguistic observations he had made in South America. He was fascinated by the local Taíno and Arawak languages and their similarity, in his view, to Hebrew and Phoenician. The English translation of what he wrote was poor and I have therefore modified the key points he made as follows:

> *"It becomes obvious that the Taíno, iti or hiti, woman, at its very origin is the Hetian woman and this is how the same term Taíno became synonymous with the Phoenician term hiti. The Hittites were among the Canaanites Joshua massacred; from which resulted their first migration to Libya (Morocco), followed by their embarkation for the island of Haiti, began at the time of Joshua; it would be more than 3300 years ago while the second migration, that of the Carthaginians for Haiti, a date of approximately 2700 years. Besides the presence in Haiti of the Canaanite race nicknamed Phoenician by the Greeks, other historical and philological evidence will confirm this"* [72]

The stories of Columbus and the Phoenicians, therefore, are linked in some important respects, as Columbus relied on Marinus of Tyre for his initial calculation of the size of the 'Ocean Sea'. In rediscovering Hispaniola, and in choosing Hispaniola as his base for coloni-

72. The Phoenicians in the island of Haiti and on the American continent, Vicomte Onffroy de Thoron 1889 translated by Matt Ferguson and Stephanie Merat. Website: https://pastebin.com/RX3N578b

sation, was he unknowingly repeating a colonisation first established by the Phoenicians and Carthaginians centuries earlier, as suggested by Vicomte Onffroy de Thoron?

After their confrontation at the Bay of Arrows (Samaná Bay), the *Niña* and *Pinta* headed back east across the Atlantic but were separated by a storm, with the *Niña* seeking refuge on the island of Santa Maria in the Azores where the altercation with the senior Spanish official on the island took place.

Another storm then meant that Columbus headed for Lisbon in Portugal, rather than Spain. This led to an awkward meeting with King John II of Portugal, who claimed that Columbus appeared to have broken the 1479 *Treaty of Alcáçovas*, which stated that the Portuguese had control of the Atlantic Ocean. Columbus spent over a week in Portugal before setting sail for Spain, which he reached on 15th March, 1493.

His need to impress Queen Isabella to keep the 'Enterprise of the Indies' moving forward, meant his letters to the royal court were huge exaggerations. His report on the first voyage omitted most negative issues and was overflowing with optimism about the riches that awaited them with further exploration. Huge amounts of gold were always just the next island away.

After arriving back in Spain, he was welcomed as a hero and rode in a carriage alongside King Ferdinand through the streets of Barcelona. His letter reporting on the first voyage to Queen Isabella was printed in Spain and quickly circulated throughout Europe. Columbus' expedition was the match that set the fire of the Age of Discovery alight in the sea-faring capitals of Europe. The starting gun in the race for the New World had been fired.

Under the terms of the *Treaty of Tordesillas* in 1494, the papacy offi-cially divided the Americas between Spain and Portugal, while ensuring the latter kept possession of its prized African outposts and the route to India. However, in reality, any nation who could plant a flag and colo-nise an area with force could now become a player on the world stage, as the British and French were to do in the next century.

As a result of the euphoria and stories about the New World, Columbus was granted his wish for a second voyage and a very signifi-cant fleet of 17 ships was assembled to colonise and settle Hispaniola. The fleet, of which Columbus was admiral, was made up of around

1000 to 1200 men. Its crews included soldiers, farmers and priests as well as prisoners who were offered the chance to settle the new lands on condition that they were never to return to Spain. Twenty horses and twenty hunting dogs, along with substantial stores of food, wine and weapons were also recorded. There were also two 'Indians' among the crew who were to act as interpreters, the only survivors of the seven that were taken to Castile on the return of the first voyage of discovery.

Second Voyage of Discovery

Columbus set sail once more on 24th September 1493 from Cadiz, and again visited the Canary Islands for a few weeks before setting a more southerly course than on the first voyage. The fleet arrived at the island of Dominica – so-called because it was discovered on a Sunday – in the Windward Islands on 3rd November and then continued to Marie-Galante, now part of Guadeloupe, as well as Montserrat, Antigua, Saint Martin, and the Virgin Islands amongst others.

Our voyage on *Phoenicia* had coincidentally followed a similar route from the south of the Canary Islands towards Guadeloupe, and then in a more gradual north-westerly direction to Santo Domingo in the Dominican Republic. From Guadeloupe, Columbus took a much more northerly course towards the Virgin Islands, before traversing the northern coast of Puerto Rico and then on to the northern coast of Hispaniola to La Navida where he had left his 39 men some ten months earlier. Although Columbus was in a hurry to reach the settlement at La Navida, he nonetheless made several stops at the islands he discovered along the way.

At Guadeloupe he sent a party of his men ashore into the villages and made an attempt to engage with the natives. Most of the villagers ran away, but they did manage to capture a boy of about 14 and some women, who all came willingly. It later transpired that they were prisoners of the Caribs and had been forcibly taken during raids on other islands.

One ship's captain and six men became lost on the island and it was several days before they re-emerged. Several further landings were made at various islands en-route to La Navida, when search parties inspected the deserted dwellings. Here they found many human bones and skulls used as water containers. The captured women confirmed that the islands were inhabited by Caribs and when they learnt that Columbus hated the Caribs because they were cannibals, they were delighted.

The Caribs wore two woven cotton bands, one below the knee and the other above the ankle, so they were clearly distinguishable from other islanders. Dr Chanca, a Spanish physician paid by Ferdinand and Isabella to accompany the second expedition, reported that the Caribs were 'beast-like' and that:

> *"They are friendly to each other as if of one family, they do not harm each other but make war against the neighbouring islands... they travel up to 150 leagues to make raids in their canoes. They have arrows tipped with tortoise shell or fish bones and dipped in a plant-based poison that can kill and do great injury with these weapons, which are not very terrible, however, to men of our nation.*
>
> *They carry off all the women they can take, especially the young and beautiful, who they keep as servants and concubines. They had carried off so many that in fifty houses we found no males and more than 20 were the captive girls. The women say they are treated with such cruelty that seems incredible. The Caribs eat the male children that they have by them, and only bring up the children of their own women; and as for the men they are able to capture, they bring those who are alive home to be slaughtered and eat those who are dead on the spot.*
>
> *They say that human flesh is so good that there is nothing like it in the world; and this must be true, for the human bones we found in their houses were so gnawed that no flesh was left on them except what was too tough to be eaten. In one house the neck of a man was found cooking in a pot. They castrate the boys that they capture and use them as servants until they are men. Then, when they want to make a feast, they kill and eat them, for they say the flesh of boys and women is not good to eat. Three of the boys fled to us, and all three had been castrated."* [73]

73. Cohen J M, 1969. *Christopher Columbus, The Fourth Voyage*, Penguin Classics, pp. 127-157.

Columbus' fleet continued island-hopping towards Hispaniola with some 10-20 women and several men from the islands who had either been captured or volunteered to join the fleet. Ill-discipline also began to break out in the way the Christians treated the 'Indians', as the account of Michele de Cuneo, one of Columbus's Italian lieutenants, records:

> *"While I was in the boat (going ashore), I captured a very beautiful Carib woman, who the said Lord Admiral gave to me. When I had taken her to my cabin, she was naked as was their custom. I was filled with a desire to take my pleasure with her and attempted to satisfy my desire. She was unwilling, so treated me with her nails that I wished I had never begun. But – to cut a long story short – I then took a piece of rope and whipped her soundly, and she let forth such incredible screams you would not have believed your ears. Eventually we came to such terms, I assure you, that you would have thought she had been brought up in a school for whores."* [74]

As the fleet made its way towards La Navida, the ships anchored at a small harbour about two leagues from their intended destination. They explored the area, which was largely deserted, and found two decaying bodies, one that had been bound by the feet and another had a noose around his neck. The next day they found two more bodies, one of which was heavily bearded.

This was a bad sign because none of the 'Indians' had beards. Later they arrived at La Navida and were not met by the welcome they expected. Columbus had told his men that they would be met by a very large number of canoes. Communicating with one of the interpreters, a couple of natives on a canoe told them that all the Christians had been killed. Initially, Columbus dismissed this account. He then ordered that some cannon shot should be fired towards the settlement expecting a similar reply from the Christians. There was no reply.

A boat party was sent ashore which found that the blockhouse that had been built for the settlers and the village had been burnt and demolished. The next day, the cousin of the local King Guacamarie

74. Ibid. p. 139.

arrived to speak with Columbus and told him that all the Christian settlers were dead and had been killed by two rival kings, King Caonabo and King Mayreni. Columbus was in two minds as to whether to believe this account and what retribution was appropriate.

Gradually, there was more interaction with the natives and bartering for gold, but they remained shy and fearful of the Spaniards. Their account of the two kings attacking the settlers was maintained, while the interpreters pointed out that the settlers had taken three or four women apiece, forming a murderous group in pursuit of gold and women. Revenge by the local Taíno people was inevitable.

Within a few days of arriving, Columbus decided to build a new settlement not far from La Navida, which he named La Isabella after the Spanish queen. Nevertheless, Isabella was a short-lived settlement and was replaced within a couple of years by Santo Domingo on the south coast of the island. This was where *Phoenicia* made landfall on 31st December 2019.

Having built the foundation of La Isabella, Columbus then explored Cuba and Jamaica, returning to Hispaniola in August 1494. By that time, two thirds of the Spanish settlers had died of disease and famine. With little gold to be found, Columbus turned to exploiting the one resource that Hispaniola did have in abundance – its human population. It was now that he authorised his colonists to buy and sell slaves.

He instituted '*Encomienda*', a Spanish labour regime that rewarded conquerors with the labour of non-Christian natives. While punishments against his own men for minor crimes could result in complete dismemberment as a warning to others, the punishments were, if anything, more severe for the enslaved natives.

Each Taíno adult was required to produce a '*hawk's bell full of gold*'[75] every three months and, if this was lacking, 25 pounds of spun cotton. The hawk's bells were originally part of European falconry, made of copper or bronze, and tied to the feet of the hawks, presumably to monitor their whereabouts when hunting. They were prized by American traders in the 16th, 17th and 18th centuries and in Columbus' time were a convenient tool for measuring the equivalent of an ounce or two of gold.

75. New Internationalist, 5 December 1991. Christopher Columbus and the Colonial Legacy. Website: https://newint.org/features/1991/12/05/keynote/

Failure to produce tributes of gold, for which they received a token to wear around their necks, was met with beatings, rape, torture, hangings and mutilations. The latter included cutting off their ears, tongues and hands, leaving them to bleed to death. Many thousands of natives preferred suicide, rather than face such barbaric oppression. Those that ran away were hunted down by Columbus' vicious hunting dogs.

The former slave owner and later bishop, Bartolomé de las Casas, in his account The Destruction of the Indies, summarised what he witnessed, writing:

> *"Such inhumanities and barbarisms were committed in my sight as no age can parallel. My eyes have seen these acts so foreign to human nature that now I tremble as I write."* [76]

One of his most graphic passages states:

> *"They [the Spanish explorers] forced their way into native settlements, slaughtering everyone they found there, including small children, old men, pregnant women, and even women who had just given birth. They hacked them to pieces, slicing open their bellies with their swords as though they were so many sheep herded into a pen. They even laid wagers on whether they could slice a man in two at a stroke, or cut an individual's head from his body, or disembowel him with a single blow of their axes. They grabbed suckling infants by the feet and, ripping them from their mothers' breasts, bashed them headlong against the rocks. Others, laughing and joking all the while, threw them over their shoulders, shouting, "Wriggle, you little perisher."* [77]

Casas wrote this in 1542, when there were only a handful, perhaps 200, Taíno left on Hispaniola. Across the Caribbean in total, he claimed the Spanish were responsible for the deaths of 12 to 15 million indigenous people.[78]

76. Casas, Bartolomé de las, Anthony Pagden 2004. *A Short Account of the Destruction of the Indies* (Penguin Classics).

77. Ibid.

78. Website: https://www.washingtonpost.com/history/2019/10/14/here-are-indigenous-people-christopher-columbus-his-men-could-not-annihilate/

Columbus' second fleet eventually left Hispaniola on 10th March, 1496, landing in Portugal in June, having been away for some two-and-a-half years. An entry in his later journal of September 1498, read:

> *"From here one might send, in the name of the Holy Trinity, as many slaves as could be sold."* [79]

With him he took some 500 Arawak slaves to Spain, one of the first recorded mass transportations of slaves from the Americas, of which some 200 died during the voyage. And so it was that Christopher Columbus, usually remembered erroneously as the discoverer of the American continent, became instead the father of the European-American slave trade.

Third Voyage of Discovery

Columbus' third voyage was a smaller affair than the second voyage. With just six ships sailing from Spain, three of which were directed to sail straight for Hispaniola, Columbus himself took the other three to search for the route to the Asian continent he had so long hoped to find. This time, he sailed even further south than on any of the earlier voyages and, on 31st July 1498, sighted Trinidad. On the following day, he reached the mouth of the Orinoco River, followed by the Paria Peninsula on 5th August, which Columbus recognised must be the continent's mainland.

After briefly visiting the Chacachacare Islands and then reaching Margarita on 14th August, while also sighting Tobago and Grenada, he headed directly for Hispaniola. Given the complete lack of knowledge of the region and the primitive navigation tools at his disposal, this voyage to Hispaniola was quite a remarkable achievement.

However, the situation that awaited him in Hispaniola was deeply troubling. Many of the settlers were in open rebellion at the harsh conditions and the lack of the riches that they had been promised. Some of his crews were equally rebellious and a number of men were hanged for disobedience. By October 1499, managing Hispaniola had become so

79. Stone, Edward T. (1975). *"Columbus and Genocide"*. American Heritage. Vol. 26 no. 6. American Heritage Publishing Company.

difficult that he sent two ships to Spain, asking for the Court of Spain to dispatch a commissioner to help him govern. However, the Court had already heard stories of Columbus' incompetence and cruelty and sent Francisco de Bobadilla as a replacement. Bobadilla was tasked with investigating the accusations against Columbus.

Columbus was away when Bobadilla arrived and was annoyed that he had been replaced. Bobadilla reported to Spain that Columbus used torture and mutilation to govern, and two of his brothers (Bartholomew and Diego) were also very unpopular. Columbus had put down native revolts by ordering brutal crackdowns in which many natives were killed and their dismembered bodies paraded through the streets to discourage further unrest.

In his report, Bobadilla quoted examples of gross brutality by Columbus and his brothers. In one case he claimed that Columbus, finding a man guilty of stealing corn, had his ears and nose cut off and then sold him into slavery. In another case he congratulated his brother Bartholomew for defending the family against a woman who had said Columbus was of lowly birth. She was paraded through the town and had her tongue cut out.

In October 1500, Bobadilla was able to challenge Columbus and Diego and had them put in chains on board *La Gorda,* one of Columbus' ships which was now bound for Spain. The captain of the ship offered to release Columbus, but it appears he wanted to be something of a martyr and requested to remain in chains. On his return, he wrote an impassioned letter to the royal monarchs explaining why he had been misunderstood by his detractors. Columbus and his brother remained in prison in Spain for some six weeks before King Ferdinand ordered their release.

They were then summoned to the Alhambra palace in Granada where they pleaded their case to the Catholic sovereigns, who restored their freedom and privileges. Nonetheless, Columbus was effectively stripped of his governorship of the West Indies, which was awarded to Nicolás de Ovando.

With an eye on future exploration and the lure of future riches and treasure ships from the New World, and after much discussion, the sovereigns agreed to sponsor Columbus' fourth voyage. However, the voyage would be a shadow of both his second voyage when he had 17 ships at his disposal, and of the 30 ships that Governor Ovando had been granted to manage Hispaniola.

The Fourth Voyage of Discovery

Columbus was funded just enough to secure four ships for his continued exploration of the New World, although he was forbidden to return to Hispaniola. The Spanish king and queen did not totally trust him, hence his reduced powers and fleet.

His activities and character appear to have changed during the preparations for the fourth voyage, when he took to calling himself "Christ-bearer" in his letters and using a mystical signature, which still puzzles historians, but may be related to freemasonry. He proceeded to write his *Book of Privileges* and *Book of Prophecies*, justifying his family's financial claims and his spiritual ambitions respectively.

Columbus sailed from Cádiz on his fourth voyage on 9th May 1502, passing by Grand Canaria and Martinique. True to form, he did not follow the instructions he had been given and headed straight for Hispaniola, arriving in Santo Domingo on June 29th, his fastest passage across the Atlantic. He was refused entry to Santo Domingo by Ovando, even though he claimed he needed shelter as a hurricane was approaching.

Having been refused entry, Columbus sheltered his ships in the mouth of the Rio Jaina and afterwards sailed west to Jamaica, before following the southern shore of Cuba to Honduras and Nicaragua. Ironically, Governor Ovando's first treasure fleet sailed straight into a hurricane, with 29 of the 30 ships being lost, along with 500 lives and an estimated $10 million worth of gold in today's value.[80] Likewise, Francisco de Bobadilla, who had been sent to investigate Columbus' activities on Hispaniola, lost his life on the return voyage and the vessel that was transporting Columbus' personal belongings back to Spain was the only surviving ship to reach its destination.[81]

80. Bergreen, Lawrence (2011). *Columbus: The Four Voyages, 1493–1504*. Penguin Group US.
81. Dugard, Martin (2005). *The Last Voyage of Columbus: Being the Epic Tale of the Great Captain's Fourth Expedition, Including Accounts of Swordfight, Mutiny, Shipwreck, Gold, War, Hurricane, and Discovery*. Little, Brown.

Off the coast of Honduras, Costa Rica and the Mosquito Coast of Nicaragua, Columbus encountered treacherous weather and hurricane-type conditions. His ability to keep his ships safe in these demanding situations is a testament to his sailing aptitude and skills. He pressed on southwards towards Panama, always probing for the elusive strait that would enable him, or so he believed, to reach Japan and India.

By February 1503, he had detected signs of promising yields of gold on the Panamanian coast and decided to establish a trading station at Santa María de Belén on the bank of the Belén (Bethlehem) River under the command of his brother, Bartholomew Columbus. Eventually the dire weather, Indian resistance and the worry of keeping his two remaining ships safe, both of which were in poor condition due to shipworm, made him abandon the trading post and return to Hispaniola.

The expedition went from bad to worse and in June 1503 he had to beach the two ships on the Jamaican coast as they were no longer seaworthy. His crew were at the mercy of local Indians for food and there was no prospect of being rescued as no one knew they were there. He was able to keep the Indians in awe of his powers by predicting an eclipse of the moon using his astronomical tables – a feat that ensured their continued support and supplies of food when he and his crews were all but castaways.

Eventually the two captains of his wrecked ships, Diego Méndez and Bartolomeo Fieschi, with some local Indians, volunteered to row the 450 miles (720km) to Hispaniola in an open-topped Indian canoe. Their chances of success were very slim but, against all odds, they made it. On their arrival, Governor Ovando was in no great hurry to launch a rescue party for he loathed Columbus. Help eventually arrived, however, in June the following year, with Columbus and his men reaching Hispaniola in August, 1504.

On 7th November, Columbus arrived back in Spain only to find that his greatest supporter, Queen Isabella, had made her will and was on her death-bed. She died 19 days later, on 26th November 1504. In some respects, Columbus' fourth voyage had been the most promising, and came closest to discovering substantial quantities of gold in central America. Unfortunately for him, he narrowly missed discovering both the Mayan civilisation in the Yucatán and also the Pacific Ocean across the Panamanian isthmus, when he had been so close.

Columbus was a man who drove himself incessantly, remaining on the fo'castle for days on end, taking very little sleep, checking the ship's course and ensuring the safety of the ship. His need to be on deck for long periods made him extremely ill, including suffering from gout and developing what we would now call 'sea blindness', the result of the sun reflecting on the water without any protection for his eyes.

He was clearly very single-minded and believed it was his destiny to extend the lands to the west for Christendom and the Catholic monarchs, while bringing back their riches for Spain. As the voyage was bedevilled by bad weather and worm-infested ships, he was lucky that he made it back to Spain at all. On 20th May 1506, aged 54, Columbus died in Valladolid, Spain, still contesting his 10% share of profits with the Spanish crown, the legal cases around which would rumble on for many decades after his death.

Unfortunately, during our own voyage aboard *Phoenicia*, we were unable to explore the Dominican Republic as much as we would have liked. We had to attend to repairs that were urgently needed on the boat and we also needed to stock up on our seriously depleted provisions.

In addition, a lot of time was taken up with the problems of obtaining US visas for the members of the crew who had been unable to arrange them before leaving. Nothing could move forward without individuals attending the US Embassy in person. For Aziz – whose name, it transpired, was the same as a wanted terrorist – it proved to be impossible anyway, and he was unable to join us for the final leg of the journey. He had been, throughout the voyage, an integral part of the crew, so this loss was sad for all of us.

Reaching the American Continent

When we were at last ready to take our leave of the Dominican Republic in mid-January, the navy had kindly prepared another ceremony for us. Not for the first time during our voyage aboard *Phoenicia*, it was once again quite a tricky manoeuvre leaving the harbour. This time because the wind was blowing us back against the pier. Luckily, the experienced navy team were very helpful and gave us three rousing cheers as we finally left the harbour.

We estimated that it would take about ten days to reach Florida and we were convinced that our most difficult challenges were behind us. How wrong we were. At the beginning, all went well. As we headed out into the open seas, the wind was in the right direction and we were greeted by a brisk Force 5 blowing us west towards Cuba. This was very pleasant and exhilarating and we had some great sailing for the first couple of days.

Unfortunately, this turned out to be only a brief interlude. As we reached the southernmost point of the Dominican Republic, we found ourselves between two small islands about a mile apart, a bit like sailing through the eye of a needle. By now the wind had strengthened, and we were concerned we didn't have much leeway. There were also currents that we were worried might carry us onto the outlying rocks of the islands on both sides of the ship.

Happily, we managed to thread the needle and pass through. This was followed by excellent progress for the next day-and-a-half, as easterly winds pushed us towards Cuba. We rounded the archipelago on the southwestern side of Haiti and headed north through the Windward Passage, a 50-mile wide strait between the two islands. This took us out of the easterly winds and into an area of calm water which really did turn out to be the proverbial calm before the storm.

About two hours later the strongest winds of the entire voyage started to blow, with visibility reduced to almost zero. By this time, it was getting dark, so we had to start the engine to keep the prow straight into the wind, otherwise the waves might have overwhelmed us. It was at this point that Steinar, who was helming, saw a white wall of water coming towards the ship as the stern was lifted up by a huge wave. For a moment it felt as if we had been tipped off a cliff.

Steinar told me later that a hundred thoughts flashed through his mind at once. Had we closed the hatch at the front of the deck? Was the water flooding the cabin? What would happen to the electronics if they were covered in water? For a moment he also thought that David Smith, who had joined us in Tenerife, had been washed overboard. Before the giant wave hit, he had seen him on deck but now, he was nowhere to be seen. In fact, moments before, David had gone down below into the cabin to get some coffee and all was well.

I'd never been at sea during either of my two expeditions on *Phoenicia* when the weather was as bad as it was that night. In fact, it was the most challenging of the entire voyage. The waves in the middle of the channel were consistently two to three metres high, and for hours the boat was being rocked violently from one end to the other. We needed to have two, sometimes three, crew on the helm to keep the ship steady and into the wind. At the same time, we needed to man both the rudders on the stern quarters.

At times, the propeller was dragged right out of the water at one end as the horse's head on the bow was plunged under at the other. There was white foam and spray everywhere, with huge amounts of water washing all over the deck. This went on for most of the night. At one point the speed of the boat was reduced to half-a-knot per hour and I was beginning to think we were in serious trouble.

I was also worried for the two new crew members, Lindsay and Vera, who had joined us in Santo Domingo. After it was over, we all chatted about it and I think it was a genuinely terrifying experience for many of the crew. Lindsay said that he had an out-of-body experience and was looking down on himself from above the deck. Sheimaa even told us that she would have felt quite happy if a wave had washed her overboard, so that it would all be over. I think her view was that this is what she had signed up for, and the elements would do their thing. Like many of the crew she was very seasick. But fate being willing, she was determined to see it through and did sterling work manning one of the stern rudders.

At this stage, I was having to think of a Plan B and was considering taking shelter in Port au Prince, or possibly one of the nearby bays. However if we did this I knew we were very likely to be apprehended by the Haiti Coast Guard. We would then almost certainly be detained and, because it is a very poor country, we would have had no alternative but to buy ourselves out of trouble. The other alternative was to take refuge in Cuba. However, if we went to Cuba we definitely wouldn't have been allowed into Florida. A Catch 22 if ever there was one.

I was very worried and trying to assess the dangers to the crew for which I was responsible. I came off watch at about 2 a.m. and was up again at 6 a.m. As luck would have it, it was now that the weather started to moderate and the winds to calm. The seas were still angry and rough, but it was clearly a lot better than it had been during the middle of the night.

The weather continued to calm as the morning progressed, and we started to make better progress. But during the height of the storm, one of the engine mounts had snapped due to the vibrations shaking the boat. Luckily, Dirman had spotted it and was able to drill a hole in one of the metal braces and fix it back in place.

By late afternoon of the following day, we were sailing beyond the Windward Passage to the north of Haiti and Cuba and towards the Bahamas. By this time we were in the central Caribbean, which has its own problems. Here, the water is very shallow, sometimes just a few metres deep, which gives very little clearance for a sailing ship, especially when the seas are really rough. Our draught was about five feet and we had to make sure we were in the deepest part of the channel if we were to avoid hitting the bottom.

This caused yet more problems, as all the larger boats and ships were congregating towards the centre of the channel as they made their way towards Florida. A storm in these waters is potentially much more dangerous than in the middle of the Atlantic where the waves are much slower and more consistent. There is certainly considerably less chance of a collision with another boat.

In these shallow waters, if you sail into an area where the wind is blowing against the current or against the tide, it's problematic. Once again it demonstrated how much less forgiving the sea is close to land, in places like the Mediterranean or the Caribbean, than it is in the middle of the ocean. In the latter, there are no rocks and no coastline, and you have plenty of time to see other ships approaching.

We were also worried that the US Coast Guard might be stopping us every few miles, thinking that we had drugs or illegal immigrants on board. In fact, a couple of coastguard cutters came within a mile or two of us. Happily, they never stopped us, and didn't seem interested. This was a great surprise, as we obviously didn't look like a normal boat. We could easily have been a group of Cuban refugees trying to reach Miami. Clearly, they had bigger fish to fry.

As we came closer to Florida, we started to see whales and Portuguese men o' war. The latter are deadly and move passively, driven by the winds, currents, and tides. These ones were huge. They looked like transparent, floating capsules, sometimes with a tinge of purple and blue in their gas-filled bladders. Floating along beside the ship with the early morning light glinting off them, they actually looked quite beautiful.

It was quite a surreal experience when we at last saw the skyline of Miami. We had emerged somehow unscathed from this terrifying experience when we had been at the mercy of the elements. And while nature can sometimes be violent, there is also a powerful sense of being an infinitesimally small part of a larger creation. And now, suddenly, we were seeing the exact opposite. Man's creation writ large across the horizon. Our voyage into ancient history really was coming to an end at last.

While all this had been going on, our former crew mate, Boyd Tuttle, had been frantically making arrangements for our arrival as we made our way from the Dominican Republic towards Florida. This wasn't easy for him. As a sailing vessel designed according to a very ancient pedigree we would only arrive when we arrived. Nonetheless, in the absence of a reliable date, a very conservative estimate was agreed for 4th February, 2020.

In the event, we made better progress than we had predicted, successfully negotiating the entrance to Port of Everglades, Fort Lauderdale's main port and home to a number of cruise liners, commercial activities and super yachts. We then made our way through a few miles of inland waterways and were able to moor up at an unoccupied berth en-route to the Coral Ridge Yacht Club (CRYC). Here the crew were able to get a shower, a good meal, and tidy up the ship before the day of our official arrival.

On the morning of 4th February, as we made our way further along the internal waterways, we were mesmerised by the countless super yachts and luxury mansions. The level of wealth on either side of us was simply astonishing. I don't think any of us had ever seen so much valuable real estate and massive super yachts, some equipped with helicopter pads and other toys. It actually felt quite mind-blowing after our journey into an ancient past and all of us experienced quite a shock to the system. We learned later that many of the super-rich owners were based in New York and flew down for long weekends or to take their yachts to the Caribbean for summer vacations.

As we made our way along the waterway, we were joined by a fire boat from Broward County, Florida, which then escorted us towards the Coral Ridge Yacht Club. The fire boat radioed ahead to request that the low road bridges along the way should be opened so as not to delay us. Here was our own special escort and the first hint that a VIP arrival was awaiting us. Finally, through the Sunrise Boulevard Bridge, we could see the outline of the yacht club. The fire boat turned on their high speed water hoses sending thousands of gallons of water cascading into the air ahead of us, creating a beautiful water fountain display.

Prior to our arrival, we had been told that we needed to get permission from the local police department to launch Yuri's drone, because of security concerns. However, we were worried that we might never get permission, or it might be denied, so I told Yuri to fly the drone anyway, that we would deal with any consequences afterwards. In the event, our arrival was such a success that hardly anyone seemed to notice his drone buzzing about overhead. This resulted in some great aerial photography as *Phoenicia* made landfall in America.

This time, in contrast to some of our previous ungainly arrivals, we were able to sail past the Coral Ridge Yacht Club and do a neat pirouette in a wider basin, before approaching the Club's jetty. Amazingly, some 200 club members had turned out to welcome us and mark our arrival. No expense had been spared and a band struck up in dramatic style as we made the final approach.

Dirman calmly took control of the helm and skilfully guided us into position between two large yachts. He was as cool as a cucumber and guided *Phoenicia* with great skill. After all our trials and tribulations of crossing the Atlantic, this was not the time to scratch one of the gleaming yachts alongside or smash into the jetty ahead of us. As we threw our lines to willing hands, spectators on the clubhouse balcony and on the club's lawn cheered our arrival. The yacht club had prepared a podium and flags and soon the loudspeakers were ringing out with messages of congratulations on our achievement.

No sooner were our lines secured than various dignitaries and members of the press descended upon us. Ironically, there was hardly any time to reflect upon the fact that my ambition to sail a Phoenician ship across the Atlantic had finally been fulfilled. I had been on the boat for some seven months since leaving the UK and it was five months since we left Carthage. Now, 6000 miles later, here we were in the heart of Florida, enjoying an incredible welcome from the members of the yacht club, city dignitaries and members of the Lebanese and Tunisian communities.

After a few minutes of frantic activity, a number of welcome speeches were made, including from the Commodore and the General Manager of the yacht club, officials from the Mayor's office and our own VIP supporters who had helped to make the expedition possible. I was then asked to say a few words and managed to thank everybody who had made our arrival such a special event. Most important of all, it was an opportunity to thank the members of the crew for putting their trust in me and making this whole incredible voyage a reality. At the same time, Charlie had been commentating on our arrival, interviewing yacht club members and streaming the whole event live on Facebook for the thousands of enthusiasts who had been following our adventure during the preceding months.

As soon as the official speeches were finished, I put out an invitation to anyone who was interested to clamber aboard to witness the basic conditions, and experience close-up the smell of well-oiled wood, rank sleeping bags and damp clothes. The most frequently heard comments were: "You mean you've just sailed this across the Atlantic, you must be crazy!" or simply "That's crazy man!" In short, we were treated with admiration and disbelief in equal measure.

There was just time to grab a quick bite to eat at the yacht club's outdoor restaurant before I was asked to make a short presentation to a hundred or so members of the club who wanted to learn more about our expedition. The audience seemed genuinely mesmerised by the story of the project and our crossing of the Atlantic.

However, the best part of the meeting was yet to come. Boyd Tuttle said a few words and then introduced Betty Lafontaine to the audience. At this point I didn't know what to expect. All Boyd had told me was that she would like to say a few words and that she had something special to give me.

Betty duly stepped forward and her spiritual presence immediately filled the room. She recited a couple of songs for our benefit and said a little bit about the beliefs of the Navajo tribe from which she comes. I was completely dumbstruck by her presence. She told us that she had written the songs herself, explaining their meaning and the context of her cultural background.

It was only now that I was overtaken with emotion. Known in her community as 'Red Ant', Betty explained that she was from the Navajo tribe – which since 1959 has officially been known as the Navajo nation – which occupies the largest part of any territory occupied by an indigenous group in the United States. Their territory spreads across parts of Arizona, New Mexico and south eastern Utah. Indeed, the area is so great that it would cover the ten US states of West Virginia, Maryland, Massachusetts, Vermont, New Hampshire, New York, New Jersey, Connecticut, Delaware and Rhode Island combined.

Had Betty been from any other American indigenous group it would not have meant quite so much to me. However, I knew a little bit about the Navajo, since in 2005 I had been able to witness some of their ancient customs at first hand. I had been invited by a Canadian, Eric Hibbert, to join a team to raft the white water of the Grand Canyon. Eric, it is not an exaggeration to say, has spent most of his life whitewater rafting and travelling the world. He had been introduced to me in 2003 and became a key crew member on the Borobudur ship expedition when we had sailed from Indonesia to Madagascar and then around the Cape of Good Hope up to Ghana in West Africa.

Eric was a skilled white-water rafter and sailor and, when I launched my own adventure travel company, Pioneer Expeditions,[82] I turned to Eric to lead our first ever trip rafting down the Matsiatra river in Madagascar in 2007.

82. Pioneer Expeditions was founded in 2006 and provides Adventure and Wildlife trips to exotic and remote destinations. Details at PioneerExpeditions.com

Given the rafting experience through the Grand Canyon with Eric and his other team members, I was captivated by Betty's story of her people. I could picture them living in the Grand Canyon and the surrounding plains, to which they later moved. Betty went on to say that Navajo folklore states that their ancestors came from the big sea to the east. In other words, Betty was telling us that the Navajo people came from across the Atlantic. Could the Phoenicians have contributed to the populations of indigenous Americans?[83]

I could hardly believe what I was hearing. It immediately reminded me that very few people once believed the real-world truth of the Vinland Sagas – the *Saga of the Greenlanders* and the *Saga of Erik the Red* – telling of the founding of Greenland in about AD 985 and the discovery of the American continent in around AD 1000. These accounts, which were handed down orally until they were written down by Icelandic scholars in the 13th and 14th centuries, disagree on some points of the detail. Nevertheless, they record accounts of the discovery of lands to the west, populated with indigenous peoples, written hundreds of years before Columbus.

The Sagas were invariably dismissed by commentators and academics as the fanciful legends and writings of Icelandic story tellers, who were themselves the descendants of Norwegian Vikings. It wasn't until the end of the 1960s that Viking sites were discovered at Aix-en-Meadows, Newfoundland, off the coast of Canada, confirming the stories of the Vinland Sagas.

Now, Betty 'Red Ant' was telling the assembled audience that she believed a similar story was true for the Navajo nation. As I was trying to process this vital piece of information, Betty proceeded to present

83. This claim may seem far-fetched but it is not without foundation. Stephen C. Jett, writes in his book Ancient Ocean Crossings (University of Alabama Press 2017): "Donald N. Yates and collaborators… characterized the mtDNA of fifty-two individuals of partial Cherokee ancestry who did not display any of the usual Native American mtDNA haplogroups A through D… identifying (in order of the frequency) haplogroups T, U, X, J, H, L and K. T, X, and J are essentially Levantine (eastern Mediterranean) in origin,"
Jett also noted that this DNA was ancient and not the result of recent European or Middle Eastern admixture in America:
"Yates' genetically remarkably diverse Cherokee sample, the unique haplotypes represented therein, and the frequencies of the haplogroups found—quite different from those of the larger US populations—are striking: 'Similar proportions of these haplogroups are noted in the populations of Egypt, Israel and other parts of the East Mediterranean … No such mix could result from post-1492 European gene flow into the Cherokee Nation.'" pp. 353.

me with a traditional drum on which she had painted a colourful picture of *Phoenicia* under full sail, on the drum skin itself.

I accepted it graciously and felt, as I still feel, that it was an important symbol of what I believe to be the truth. Which is that before Columbus and the Vikings, other ancient sailors from Europe and the Middle East reached the Americas. The crew of the *Phoenicia* had now conclusively proved that it was physically possible. Now Betty's presentation gave me renewed hope that one day we would find the needle in the haystack: the archaeological or scientific evidence[84] that ancient sailors really did arrive in the Americas thousands of years before Columbus.

Following the success of the voyage and the publicity generated, we were invited by Harry Horgan, the Founder and President of the Shake-A-Leg Foundation to visit them in Miami and share our experiences. So, the *Phoenicia* and crew made the short journey to Miami and spent the next three weeks moored at their centre in Coconut Grove, where we were able to share our experiences with the Shake-A-Leg members who are made up of disabled children, military veterans and families. Various events in conjunction with the Shake-A–Leg foundation were organised by Tom and Norma Jean Abraham and Doumit Shmouni. It was therefore a great end to our 6000-mile voyage, to share the highs and lows of what we had done and help to inspire this incredible group of budding sailors and water-sport enthusiasts. With the pandemic causing countries around the world to close their borders, hasty plans were then made for the crew to return to their home countries to reflect on an incredible voyage and their contribution to the on-going debate as to whether the Phoenicians came to the Americas before Columbus.

84. This scientific work is well underway and whilst not generally accepted by the academic community at large, the evidence is being gathered and many believe we are at a tipping point. An example of additional scientific evidence can be seen in the work of John Sorenson and Carl Johannessen in "World Trade and Biological Exchanges Before 1492", 2nd Edition, iUniverse, 2013 New York. Sorenson and Johannessen present nearly 200 floral and faunal species, some confirmed and others possibly identified, in both the Old World and New. This epic work reflects decades of research studying such exchanges.

Acknowledgements

I would like to express my sincere thanks to all those who have helped in the creation of this book. I would particularly like to thank Richard Madden for his tireless work in the writing of it, without which it would never have happened; Irene Goodacre for her advice and editing of the manuscript, Deborah Wood for the book design and layout, and for proof reading the manuscript; Rosie Johnson, Colin Moore, and Tracey Whalley. The front cover of the book was created by Robert Onion and Betty Onion, which I am most grateful for.

Also, I would like to thank all those who have read the manuscript and given their comments and advice. I would also like to thank Sir Ranulph Fiennes, Col John Blashford-Snell, Benedict Allen, Pen Hadow, Mark Beaumont, Levison Wood and Dr Habib Chamoun-Nicolas, for their commendations regarding the book.

In terms of the expedition, I would like to thank the following individuals for organising key parts: Clary Hughes as Project Manager, Rémi Kahwaji, Sheimaa Oubari, Eryj Ben Sassi, Dr Habib Chamoun-Nicolas, André Azoulay and Boyd Tuttle. I would also like to thank Colin Moore, Robert Foote, Rikki and Juliet Johnstone, Edwin Messenger and Ian Bond for helping to prepare the *Phoenicia* for the Atlantic and other supporting activities. I would also like to give special mentions to Viking Life Saving Equipment who provided our life rafts, the Captain Scott Society for their award, the Shake-A-Leg and Anthony R. Abraham Foundations in Miami and the Coral Ridge Yacht Club who rolled out the red carpet for us on our arrival in Florida, USA.

I would also like to thank Ray Korpan, Hicham Aboutaam, Salem Ayoob, Hugh and Natalie Lumby, for their valuable contributions in supporting the expedition.

Last but not least I would like to thank Laurenne Mansbridge, my co-director at Pioneer Expeditions, for graciously allowing me to take time out to undertake this expedition. A full list of supporters, friends, donors and sponsors of the expedition is below, with apologies for any omissions.

Adam Rosen *(USA)*

Admiral Hector Juan Martinez Roman *(Dominican Republic)*

Agence de Mise en valeur du Patrimoine et de Promotion Culturelle *(Tunisia)*

Alfred Malek *(Dominican Republic)*

Ali Wild *(USA)*

Allen Shaheen *(USA)*

André Azoulay *(Morocco)*

Andy and Rosie Johnson *(UK)*

Anis Zarrouk *(Tunisia)*

Annie Totah *(USA)*

Anthony R. Abraham Foundation *(Miami USA)*

Antoine Menassa *(France/Lebanon)*

Association Didon de Carthage *(Tunisia)*

Association Essaouira Mogador *(Morocco)*

Association Tunisienne des officiers de la Marine Marchande *(Tunisia)*

Aventuras Produções e Edições Educativas Ltda

Dr Bassem Al-Masri *(USA)*

Captain Scott Society *(UK)*

Carmen Khoury *(Dominican Republic)*

Charlotte Lumby *(UK)*

Circle Brands *(UK)*

Clary Hughes *(UK)*

Club Libanes-Sirio-Palestino *(Santo Domingo, Dominican Republic)*

Club Naval Santo Domingo *(Domincan Republic)*

Col John Blashford-Snell *(UK)*

Colin Moore *(UK)*

Coral Ridge Yacht Club *(Fort Lauderdale, USA)*

Danielle Eubank *(USA)*

Daphne Villalba Sajiún *(Dominican Republic)*

David Wardrop *(UK)*

Dominican Republic Navy

Don Jose Attias *(Dominican Republic)*

Doug and Rita Smith *(UK)*

Doumit Shmouni (USA)

Edward M Shiner *(USA)*

Egyptian Bureau for Cultural & Educational Affairs

Elizabeth Belfer *(USA)*

Elvis Alam *(Dominican Republic)*

Fatma Bouhlel *(Tunisia)*

Fernando Pineiro *(Spain)*

George Faddoul *(Lebanon)*

Ghida Akoum *(Lebanon)*

Gisele Khoury *(Lebanon)*

Dr Habib Chamoun-Nicolas *(Mexico/Lebanon/USA)*

Harry Horgan *(USA)*

Henrietta Thorpe *(UK)*

Hiba Faour *(Lebanon)*

Hicham Aboutaam *(USA/Lebanon)*

Hugh and Natalie Lumby *(UK)*

Ibtissam Khoury *(Lebanon)*

Ines Hassoumi *(Tunisia)*

International School of Carthage *(Tunisia)*

Jacqui Smith *(UK)*

Jamel Barouni *(Tunisia)*

James Lumby *(UK)*

Jamila Bennour *(Tunisia)*

Dr Joel and Pam Klass *(USA)*

Jonathan Tubb *(UK)*

Joy Raymond *(UK)*

Dr K Harb *(Lebanon)*

Laurenne Mansbridge *(UK)*

Maha Chalabi *(Lebanon)*

Majdi Ramadan *(Lebanon/USA)*

Mariza Avogadra Thomé *(Argentina)*

Mark Harriman *(UK)*

Miami Yacht Club *(USA)*

Mike and Betty LaFontaine *(USA)*

Ministry of Tourism in Tunisia

Ministry of Transportation in Tunisia

Mohamad Osman *(UAE)*

Mohammad Ghassen Nouria *(Tunisia)*

Mourad Jebali *(Tunisia)*

Municipality of Carthage *(Tunisia)*

Nadim Ghantous *(Lebanon)*

Dr Naji Karam *(Lebanon)*

Nandra Mansaram *(USA)*

Nathaniel Merrill *(USA)*

Nick Kahwaji *(Canada)*

Nick Swallow *(UK)*

Norma Jean Abraham *(USA)*

ONTT Office National du Tourisme

Tunisien *(Tunisia)*

Paul Bayly *(NZ)*

Philip Searles *(UK)*

Phoenician International Research Centre *(USA)*

Port of Essaouiria, Morroco

Prof Reem Bahgat *(UK/Egypt)*

Raymond Debbane *(USA)*

Rikki and Juliet Johnstone *(UK)*

Rita Zehenni *(USA)*

Rob and Trish Foote *(UK)*

Romero Britto *(Miami USA)*

Salem Ayoob *(USA)*

Salim George Khalaf *(USA/Lebanon)*

Sarah Taylor *(UK)*

Save Tyre Foundation *(Lebanon)*

Scientific Exploration Society *(UK)*

Shelby White *(USA)*

Simon and Greta Duff *(UK)*

Sir Robin Knox-Johnston *(UK)*

Skander Malek *(Tunisia)*

Stirling and Son *(UK)*

Tariq Othmani *(Morocco)*

Terry and Lynne Kerley *(UK)*

The Lebanese Cultural Union

Tom Abraham *(USA)*

Viking Life Saving Equipment *(UK/Denmark)*

Will Stirling

Zarna Mannix Beale *(UK)*

Illustrations

I would like to thank the following for the use of their illustrations and images.

The book cover design: Robert Onion and Betty Onion of Circle Brands, **www.circlebrands.co.uk**

Prof Clive Finlayson: Ancient Ship Rock drawings from Laja Alta Cave, Spain.

Salim George Khalaf: Carthaginian Gold stater illustration from **www.Phoenicia.org**

Danielle Eubank; Phoenicia under Sail **www.danielleeubankart.com**

Map of the Phoenician Influence in the Mediterranean, courtesy of the **Biblical Archaeology Society**.

Expedition Crew List

Expedition Crew Members	Participation from/to
Abdul Aziz *(Indonesia)*	Tunisia - Dominican Republic
Boyd Tuttle *(USA)*	Tunisia - Cadiz
Carson Petty *(USA)*	Tunisia- Gibraltar
Charlie Mannix Beale *(UK)*	Tunisia - Florida
David Hoskings (UK)	Essaouira -Tenerife
David Smith *(UK)*	Tenerife - Dominican Republic
Diderik Cappelen *(Norway)*	Tunisia - Florida
Doug Petty *(USA)*	Tunisia- Gibraltar
Edwin Messenger *(UK)*	Tunisia - Cadiz
Habiba Mechichi *(Tunisia)*	Essaouira -Tenerife
Ian Bond *(UK)*	Cadiz-Essaoira
Lindsay Mcauley *(Australia)*	Dominican Republic - Florida
Maran Fazzi *(Netherlands)*	Gibraltar to Florida
Max Cattini *(UK)*	Tenerife - Dominican Republic
Rémi Kahwaji *(Lebanon/Canada)*	Tenerife - Dominican Republic
Sheimaa Oubari *(Lebanon/France)*	Tenerife - Florida
Steinar Lillås *(Norway)*	Tunisia - Florida
Surdirman *(Indonesia)*	Tunisia - Florida
Tom Westcott *(UK)*	Tunisia - Gibraltar
Vera Sanada *(Brazil)*	Dominican Republic - Florida
Yuri Sanada *(Brazil)*	Tunisia - Florida

Delivery Crew Members
from UK to Tunisia (or part of)

Aaron Barrett *(UK)*

Carmen Lopez Franco *(Mexico)*

Charlie Mannix Beale *(UK)*

Christopher de Sadeleer *(Belgium)*

Dave Lamb *(Australia)*

Eikka Huhtala *(Mexico)*

Fred Kingdon *(UK)*

Isabel Kelly *(UK)*

Jean-Hugues Gooris *(Belgium)*

Joff'rey Kowalski *(Belgium)*

Joshua Carille *(New Zealand)*

Lucy Weller *(Germany)*

Marcus Bond *(UK)*

Rémi Kahwaji *(Lebanon/Canada)*

Sally Welburn *(UK)*

Sheimaa Oubari *(Lebanon/France)*

Sherman Jones *(Canada)*

Ship Design Plan and Statistics

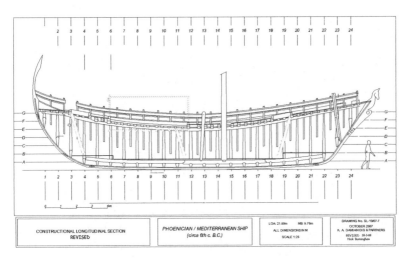

Phoenicia's Facts and Figures

Length	20m
Beam	5.8m
Mast height	15m
Freeboard	1.3m
Draft	1.5m
Gross tonnage	50 tonnes
Ballast	20 tonnes
Rig	Single square sail
Size of sail	12.5m x 8.5m
Average speed	2.5-3.5 knots
Top recorded speed	10.6 knots (with very strong current)
Distance sailed since launch in 2008	Over 30,000 miles
Minimum crew required	6
Ideal crew number	12

TIMELINE

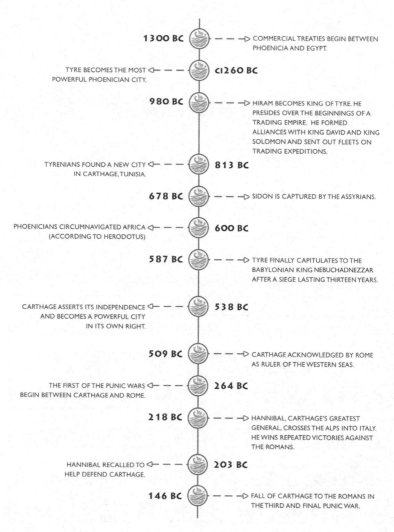

1300 BC — — ▷ COMMERCIAL TREATIES BEGIN BETWEEN PHOENICIA AND EGYPT.

TYRE BECOMES THE MOST ◁— — **C1260 BC**
POWERFUL PHOENICIAN CITY.

980 BC — — — ▷ HIRAM BECOMES KING OF TYRE. HE PRESIDES OVER THE BEGINNINGS OF A TRADING EMPIRE. HE FORMED ALLIANCES WITH KING DAVID AND KING SOLOMON AND SENT OUT FLEETS ON TRADING EXPEDITIONS.

TYRENIANS FOUND A NEW CITY ◁— — **813 BC**
IN CARTHAGE, TUNISIA.

678 BC — — — ▷ SIDON IS CAPTURED BY THE ASSYRIANS.

PHOENICIANS CIRCUMNAVIGATED AFRICA ◁— — **600 BC**
(ACCORDING TO HERODOTUS)

587 BC — — — ▷ TYRE FINALLY CAPITULATES TO THE BABYLONIAN KING NEBUCHADNEZZAR AFTER A SIEGE LASTING THIRTEEN YEARS.

CARTHAGE ASSERTS ITS INDEPENDENCE ◁— — **538 BC**
AND BECOMES A POWERFUL CITY
IN ITS OWN RIGHT.

509 BC — — — ▷ CARTHAGE ACKNOWLEDGED BY ROME AS RULER OF THE WESTERN SEAS.

THE FIRST OF THE PUNIC WARS ◁— — **264 BC**
BEGIN BETWEEN CARTHAGE AND ROME.

218 BC — — — ▷ HANNIBAL, CARTHAGE'S GREATEST GENERAL, CROSSES THE ALPS INTO ITALY. HE WINS REPEATED VICTORIES AGAINST THE ROMANS.

HANNIBAL RECALLED TO ◁— — **203 BC**
HELP DEFEND CARTHAGE.

146 BC — — — ▷ FALL OF CARTHAGE TO THE ROMANS IN THE THIRD AND FINAL PUNIC WAR.